FENTON BRESLER

ƒð

STEIN AND DAY/*Publishers*/New York

First published in the United States of America in 1981
Copyright © 1980 by Fenton Bresler
All rights reserved
Printed in the United States of America
Stein and Day/*Publishers*/Scarborough House
Briarcliff Manor, New York 10510

Library of Congress Cataloging in Publication Data

Bresler, Fenton S
  The Chinese Mafia.

  First published in 1980 under title: The trail of
the Triads.
  Bibliography: p.
  Includes index.
  1. Narcotics, Control of — Hong Kong.   2. Narcotics,
Control of — Asia, Southeastern.   3. Hung men.
4. Heroin. I. Title.
HV5840.H6B73   1981   364.1'77'0959   80-5797
ISBN 0-8128-2752-X

Contents

Illustrations

Heroin factory seized in Hong Kong *(photo: Superintendent Leonard Williamson, Royal Hong Kong Police)*

· Preparing heroin for smoking, Hong Kong style *(from* Heroin Manufacture in Hong Kong, *by courtesy of the Royal Hong Kong Police Narcotics Bureau)*

Tattoos used as identification marks by Triad members in Singapore *(from* Police Life Annual 77, *Singapore Police Force)*

The altar used by a Triad during the initiation ritual for new members *(from* Police Life Annual 77, *Singapore Police Force)*

General Tuan Shih Wen, one of the ex-KMT drug warlords, 1967 *(Sunday Telegraph)*

Part of General Tuan's force of 2000 men on parade in north Thailand *(Sunday Telegraph)*

The basis of General Tuan's army – an opium poppy *(Sunday Telegraph)*

General Kriangsak Chamanand, then Thai Prime Minister, at the ceremonial burning of £120 million of heroin, January 1979 *(Express Newspapers)*

Georgie Pai, who, as a 'Red Pole', became the scourge of London's Chinatown *(Press Association)*

May Wong and her lover, Li Jafar Mah, jailed at the Old Bailey for heroin trafficking, January 1977 *(Press Association)*

Chung Mon, first 'Godfather' of Amsterdam in the days of his glory *(photo: AB Koers)*

Chung Mon gunned down in the streets of his adopted city *(De Telegraaf)*

South-East Asia

Opium growing areas making up the Golden Triangle

Undefined area of Red China making up the Golden Quadrangle

--- National boundary · · · · · Provincial or state boundary

0   500 MILES

TIBET

SZECHWAN

INDIA

TIBET

CHINA

HUNAN   FUKIEN

YUNNAN

KWANGSI   KWANGTUNG

Kowloon

Macao

Lashio

NORTH
VIETNAM

Hong Kong

Kengtung

BURMA

Ban Houei Sai

Chiangra

Long
Tieng

Chiangmai

Gulf
of
Tonkin

HAINAN

Lampang

Rangoon

Vientiane

LAOS

THAILAND

Pakse

Danang

Bangkok

Paknam

KAMPUCHEA

Pleiku

Uttapao

Andaman
Sea

Phnom Penh

Nha Trang

South
China
Sea

Saigon

SOUTH VIETNAM

Gulf of
Siam

PHILIPPINES

BRUNEI   SABAH

KualaLumpur   MALAYSIA

SARAWAK

Singapore

SUMATRA

INDONESIA

BORNEO

Acknowledgments

It would have been absolutely impossible to write this book without a great deal of help and co-operation from all manner of people who were prepared to talk to me. To all of them I must express my deep appreciation and gratitude for the time they have spent with me – even if I have not been able to accept all that they have told me.

I am not in a position to name all those who have spoken to me. Furthermore, the United States Drug Enforcement Administration special agents talked to me on the basis that I could name them *en bloc* 'at the front of the book' but that I could not identify their individual locations of duty. Certain officers of the Royal Canadian Mounted Police preferred that I express my debt of gratitude solely to the RCMP Criminal Intelligence Service Canada without specifying names.

However, I am happy to make public expression of my thanks to the following named persons:

US Drug Enforcement Administration: Administrator Peter Bensinger; senior executives John Warner, Richard Bly, Peter Fong, Vernon D. Meyer and Daniel Addario; public affairs spokesmen Con Dougherty, James Judge and Joe Flanders; and special agents John Feehan, Terry Burke, Paddy Maher, Eileen Hayes, Kevin Gallaher, Tom Cash, Greg Paasic, Allan Maclain, Michael Long, James Beckner, Robert J. Furie, Arthur Johnson, Peter Wang, Peter Niblo, Bill Dwyer, Melvyn Young, Lionel Stewart and Richard Logan.

US Customs Service: John Cusack.

New York City Police Department: Captain Allan Hoehl and Detective Neil Mauriello of the 5th Precinct; Lieutenant Martin Kennedy, Sergeant Jim Sordi and Detectives Lloyd Hutchens and Fred Elflein at Police Headquarters; and Detectives Charles Henry and John Chartrand of Homicide, 13th Precinct.

Chicago Police: Sergeant Kenneth Brandt, Investigator Barney O'Riley.

San Francisco Police: Sergeant John McKenna, head of the Asian Task Force.

Los Angeles Police Department: Ross Arai, team leader of the Asian Task Force, and Ernie Lopez, a member of his force.

Canadian Police: Vancouver – Inspector Lew Dempsey, Inspector Ray Peterson, Superintendent Eddie Makins and Corporal Derk Doornbos; Toronto – Sergeant Bill Holdright, Constable Michael J. King; Ottawa – Staff Sergeant Don Devine.

Royal Hong Kong Police Force: Police Commissioner Roy Henry, Assistant Commissioner Peter Law, Detective Chief Superintendent John Thorpe, Superintendents Douglas Lau, Lionel Lam, Peter So, Gordon Brooke and Leonard Hill, Chief Inspector Keith Francis.

Independent Commission Against Corruption (Hong Kong): Sir Donald Luddington and G.A.Harknett.

Hong Kong Customs: Douglas Jordan.

Macao Police: Margharita.

Royal Thai Police: Police-Major-General Pow Sarasin, Police-Colonel Damrong Vaivong and Aran Suwanbubpa, chief of the Co-ordination and Evaluation Division of the Office of the Narcotics Control Board.

Royal Malaysian Police: Jerry Lieuw, deputy-head of the CID and David Khoo, one of his officers.

Singapore Police: Michael Chai, Director of the CID, and Poh Geok Ek, Deputy Director, Central Narcotics Bureau.

Metropolitan Police: Detective Chief Superintendent John Smith, head of the Drugs Squad, Superintendent William Taylor, deputy-head of the Drugs Squad, Sergeants Ken Beever and Bill Thomas, Superintendent Fred Luff, Detective Chief Superintendent Michael Huins, Detective Chief Superintendent Algernon Hemmingway and ex-Detective Chief Superintendent Gwyn Waters.

Manchester Police: Detective Chief Superintendent Nigel Hill, Detective Sergeant Derek Boone, Detective Constable Frank Hayden.

Liverpool Police: Assistant Chief Constable Frank Jones, Superintendents Owen and Anderson.

Hampshire Police: Superintendent John Wright of the CID.

Dutch Police: Jan van Straten and Age Moeke of the Central Criminal Intelligence Unit at The Hague; Commisaris Gerard Toorenaar of the Amsterdam Police.

West German Police: Erich Strass and Manfred Bolte of the Criminal Investigation Department, Wiesbaden.

French Police: François Lemouel, head of the Drugs Squad, Paris.

Interpol: Detective Chief Superintendent Raymond Kendall and Superintendent John Morris.

I must also thank US Congressman Lester Wolff, whose outspokenness on the subject of South-East Asian heroin has made him unpopular in certain quarters, Mr Man Bun Lee, former 'uncrowned Mayor' of New York's Chinatown, Mr Stan Shillington, of the Co-ordinated Law Enforcement Unit, Vancouver, Canada, Mr Douglas Chalmers, a personal friend in Hong Kong who has manfully kept me abreast of developments in the colony with frequent supplies of media information, Mrs Elsie Elliott of the Hong Kong Urban Council who is probably the most outspoken local critic of the authorities there, ex-Hong Kong Detective Inspector Walter Easey, Mr Brian Tisdall in legal practice in Hong Kong, Mr Nico Polak, a Dutch journalist who has made a special study of the Triads in his own country and Miss Ellen Moerman, without whose splendid translations of material, only available in the Dutch language, I would have been deprived of valuable information.

Finally, it would be churlish of me not to acknowledge my indebtedness to Miss Blanche Osborn who has proved an indefatigable typist of a manuscript not always easy to decipher and, above all, to my wife Gina who has had a lot to put up with during the sometimes arduous over two years that I have spent in researching and writing this book.

London, March 1980

Introduction

In 1963 Interpol headquarters in Paris sent out a top secret circular to the police of its member states:

Since 1959 the General Secretariat's attention has been drawn – more especially by the authorities in Hong Kong – to the arrival of a certain number of Chinese in Europe. Supplied with passports, and claiming to be tailors or representatives for genuine or non-existent clothing manufacturers with headquarters in the Far East, they make numerous journeys in all European countries, in particular staying in large ports to contact American sailors stationed in the area or just calling there. Officially, their purpose is to sell clothes for both men and women, but their criminal record has led the police authorities who warned us about them to believe that their real purpose is to establish contact and relationships with certain suspicious characters in an attempt to set up a system of drug traffic and distribution, aimed ultimately at the United States of America.

The Hong Kong authorities have singled out four of these Chinese as being particularly dangerous because they belong to a Chinese criminal society called the 'Green Pang Triad Society' which, before 1949, operated in North China. The more important members of this society, which concentrates mainly on prostitution rackets, trafficking in drugs and extortion, have moved to Hong Kong and the society has been re-established there under the name 'The Thin Blade Gang', taken from the weapon used by its members.

This circular, reading like something out of a James Bond movie, then went on to name no less than eighty-five suspects whom the free world's police forces were advised to keep under surveillance.

Two years later, in 1965, Interpol repeated its stern warning in two leading articles which appeared in their official publication *The International Criminal Police Review* and which dealt in detail with Triad Society operations in Singapore.

For all the notice that the world's police forces seem to have taken of these warnings, Interpol need not have bothered. Today, nearly twenty years after the first circular, many police officers claim that criminal Triad Societies do not exist and even the most informed sources at Interpol itself are uncertain of the exact nature of Triad operations. According to Detective Chief Superintendent Raymond Kendall, a senior Scotland Yard man now head of Interpol's Police Division, the Triads are 'hoodlums, criminal elements that gang together – then sometimes fight viciously with each other. There is no real link between them despite their so-called "blood brotherhood". If you have 500 Triads, you have 500 leaders.'

But are they more than just that? Indeed, do they exist at all?

The 1970s saw a vast increase in the numbers of predominantly young ethnic Chinese, primarily from Hong Kong, coming into Europe and, even more, into the United States and Canada. The same years saw a veritable explosion in the international trafficking and consumption of heroin. The United Nations Commission on Narcotic Drugs reported in February 1979 that heroin seizures (accepted to be at best about ten per cent of the amount in circulation at the time) had escalated from a yearly average of a mere 84 kilos in the years 1947–51 to a staggering 2337 kilos in 1977 alone. Huge sums of money are involved: according to declassified Drug Enforcement Administration (DEA) information, the street value of all heroin sales in the United States in the mid-1970s was about $8 billion a year, which put heroin fifteenth in the comparative listings of sales of the 500 largest United States business corporations for that year, as recorded by *Fortune* magazine. This ranks it just below Shell Oil and ahead of Du Pont, Western Electric, Goodyear Tyre, the Xerox Corporation and the Campbell Soup Company. Profits are astronomic: a DEA special agent in Thailand's capital of Bangkok told me that one kilo of South-East Asian heroin would be worth at least *one hundred thousand times* more when it was eventually sold in the streets of New York.

Is there a causal connection between the numbers of ethnic Chinese moving into the West and the huge increase in heroin trafficking?

Although by no means all the world's supply of heroin comes from South-East Asian sources – opium, from which heroin is refined, is grown in Lebanon, Iran, Pakistan, Afghanistan, Turkey and Mexico – South-East Asia nevertheless remains and is likely to remain in the 1980s the single major source of supply. In Western Europe in 1978, 397 kilos of South-East Asian heroin were seized as against 106.7 kilos of all others and although there was a vast increase in the flow of Iranian heroin into Western Europe and the United States after the overthrow of the Shah in January 1979, this is unlikely to remain a permanent feature of the narcotics scene. In December 1979, the Ayatollah Khomeini, Iran's post-revolutionary leader, banned all future heroin traffic in and out of his country in a deliberate attempt to reimpose the tight controls formerly operated by Savak, the Shah's notorious secret police;* but in any case it had been reaffirmed three months earlier, at an international anti-narcotics conference in Bangkok, that more than half the world's illicit heroin supply still came from South-East Asia – with an inevitable ethnic Chinese involvement.

In January 1978 I set out to try and uncover the truth about the Triad element in this new major drugs scene. My researches began with a visit to Interpol headquarters in Paris and have taken me to thirteen countries, several of them more than once, and across many thousands of miles. Armed with a valuable letter of introduction from Eric Wright, an old friend and the head of the News Division at Scotland Yard, police doors were opened to me all over the world and I have had the full co-operation of Peter Bensinger, Administrator of the DEA, Washington, DC. I have spoken to both 'injuns and chiefs'; I have had discussions with Mr Roy Henry, Commissioner of the Royal Hong Kong Police and gone out on night-time raids with an 'anti-Triad action squad' in the back streets of Kowloon. I have had a night on the town with young Hong Kong policemen which taught me more than many an hour in a police library ever could. I have gone along with CIA-type antics by New York cops and DEA men – and I have had a few unpleasant, even scary, experiences of my own. Also, I have been fortunate

* After this book went to press, Khomeini's decree was followed up by the establishment in May 1980 of a special drugs court under the religious judge, Ayatollah Sadeq Khalkali. He soon showed he meant business. By mid-July about 200 offenders had been executed.

enough to interview three Triad Society members myself: one of them in Arnhem Jail in Holland and the other two in typically anonymous plastic modern hotel rooms in Hong Kong and Toronto.

I promised to make no judgements until I finished my task and could reflect on the mass of information I had collected. As a barrister, I am trained to assess the evidence impartially. The only difference from my normal courtroom activities is that this time I went out to collect the evidence as well, something that in English law, as distinct from American, I am never allowed to do.

After some two years of research and on a fair assessment of the evidence, I believe that the Triads not only exist as Chinese criminal secret societies but that they constitute the most frightening new development in international crime since the Mafia ceased to be a patriotic Sicilian organization dedicated to fight for their oppressed homeland and turned to more lucrative, if less honourable, activities.

My investigations have often met with official complacency, ignorance and, at times, corruption, as well as the concern of dedicated law enforcement officers risking their lives in undercover work and the frustration of young officers faced by the bland contentment of their superiors. A senior Customs officer in London told me: 'We have never, as far as I can find, had any smuggling of drugs detected . . . where at any stage any person has said either he is a Triad, referring to himself, or indeed [said] "That man there is a Triad".' He ignored the fact that a Triad, as a member of a secret society, is hardly likely to disclose his secret to the authorities, any more than members of the Mafia would if interrogated, and his approach is typical of the upper echelons of the law enforcement agencies in Britain.

Detective Chief Superintendent John Smith, then head of Scotland Yard's Drugs Squad, stated on television in January 1979: 'While [heroin trafficking] stays at its present manageable level, we can happily detect offences against that area of the law in the way that we are doing at the moment.' On the same television programme Peter Cutting, chief of British Customs and Excise anti-drugs operations, said, 'We've got superb relationships with the sixty-odd police forces in this country and I think our approach is largely a national approach and certainly it stands in very high esteem internationally as to our success.' – an observation reminiscent of the late Lord Hewart's, when Lord Chief Justice at a particularly bad time for the English Bench: 'Her Majesty's Judges are satisfied with the almost universal admiration in which they are held.'

Six months after the television programme, Home Office statistics were published which showed an alarming increase during 1978 in drug addiction in Britain, with a nineteen per cent rise in the number of registered addicts and more than double the annual amount of heroin seized, most of which came from South-East Asia.

Meanwhile, Interpol in June 1977 had again warned the world's police forces of 'crimes of violence committed in various countries by offenders of Chinese origin (mainly from Hong Kong) against their compatriots'. The top secret circular stated that in Europe the Netherlands was the main country concerned but that there were isolated cases in Belgium, the United Kingdom, Spain and West Germany. Amsterdam was already well established as 'the heroin capital of Europe'.

Unlike the British, the Americans are at least aware of the problems that face them and do accept Triad secret societies as a reality of modern criminal existence. In September 1978 I attended a secret conference on Triads which had been called by the New York City Police Department for other police forces in the United States and across the border in Canada. A month later in Washington DC, Peter Bensinger of the DEA expressed deep concern 'as to whether South-East Asian heroin may fill the gap in United States domestic supply caused by the success of the Mexican eradication campaign over the past two years'.

A DEA special agent in Bonn, West Gemany, told me that he had not yet met a Chinese involved in criminal narcotics activity who was not a Triad, and another agent, stationed in London, said that the trafficking of South-East Asian heroin is basically under the aegis of the Triads. According to a recently retired DEA special agent and one of the most experienced of all operators in this field, Triad involvement in the trafficking of heroin into the West Coast of the United States goes back to the earliest days of the importation of the drug.

In February 1979 DEA's official magazine stated: 'South-East Asia's annual production of approximately 400 metric tons of opium, apart from local consumption and delivery elsewhere, is still a potential dagger that could strike the heart of the

American market.' When I talked to Peter Bensinger, he fully concurred with my fears that the Triads and their involvement in the world-wide trafficking of heroin from South-East Asia formed the greatest potential threat to law and order on the international front for the 1980s.

This book is about that threat, a book about dedicated police officers and lazy ones, intrigues and double-talk, jargon and the blurr of official statistics – and lies. It is about violence and death, whether the sordid death of a heroin addict found in the cubicle of a public lavatory with a syringe still sticking in his emaciated arm or the ruthless contract killing of someone involved in this dangerous and evil criminal network. Some matters that I have ascertained I am not at liberty to disclose: confidences must be honoured. Some of the secrets I have been told could lead to death for those telling them to me. My notebooks and the sixty-five cassettes containing all my recorded interviews, together with their transcripts, have been placed in a safe deposit box at a central London bank in order to preserve that secrecy and to have the evidence available should anyone claim that I have misquoted him. Where remarks are quoted in the following pages and it is not specified to whom they were made, they were in every case made to me and recorded in my notebooks or on my tape-recorder. By the time of publication, some of the ranks or positions of those mentioned in the book may well have changed but, unless stated to the contrary, I have used those that were current at the time of writing.

PART I

The Heroin Background

1 What is Heroin?

The Triad involvement in the drugs scene is exclusively a heroin involvement. Cocaine, LSD or marijuana have no part in it. Even more specifically, it is concerned only with the marketing of heroin that originates in the Triads' own home area of South-East Asia. But before investigating the exact nature of that Triad involvement, we need to examine what the drug itself actually is.

The story of heroin has roots deep in history, for heroin is a chemical derivative of opium and is almost as ancient as civilized life itself. The euphoriant effects of the opium poppy are implied in Sumerian records of 4000 BC and Greek and Roman records are full of historical references. Homer wrote in the *Odyssey* of 'a drug which quenches pain and strife and brings forgetfulness of every ill'. Allusions to opium abound in the works of Shakespeare:

> Look where he comes! [says Iago of Othello] Not poppy,
>   nor mandagora
> Nor all the drowsy syrups of the world,
> Shall ever medicine thee to that sweet sleep
> Which thou ow'dst yesterday.

Indeed, opium (from the Greek word *opion,* meaning poppy juice) has almost from time immemorial been the classic way of obtaining merciful oblivion from misery, aptly pointed out in Karl Marx's famous line, 'Religion is the opium of the people'. However, what may come as a surprise to most people is that opium did not originate in the Far East, despite the popular Western image of the Chinese puffing on his hookah or opium pipe.

The opium poppy, botanical name *Papaver somniferum*, grows best in moist climates at elevations above 2000 feet. It was first cultivated in the Middle East and thereafter in India and in fact did not appear in China until as late as the seventeenth and eighteenth centuries when it was shipped in by the Portuguese. The Ch'ing Emperor banned its sale in 1729 but failing imperial power proved ineffective to enforce the ban. British merchants took over the trade and in 1773 the government of British India granted the East India Company an exclusive monopoly over the entire Indian poppy crop.

As opium imports into China kept rising, in the name of British commercial enterprise and free trade, successive Emperors pronounced further bans on the traffic in 1796, 1800, 1813 and 1815 – but all to no avail. The situation became intolerable. The Chinese government demanded the right to regulate trade into its own country and protect its own subjects, the British demanded recognition of the right to do exactly what they wanted. Not for nothing do Chinese people, between themselves, still refer to Englishmen and Westerners in general as '*gwailo*', white devil!

The situation led to the First Opium War (1839-42) in which China's defeat threw her wide open to British commercial interests, including an unbridled opium trade, and forced her to cede Hong Kong island to British colonial rule – to be followed later, after the Second Opium War (1856-58), by the cession of Kowloon on the mainland and finally, in 1898, by the granting of a ninety-nine-year lease of the 366 square miles of land – the 'New Territories' – at the back of Kowloon.

Meanwhile, in 1806, Friedrich Wilhelm Serturner, a pharmacist in Westphalia, Germany, poured liquid ammonia over opium and obtained a white powder which he found to be the basic cause of the soporific properties of opium. He called this new drug '*morphium*' after the Greek god of dreams, Morphius, and so the modern pain-killer of morphine was born: ten parts of opium refined down to one part of morphine.

Morphine's addictive properties came to prominence during the American Civil War. In 1856 the hypodermic needle, invented thirteen years earlier, was introduced into the United States and was used extensively to administer morphine to the war casualties. It was also used in the treatment of dysentery amongst the soldiers. Vast numbers of them became addicted to the drug – so much so that morphine addiction became known as 'the soldiers' disease'.

It was not until 1874, and in London, that a British research chemist, C.R.Alder Wright, first carried on the morphine process to develop the drug that today we call heroin and whose scientific name is *diacetylmorphine*. Compiling a catalogue of the actions of organically derived acids on morphine, Wright boiled some morphine over a stove for several hours with acetic anhydride, a pungent chemical liquid closely related to the familiar acetic acid that we find in vinegar – and obtained a strange new substance that he faithfully recorded. After biological testing on dogs showed that this substance induced 'great prostration, fear, sleepiness, speedily following the administration . . . and a slight tendency to vomiting', he wisely decided to discontinue his experiments.

Commercial promotion of the new drug had to wait until 1898 when the highly respectable German pharmaceutical combine Bayer, in perfectly good faith but perhaps without sufficient prior care, launched upon an unsuspecting world public this new substance, for which they coined the trade name 'heroin' and which they marketed as – of all things – a 'sedative for coughs'.

This one-time trade name has now passed into virtually every language in the world, but it was soon realized that, despite its great medical value (it is, for instance, according to some doctors, the only drug that can control the intense pain suffered in terminal cancer), its potential for evil was tremendous. Unrestricted distribution by physicians and pharmacies created an enormous drug abuse problem and by 1924 Federal narcotics officials were estimating that there were 200,000 heroin addicts in the United States alone. In that year, both Houses of Congress unanimously passed legislation outlawing its import or manufacture in the United States, and nowadays heroin is lawful, and then solely for restricted medical uses, in only nine of the 188 countries and territories whose requirements for opiates and cocaine are compiled and published every year by the International Narcotics Control Board, an organ of the United Nations, in Geneva. Britain is one of those nine countries where limited medical use of heroin is allowed.

But if heroin is so dangerous that even its curtailed use for medical purposes is prohibited in most countries of the world, why does anyone want to take it? I assumed that it must be the most marvellous kind of aphrodisiac, giving an immense added thrill to existence. But this is not so. In a sense it is quite the opposite, as I found out from a young ex-addict in London, who incidentally had cured himself the 'cold turkey' way, after two of his university friends had died as a result of heroin, by locking himself up and forcing himself not to touch the drug for a month.

He had first taken it with a group of college acquaintances who had already experimented with heroin and he thought of it as a new experience for him. He described the first effect 'as a sort of floating feeling. Cloud Nine is a good description of it. No worries at all about anything. You just don't give a damn. You just sit and go through it. You feel a slight bit of nausea in your stomach and sometimes people are really sick on the first time if they take a lot of it.' But it certainly did not act as an aphrodisiac. 'It makes your head feel very large and sounds are a bit more echoey and mellow, and it is very, very relaxing, that's all.'

Heroin can be taken in different ways – smoked, injected or sniffed up the nose, like cocaine and the amphetamines. When it is injected, rather than sniffed, this young man explained, the effect is more immediate – 'a rush of that complete spacey feeling'.

His descriptions helped me understand how the recent 'heroin explosion' began with the United States servicemen in the Vietnam war. For them, heroin was not the equivalent of a World War One official ration of whisky or rum to give them 'liquid courage' to clamber out of the trenches and charge at the enemy across a no-man's-land raked by gunfire. It was not 'the kick' that the drug gave that first opened this particular Pandora's box but rather the sensation of ease and contentment, and 'what the hell!'. 'The impact on American troops – most of them bored, frightened, resentful, ignorant – was immediate,' a US Army psychiatrist is quoted as saying in Dr David E. Smith and Dr George G. Ray's *Heroin in Perspective,* which reports that the first large influx of heroin to be introduced directly into American military units in Vietnam was in 1968 when a detachment of soldiers, coming from Thailand to South Vietnam to assist American combat forces, brought a supply with them.

'I just wanted to get out of Nam, and "scag" [US Army slang

for heroin] just took me out for a while at least,' related one soldier. A returning GI told army doctors: 'My first tour there in '67, a few of our guys smoked grass. Now the guys walk right in the hootch with a jar of heroin or cocaine. Almost pure stuff. Getting "smack" [another slang term for heroin] is like getting a bottle of beer. Everybody sells it. Half my company is on the stuff.'

And when US servicemen began to be pulled back from Vietnam in 1971 and the local dealers – all overseas ethnic Chinese – found their market vanishing, it was only natural that they should turn to two areas in particular – the domestic market in the United States where those servicemen originally came from (but where at that stage the Mexicans were already becoming entrenched) and to Western Europe, where there was another potentially lucrative market: the US servicemen stationed in West Germany. The Chinese had no existing links with which to seek to set up operations in West Germany but in Holland, just across the border, there were flourishing Chinese communities in Amsterdam and Rotterdam. That, plus the relaxed 'Do your own thing, man!' hippy-type philosophy already prevailing in Amsterdam made the otherwise seemingly unlikely Dutch an appropriate guest nation for this new outpost of the narcotics industry.

But what is not generally appreciated is that the heroin which was, in DEA jargon, 'the drug of choice' of the US servicemen in Vietnam and is still today the preference of addicts in the United States and of US servicemen abroad is not the same kind of heroin as that which is 'the drug of choice' in Western Europe or even in South-East Asia itself.

I had naively thought that heroin was simply heroin but there are, in fact, several different kinds, of varying strength and purity. It is like chocolate, which may be milk, plain, bitter, cooking chocolate, of good or poor quality.

The two main types of heroin are known as No.3 and No.4 depending on the source of supply. Mexican and Turkish heroin, for instance, is always No.4, i.e. a powder easily dissolved in water and, therefore, eminently suitable for injection. South-East Asian heroin can be either No.4, which is always white and hence is often called 'Chinese White', or No.3, which is not a powder but a sort of 'rocky' granular substance, popularly nicknamed 'Chinese Brown Sugar'.

No. 4 is virtually a 'pure' drug containing well over ninety per cent neat heroin (at least when originally manufactured) and is always more expensive than No. 3, which is a 'cocktail' of various chemicals with raw heroin merely serving as a base. The colour varies between light brown, grey and red, according to the mix of the 'cocktail' and, to the connoisseur, each specific kind of No. 3 has its own distinctive flavour. No. 4 heroin also has its own individual 'explosion in the head' depending on how much it has been adulterated.

The method of taking heroin also varies. No. 3, in all its varieties, is usually smoked – both in the Far East and in the Western world – so that its immediate impact, and indeed its deleterious effect, upon the human body is not so great as No. 4, if only because it does not enter direct into the bloodstream. No. 4, however, is nearly always injected direct into the blood supply: the addict 'mainlines it', as the jargon goes.

Incidentally, a Chinese addict, wherever he may be in the world, generally only smokes his heroin, and his 'heroin of choice' is usually No. 3. His probable way of smoking it is first to place a few grains of the drug on a piece of tinfoil, which is then heated over a candle. The smoke given off by the slowly warming heroin is then inhaled either through a paper tube, which is called 'chasing the dragon', or through a matchbox cover, which is called 'playing the mouth organ'.

Because No. 4 heroin is nearly always injected direct into the bloodstream, it tends to kill faster than any other form of the drug; although *any* heroin, taken with a needle, will kill sooner or later in accordance with its strength – unless somehow the addict can be persuaded to submit to treatment. And it is No. 4 heroin that was 'the drug of choice' for Americans in Vietnam and is still the preference of addicts in the United States now. A DEA man in The Hague explained the two major reasons for this. The first is historical – before 1972, when the Turkish government cracked down on illicit opium growing, it was Turkish heroin that was the major source of supply for the American domestic market and the Mexican heroin that largely took its place (along with *some* 'Chinese White') in the mid- to late-1970s was another variety of No. 4, attractive because of its strength and its easy solubility. The second reason is that the trafficker can make much greater profits from it.

'If you get [No. 4] heroin and you "cut" it, you can "cut" four or five times. That means you make four or five kilos out of one at no extra cost and at much greater profit.' This 'cutting' or adulterating by adding more caffeine or lactose may well mean that when heroin is finally bought on the streets it may be only four or five per cent pure.

Why many heroin users die, when they come to Holland, the DEA man told me, is because the 'heroin of choice' here and throughout Western Europe is No.3, which is much more difficult to cut than No.4 and so, although No.3 is usually only about forty per cent pure to start with, the strength of the heroin sold here is far greater than that back in the States. 'They buy the kind of No.3 that is most soluble in water, or they break it down themselves and then inject it. And, Jesus, it just blows them to pieces! It kills them outright.'

'Mexican Brown', although as its name implies a brown powder rather than a white, is, like South-East Asian No.4, injected direct into the bloodstream. After the Turkish supply dried up with the breaking of the 'French Connection', this became the 'heroin of choice' in the United States, but in the early 1970s, just before its emergence on the US market, there was a period of about two or three years when 'Chinese White' and 'Chinese Brown Sugar' flooded in to the West and East Coasts of the States. The DEA man reminisced about a street-level dope dealer during this period. To satisfy his customers, he had to sell them 'rocks' – 'Chinese Brown Sugar' – but he found that he could not make much money because he could not cut the rocks he was supplied with without being left with a lot of powder. His answer was to make a ball out of other things, put molasses or syrup over it or anything to give it a brown colour, then roll it in heroin. Junkies would stare in awe at this 'big rock', which he told them came from a heroin mine in a big mountain over in Asia somewhere! He was caught and given a fifteen-year prison sentence.

The Mexican heroin that came on to the United States home market by the mid-1970s was fairly strong, and popular for that reason. In response to this increasing illegal trafficking, the Mexican government with DEA backing began a successful eradication programme, hitting at its source in the Mexican poppy fields in the years 1976 to 1978. But as one door closes, another opens. As the DEA official magazine stated in 1979: 'While heroin availability in the United States has now reached its lowest point in the last ten years, we must understand current trends of the narcotics traffic in anticipation of importations from areas other than Mexico.' And to appreciate the enormity of the threat posed by those 'current trends of the narcotics traffic', some idea of the criminal mentality behind South-East Asian heroin trafficking is necessary.

2 Tricks of the Trade

The international heroin trade from South-East Asia has effectively been in existence for only about a decade and the escalation into a multi-billion US dollar enterprise has come only within the last few years. Yet the sophisticated, intelligent – and ruthless – minds of the trafficking bosses have already evolved a complex criss-cross of methods to get their illegal goods to the customer. These are no punk criminals but highly specialized operators with a style all their own. To the heroin trafficker, the drug is just another commodity like baked beans, except that it has the special attraction of its scarcity value. The fact that a single successful deal will almost inevitably result in the death of at least one person somewhere around the world is a matter of irrelevance.

As an ethnic group, the Chinese are extremely intelligent: not for nothing does Chinese civilization antedate the Western variety. Furthermore, like many other human beings, of whatever race, colour or religion, who live out their lives for the most part in almost intolerable circumstances of poverty and squalor, many of them possess a cold indifference to the sufferings of anyone not within their concept of 'family'. One's 'family' is all. Loyalty is owed almost exclusively to the natural family and to the extended 'family' of the original village or district of the town where one now lives. Amid the vast stretches of mainland China, loyalty and patriotism could not take in a feeling of brotherhood and love for those living 2000 miles away across unknown deserts and mountains, even though they might be of the same skin colour and belong, according to anthropologists, to the same overall ethnic group. This attitude to outsiders can become a streak of utter ruthlessness when allied to criminal endeavour.

Around the Haadyai area in southern Thailand in the early months of 1979, for instance, the authorities came across a particularly gruesome method of smuggling heroin across the border into Malaysia. Babies were kidnapped or occasionally bought from their parents – who were unaware of the real purpose of the buyers. The babies were then killed, their internal organs removed and their bodies stuffed with bags of heroin. Then they were carried over the border as sleeping babes in the arms of their affectionate 'mothers'.

Nor was that all. As a news item in the *Far Eastern Economic Review* specifies: 'The infants had to be less than two years old so that the long period of "sleep" did not seem unnatural, and they had to be used within twelve hours of death while the faces retained their colour.'

This chilling combination of brilliant planning and remarkable evil is shown in all three aspects of the heroin traffickers' 'tricks of the trade': couriers, routes and smuggling methods.

Let us first look at couriers: 'On every flight on which a courier is placed, there is generally a "controller" unknown to him flying as an ordinary passenger with no drugs on him and overseeing the operation,'says a Chinese-born DEA special agent in Hong Kong. 'The "controllers" are usually *Chiu Chao* Chinese out of Hong Kong, Singapore or Malaysia. They buy the ticket, they recruit the courier and pay him. They pay the hotel bill and all travel expenses. When it is a syndicate operating at both ends, they get the merchandise free from the supplier: they know each other, they trust each other absolutely. The supplier will usually have a connection of some sort or have someone to represent him at the destination. They get sixty per cent of the profit and the "controller" gets forty per cent – maybe they share it fifty/fifty.

'The "controller" is responsible for the operating costs – if a courier or anyone else along the line is caught, the "controller" pays for his family or his legal expenses out of his share of the profit.'

That may be so as a general rule but I have also been told of cases where 'controllers' have deliberately leaked information to the police or Customs service so that a courier has been arrested – to facilitate the passage through airline formalities of *another* courier on the same flight with a far more valuable package. 'And they'll even make a double profit on the deal by claiming an informant's "tip-off money" as well,' a British Customs investigator has told me.

Originally the South-East Asian heroin couriers were nearly always ethnic Chinese like the men running the syndicates behind them but the bosses have since learned that this was inadvisable: too many couriers were being arrested. 'So the pattern has changed. Nowadays there are no rules,' a British detective inspector whom I cannot name has told me. 'They will use anyone whose services can be bought by an air ticket to somewhere in the world they want to go – plus a very nice dollop of spending money into the bargain.

'It's not only Orientals. They now use more black and white people than they do their own. It's not even only young hippy types, perhaps addicts themselves, with an easy attitude to law-breaking. Don't you believe it! We've made arrests of nice respectable old-age pensioners, retired army officers and even one sweet old lady who badly wanted to get to Canada to visit her married daughter.'

Money may be the spur for joining the courier ranks, but some Triad organizations also provide a strong back-up incentive: *fear*. John Warner, DEA Regional Director in Paris, has told me how young, disaffected Westerners far from home in Kuala Lumpur, Malaysia, are brought into the gang:

'A young Dutchman or any Western European or American, with his rucksack, hanging around the streets of Kuala Lumpur, sleeping in a hostel, can be spotted and approached by someone. The initial approach will be very simple, "Hello! How are you?" Friendly, without any actual identification, just to find out where he's going, where he comes from, what his plans are. Then this person will perhaps drop a hint: "Well, you know, if you're short of money and you don't know how you are going to get back would you like to make some money taking a little package with you?"

'They get the kid listening to them. Then they say: "If you're interested, we'll contact you." Then later the person is told, either through a note or by telephone: "Be at a certain place at a certain time." This may be a motel room or a hotel room. "Take your passport with you and just ask for the key to room so-and-so at such-and-such a place, and go up to the room".'

Then it becomes like a scene from a spy film. The youth takes his passport with him to the hotel or motel, gets the key to the numbered room and finds it completely empty except that on the bed is a blank form with typewritten questions on it and a plastic folder lying beside it. John Warner gave me a copy of this form:

Important notice: Before you fill in this form, make sure that you (i) intend to carry out this venture of your own free will and that you are willing to face any results that will occur, (ii) that all particulars given below are correct for we shall check them thoroughly and if found to be untrue, the consequences will be very serious.

Full name: _____ Sex: _____

Full home address: _____

Other addresses where we can contact you: _____

_____

Telephone No.   _____

International Passport No.   _____

Who recommended you: _____

Present age: _____ Identity Card No. & Colour: _____

Your next of kin address: _____

Answer the following questions (Yes or No):

    a) Can you read instructions and maps in English?   _____

    b) Are you willing to travel to any part of the world?   _____

    c) Are you willing to take a test to prove your ability?   _____

    d) Have you been in this venture before?   _____

    e) How much do you expect to gain per venture? M$ _____

    f) Are you willing to pay M$200 to join this venture?   _____

    g) Are you at present a member of the police and/or Customs?   __

    h) Are you willing to accept our terms (free transport to and fro, accommodation, general expenses, food and drinks and an agreed fee) for this venture?   _____

_____

Usual signature

Instructions:

Fill this form correctly, fold it up and leave it here with your international passport, identity card, your recent photograph for our checking, inside the plastic wrapper. They will be returned to you soon. Wait for instructions, you may leave now. Good luck.

Notice the chill behind those opening words: 'We shall check [all particulars] thoroughly and if found to be untrue, the consequences will be very serious' and the quiet menace of the final: 'Wait for instructions, you may leave now. Good luck.'

'These organizations have the power to back up those words,' says John Warner. Once the youth has filled in the form and left his passport, he is locked into a system from which only rejection as 'unsuitable', due performance of his duties – or arrest can release him.

'They'll contact him after they've checked him out,' says Mr Warner, 'and if he's OK, they'll say: "Go to such-and-such a place and pick up a suitcase that'll be waiting for you", or they'll give him the money and tell him to buy a suitcase of a particular kind for himself, which they will then adapt to their own purposes with a double-bottom or whatever. In some way, they'll get the stuff to him and prescribe their own method of concealment.'

How much will the youngster be getting for all this? 'A girl or a fellow bringing in stuff from Malaysia by air to Europe will usually get his ticket paid plus up to £10,000 [US$20,000] depending on how much they are bringing in. They'll be given an advance payment when they are handed over their airline ticket with the balance payable on delivery of the merchandise.

'On a large shipment, there are sometimes two or three couriers. In a case in Vienna, there were as many as ten – to cover themselves should any one or more couriers get stopped.

'The "controller" will fly with the courier, although he is totally unknown to him, of course, and he'll keep an eye on him and will make the arrangements at the other end for him to be contacted. He'll have been given a telephone number perhaps which he has to call, or, say, if he arrives at Charles de Gaulle airport in Paris, he'll be told to get a cab and go to the Gare du Nord and take a train to Amsterdam and when he gets to Amsterdam he's got to call a certain number. The permutations are infinite.'

Originally, there would only be one courier who would make the entire journey from South-East Asia to his ultimate destination but nowadays that has changed. Often, on a major consignment, there will be a network of couriers: one taking the stuff into Zurich by air who then hands over to someone who takes it by train to Frankfurt who then hands it over to someone who takes it by car to Amsterdam.

It is a never-ending game. When in 1976 a vigilant-eyed Soviet Customs officer made his first seizure of South-East Asian heroin at Moscow airport *en route* to Rome from, of all places,

Japan, it may well have been a matter for considerable congratulation. But one wonders for how long that particularly circuitous route had been in existence before – and just how often it has been used since, with perhaps the original point of departure South Korea or the Philippines instead of Japan.

And, of course, the air passenger courier is only part of the network. Seamen, and again not necessarily only ethnic Chinese seamen, have been couriers of illegal narcotics ever since the whole business started centuries ago with the original opium trade.

As for the routes, they have changed, changed again and changed back many times over in recent years. Says the DEA special agent in charge at The Hague office: 'There is a constantly altering pattern to their routes. We see this in the interrogation of their couriers after arrest. They tell us that it's not only drugs control that has made them chop and change their airports. It's also police anti-terrorist activity, which has zapped up security at some airports.

'Then it also depends to some extent on the time of year. Spain and Italy are very popular, for instance, in the summer as points of entry to Europe because of the seasonal boom in tourist travel.' They choose their time of day carefully as well. With the best will in the world, Customs officers shortly before going off duty at the end of a night shift are not likely to be as vigilant as those at the start of a new morning shift.

The syndicates adapt to their advantage every fresh development in methods of transportation. Hr Jan van Straten, head of the Dutch Central Criminal Intelligence Unit, says: 'One can be sure that using containers as a means of smuggling from Asia to Europe by ship has been done in the past several times already and will be done in the future more and more. As far as Holland is concerned, it will be very difficult to discover when containers are used for smuggling without reliable information, Rotterdam being the biggest seaport in the world. Predictable targets in container smuggling in Europe are major seaports in France, Belgium, Holland, the United Kingdom, West Germany and Scandinavia.'

Says the DEA special agent in charge at The Hague: 'I think the Chinese are beating the pants off us in Rotterdam. They are sending in great consignments, and it's not only the containers. The other day, a guy got caught with a package out of Penang –

PART II

Triads in South-East Asia

3 Triad Origins

Mainland China comprises 3,657,765 square miles and has an estimated population of no less than 973 million people, a territory and a population so vast that it is impossible to talk about 'the Chinese' having racial or national characteristics in the same way as Westerners might talk of the French, German or English. Mandarin is the 'official' language but the people of China speak a myriad of dialects split up into ethnic groups spread out over the whole area of the subcontinent, with many totally different tongues spoken even within the confines of one of the twenty-nine provinces of the modern state. The climate is equally varied, from an annual rainfall of four inches in Kashgar in the north-west to eighty-five inches in Hong Kong, and from a January average temperature of $-21\,°C$ in Harbin in the north to $13\,°C$ in Canton in the south.

When most Westerners think of the 'Chinese', they are, in fact, thinking of those people who come from only two of China's provinces – those of Kwangtung and Fukien in the south-east of the subcontinent. The reason is that these are the two major coastal provinces of southern China where the four principal migrant ports of Amoy, Swatow, Kiungchow and Hong Kong were situated in the second half of the nineteenth century, the time when the great wave of peaceable Chinese emigration occurred.

It is not without significance to an appreciation of the Triads and of their history, both in mainland China and overseas, to discover that their origins lie in Fukien, one of those two southern gateway provinces to the outside world.

Just as the Mafia was founded by Giuseppe Mazzini in Palermo, Sicily, in 1860 as a guerilla force to drive out a foreign ruler and unite with mainland Italy in the name of patriotism and liberty, so the earliest Triad Societies came into existence in Fukien province in the latter part of the seventeenth century as valiant resistance fighters against the alien oppression of the Manchus, 'barbarian' tribesmen who had swept across the Great Wall of China and in 1644 defeated the ruling native Ming Dynasty of Emperors to set up their own Ch'ing Dynasty.

For the first forty years after they had established their capital at Peking, the Manchus controlled only the northern half of China. In the south, they faced resistance, rebellion and hatred; and legend dates the founding of the first Triad Society to a militant group of 128 (some historians say 108) Buddhist monks at a monastery near Foochow in Fukien province in 1674.

Their monastery was a rallying-point against the Manchus and the monks practised a highly specialized form of physical self-defence that they had perfected for themselves: they called it Kung Fu. (The same form of combat is equally highly valued by the Triads today: the Triad Society member whom I interviewed in my hotel room in Hong Kong in October 1978 was a Kung Fu specialist and told me proudly that he owed his comparatively high position in his Society – as a 'Red Pole' or 'Enforcer' – to his prowess at Kung Fu. Alongside his Triad activities, he also earned a legitimate existence as a stunt man in Kung Fu films and, when I asked for some beer to be brought up to my room for us, he gave me an impressive *machismo* demonstration of Kung Fu fitness by biting the metal tops off the bottles with his teeth!)

But skill at Kung Fu was not enough to save the noble monks of the Foochow monastery. According to legend, the then-reigning Ch'ing Emperor sent armed troops to destroy them. One monk proved a traitor and only eighteen of his brethren escaped alive. They were hunted down until only five were left, and it is these five who are credited with founding, under the slogan 'Overthrow the Ch'ing and restore the Ming', a secret society that has been variously named the Heaven on Earth Society, the Hung Mon or Hung League (from 'Hung', the name of the first Ming Emperor) and the Triad Society, from its symbol, an equilateral triangle with its three equal sides representing the three basic Chinese concepts of Heaven, Earth and Man.

Secret societies have long played an integral role in the history of China. 'The officials draw their power from the Law, the people from the Secret Societies' is an old Chinese saying. But of all the many societies that have existed, none has wielded greater power than the Triad group of societies. They are mentioned in nearly every history book of the Chinese peoples. With great bravery, they led many abortive uprisings against the Manchu Emperors, all put down with even more than usual Oriental ruthlessness.

Their members were bound together by an intricate system of secret rituals, oaths, passwords, ceremonial intermingling of their blood. They really were a brotherhood, and a brotherhood for freedom. But even from earliest times, there was also a darker side to their activities. As Professor Stanford M. Lyman writes in his book *Chinese Americans*:

Secret societies also attracted adventurers to their ranks. Those who felt that the legitimate avenues to wealth or power were blocked against them or too slow to suit their ambitions found that thievery, extortion and the control of vice offered advantages. Much of the gambling, robbery and prostitution enterprises in China and in overseas Chinese communities were under either the direct ownership or the tributary control of secret societies. A career was possible in a secret society – either a brief, exciting life of adventure and thrills or, if fortune smiled, the chance to overthrow the empire itself and participate in the establishment of a new dynasty.

The political activities of secret societies have been a basic factor in the establishment of dynasties and in the political fortunes of the republic. In Imperial China, the secret society was the principal instrument for the expression of political grievances. Angered and alienated peasants, workers and ex-officials would form a society of outlaws or join an already existing one. The popularity so often enjoyed by these bandits stemmed from their actual or imputed identification with the impoverished masses and their opposition to Imperial subversion of local institutions and customs.

As a body of mercenary thugs, secret societies were often used to make sure that peasants and other exploited poor, such as artisans, craftsmen and petit shopkeepers, did not translate their accumulated grievances into armed violence. In the cities of China and in the overseas Chinese settlements secret societies 'protected' the various kinds of vice and crime that thrived among homeless sojourners.

Even so, it was – on the whole – a tale of honour. When in 1842 the British established the Crown Colony of Hong Kong over the tiny island bearing that name in the delta of the River

Pearl, facing the second 'gateway' province of Kwangtung, they found Triad Societies already active there: driven by Manchus into the extremities of the sprawling reaches of the mainland. There was a surge of opposition to the British by the local Chinese population and Hong Kong quickly became an even more fertile breeding ground for Triad Societies. In 1845, only three years after the arrival of British rule, there were already laws which made them a proscribed organization – which they still are to this day.

As Chinese communities from the two southern gateway provinces, fleeing oppression and poverty, spilled out into the adjoining reaches of South-East Asia and migrated across the Pacific to the West Coast of the United States and Canada, they took their Triad Societies with them. And again, even in those early overseas days, there was a black side to their activities. Victor G. and Brett de Bary Nee write in *Longtime Californ'*:

> One of the most powerful of the secret societies in Kwangtung province, the Triad Society, took part in the devastating and unsuccessful Taiping Rebellion (1851–64). Members of the Society led a series of rebellions known as the 'Red Turbin Uprisings' in the Pearl River delta between 1854 and 1864. After the suppression of the Taiping rebels, Triad members became involved in illegal activities, such as piracy and smuggling. Some fled to America, where they established branches of the Triad Society known as the Chee Kung Tong. There are scattered reports of Chee Kung Tong extortion attempts in the early 1850s and of feuds between rival branches of the secret society for spheres of influence.
>
> Along with its illegal activities, however, the Chee Kung Tong remained dedicated to its political goal of the overthrow of the Manchus' Ch'ing Dynasty and the restoration of the Ming Dynasty, and continued to function as an international revolutionary network.

When in 1911 the Manchus were at last deposed and, in the following year, the Westernized Dr Sun Yat Sen proclaimed the modern Republic of China, it was entirely appropriate that Sun Yat Sen should himself, according to his biographer Harold Z. Schiffren, have been a 'Red Pole' enforcement officer of a Triad Society. The overseas Triad Societies had welcomed Dr Sun and provided him with their own centres as bases for his operations. The money for the new republic was even printed in San Francisco's Chinatown – with the Chee Kung Tong's blessing.

On 15 February 1912, Dr Sun visited the Ming Tombs at

Nanking and there made a public declaration to the deceased Emperors that the Manchus had been finally overthrown. This was the traditional Triads' finest hour: they had finally achieved the principal political objective for which they were originally created – but with their glory came also the beginning of their ultimate degeneracy.

The assistance given by the Triad Society to the Republicans [writes former Hong Kong police officer W.P.Morgan in his *Triad Societies in Hong Kong*] resulted in its virtual official recognition by the new government and, free from restrictions, it expanded to an even greater extent than before. Its power as a lobbying force became such that ambitious civic and military officials were usually bound to join the society in order to further their ends, and merchants and traders found membership and subscriptions to the society greatly eased their commercial ventures.

As power always corrupts, so the society became increasingly corrupted. It accordingly degenerated all the more easily into far-flung criminal organizations.

Sun Yat Sen's successor, General Chiang Kai Shek, also himself a member of an old-style Triad Society, in his long and finally losing battle against Mao Tse Tung Communism, relied heavily on Triad 'generals' and the support, money and power of Triad Societies and groups. As Superintendent John Morris, a young officer of the Royal Hong Kong Police seconded to Interpol, told me: 'As Chiang's control waned, so Triad power grew. The Triads were the strong-arm wing of his party, the KMT. They were used by Chiang for jobs his official army could not do.'

The most famous of these 'jobs' was the virtual massacre in one day in April 1927 of the Communist-led labour unions in the northern seaport of Shanghai, by then the country's largest and most modern city. Chiang Kai Shek had emerged as the commander of the new post-Sun Yat Sen Nationalist Army and had embarked on his famous northern campaign to establish the authority of the Nationalist KMT government over the Communists in northern and central China. The fall of Shanghai was essential to him. The city underworld was controlled at that time by a Triad Society called the Green Pang (the same notorious society later to be named in the 1963 Interpol circular) under a brilliant young villain named Tu Yueh Sheng, who had already built up a considerable reputation for himself as boss of an opium syndicate. Unable to rely on his own troops, many of whom were sympathetic to the Shanghai workers, Chiang met with Tu soon after he arrived in the city and, as a result, on the morning of 12 April 1927, thousands of Green Pang thugs stormed out of the French concession in Shanghai into Chinese sections of the city and began a reign of terror which ultimately decimated the Communist labour unions.

Tu was rewarded officially with the rank of major-general in the KMT Army and unofficially was allowed to consolidate his position as the 'Opium King' of Chiang Kai Shek's China. Alfred W. McCoy in his monumental study, *The Politics of Heroin in South-East Asia,* quotes a Chinese historian as commenting: 'Perhaps for the first time in Chinese history, the underworld gained formal recognition in national politics.' The Triads became the strong-arm men of Chiang Kai Shek's rule: generals, soldiers, intelligence workers, villains, gangsters, drug traffickers, businessmen, murderers, a mixture of the honest and the criminal. They and many thousands more of Chiang's supporters fled when Mao Tse Tung and his Communist party finally crushed Nationalist power and in October 1949 formally inaugurated the People's Republic of China. Some joined Chiang in exile on the island of Formosa (Taiwan), many poured into the beleaguered, tiny colony of Hong Kong and some of the more fortunate sought refuge in the United States in the two leading Chinese communities of San Francisco and New York.

General Tu Yueh Sheng and his Green Pang Triads from Shanghai fled to Hong Kong, as did their greatest rivals in pre-Communist China for control of the vastly successful opium and to a lesser extent heroin traffic out of Shanghai, the Sun Yee On and Fuk Yee Hing Triads. The latter were of different ethnic origin from the Green Pang. They and five allied smaller Triad Societies came from the same comparatively small region of mainland China, the area around Swatow, a city about 170 miles up the coast from Hong Kong on the border between Kwangtung and Fukien provinces, and all were members of the same *Chiu Chao* dialect group. This was the group that as far back as the 1840s had moved into Shanghai, then the British centre of the opium trade, to obtain a slice of the very lucrative opium pie. It was also the *Chiu Chaos,* from their geographical

in Hong Kong in 1960, Police Commissioner Henry Heath wrote in the preface:

Of the approximately 3,000,000 inhabitants of Hong Kong it is estimated that about one in six is a Triad member. The vast majority are, of course, inactive members, but it should always be borne in mind that all organizations, however large, are normally controlled by small groups of active officials. The rank and file follow, willingly or otherwise, as directed by their leaders.

Legal enactments alone cannot destroy an organization of this magnitude. Haphazard arrests of individual members cannot seriously weaken the societies which are continually recruiting new members. All available resources must be concentrated on curbing its potential for evil and assisting to speed up its own process of self-destruction.

In the late 1960s and early 1970s there was a second wave of migrations from the Far East into the Western world: from Hong Kong, bursting at the seams with its post-1949 intake from mainland China, first to Britain and then, when immigration controls slammed the door in the face of many would-be entrants, to the Netherlands – where there was already a traditional link with the East from one-time Dutch rule in the East Indies – and later, as the United States eased its immigration controls in 1965 and Canada followed suit in 1967, to the old-established, traditionally law-abiding Chinatowns of North America.

Within the ranks of these legitimate and entirely honourable emigrants was, inevitably, a hard-core Triad criminal element: protection men, illegal gamblers, prostitute operators, loan-sharkers, racketeers, blackmailers – and drug traffickers. As Detective Chief Superintendent Raymond Kendall at Interpol headquarters points out: 'The Triads, though in so many ways different from the Mafia, are like them in this: if things are going slowly in other areas of organized crime, then they'll profit by whatever else is going. If drugs are available, they'll go into that.'

But how stands the record in Hong Kong? What has happened to the Triad Societies which the Hong Kong police chief himself admitted twenty years ago existed in his minute colony as a 'potential for evil'?

4 The Hong Kong Police and Triad Connections

There is nothing new about policemen who are fools – or crooks. The founder of the French Sûreté, Eugène François Vidocq, owed at least part of his brilliant track record in apprehending villains to the fact that he himself was the originator of many of the burglaries he so astutely investigated – a truth which eventually dawned on his colleagues. Corruption within a police force is certainly not unknown, as any informed person living in London or New York in the 1970s would testify, but the degree to which the Royal Hong Kong Police Force became involved in corruption – not only in accepting bribes from criminals but also in actually having major criminals within its own ranks – must make it a group of law enforcement officers unique in the annals of crime. It is somewhat embarrassing to write about this after having received a welcome fit for royalty on my arrival in Hong Kong, most efficiently organized by Drew Rennie, head of police public relations; a welcome, however, that seemed to me to become rather less royal when I began to ask awkward questions but which was always friendly and courteous.

Unlike other police forces in the world, the Royal Hong Kong Police Force is a law enforcement agency where I truly believe the real power lies not with the senior officers, resplendent in their bemedalled uniforms, puffing their pipes and lunching in a Mess beneath a large portrait of the British Queen, but with the lower ranks, the 'rank and file'. It is the tail that wags the dog. Out of the force's total established strength in 1977, the latest year for which I have official figures, 1809 were officers, of whom the overwhelming majority were white and mainly British, whereas the 'rank and file' constituted a staggering 16,770 of whom all were ethnic Chinese. No Caucasian, to use that unpleasant word, can hold any rank lower than that of inspector. These lower ranks are poorly paid, under-educated – and temptable. They do not even have to be born in the colony and only about ten per cent of them speak good enough English to qualify to wear a red tab on their sleeve indicating that they are English speaking.

Hong Kong may be a British colony but notions of colonial rectitude tend to have disappeared. When I lunched with Sir Donald Luddington, head of the Independent Commission Against Corruption, we went to the splendidly traditional Hong Kong Club. Because of an error, the table had not been booked and Sir Donald's enquiries failed to get us a place in the upstairs restaurant. (In fact we had a perfectly good lunch in the bar downstairs.) However, the next day I had lunch with a local lawyer, who also took me to the Hong Kong Club and who also discovered on arrival that no table had been booked – 'But not to worry. We've got our table. Just a little honest corruption!'

Another instance that gave me the flavour of the reality of existence in Hong Kong was when I went out one night with an anti-Triad action squad in the back-street clubs, bars and ballrooms of Tsim Sha Tsui, the main tourist area of downtown Kowloon. At about two o'clock in the morning, the Chinese sergeant at the head of the patrol pushed open the door to a ballroom on the first floor of a decrepit looking building and announced that this was a police raid. In the questioning that ensued, the Chinese manager of the ballroom became increasingly agitated by my presence. It turned out that he was an ex-policeman dismissed for corruption and was very suspicious of what I – an unknown white man – was doing raiding his club.

The first indication of any large-scale villainy in the force came in the late 1960s. As Alfred W. McCoy wrote in *The Politics of Heroin in South-East Asia*: 'While the police offensive [which began in the mid-1960s] in no way inhibited the growth of the narcotics trade, it made many Chinese police sergeants millionaires. The corruption was so pervasive that in August 1969 the mere hint of an anti-corruption campaign produced a wave of resignations by senior Chinese detectives and sergeants.'

One such resignation came from a staff sergeant named Lai Man Yau, then aged fifty-two and with a string of commendations to his credit after thirty-three years in the service. Two years later, in 1971, it was authoritatively estimated that his assets were worth US$5,850,000. Such is the nature of justice in Hong Kong even today that Lai was not arrested on a charge of having 'unexplained assets disproportionate to his official income' until January 1977 and when he was finally convicted in October 1978 he was jailed for only two years. Admittedly, he was also ordered to pay compensation to the Crown of HK$60,000,000 (about US$3,120,000) but inflation and shrewd investments as a 'merchant' over the years enabled him to pay over immediately a sum of HK$12,000,000 (US$2,340,000) and to promise the balance within a short time by arranging some mortgages on his property. And Lai was not even a major figure among the Chinese millionaire sergeants!

However, the world's attention was first brought to the quite astonishing degree of corruption within the Royal Hong Kong Police Force in July 1973 by the case of Chief Superintendent Peter Godber. 'What was new about Godber,' I have been told, 'is that he was the first high-ranking British police officer to take a leaf out of the Chinese sergeants' book and set up his own corruption network instead of just taking handouts from the Chinese.' The bubble of corruption finally burst when greed had seeped *upwards* from the lower levels to almost the highest. Godber was told that he was under suspicion for accepting bribes on a massive scale and would be given seven days in which to explain how he had acquired some £300,000 in various bank accounts. He was allowed to leave police headquarters, go home to collect his wife and their passports and get on the next plane to Britain.

In the following month came the news that Superintendent Ernest Hunt, a former Welsh policeman who had risen to command the colony's Murder Squad, had been charged under an anti-bribery ordinance that makes it an offence 'to maintain a standard of living above that commensurate with present or past official emoluments'. Hunt was charged as he lay in the private ward of a Hong Kong hospital and, when the magistrate remanded him on bail of HK$20,000 (£1,575), he is said to have produced the money from a bedside drawer in HK$500 bills.

Subsequently, Godber, extradited back to the colony from Britain, was jailed for four years on one count of conspiracy and on another of corruptly accepting HK$25,000, although I have been told that the real amount he stashed away was four million English *pounds*, not even Hong Kong dollars. Hunt was also jailed – for an amazingly lenient one year – for failing to give a satisfactory explanation of how he was able to spend HK$207,404 (£16,726) when his official income for that period was only HK$156,599 (£12,626).

Walter Easey, a member of the Hong Kong Police Force from 1962 to 1968, two years of which he spent in its Anti-Corruption office (who incidentally openly admitted that he was the secretary of a private 'Hong Kong Research Project' aimed at ending British domination in the colony), told me in London: 'The apparent suddenness of the surfacing of Triad violence in Western capitals *circa* 1974 occurred as the worldwide co-ordinating centre for Triads – a group of about forty senior Chinese detectives in the Hong Kong Police – fled in the wake of the corruption purge that followed the scandal of Godber's escape and subsequent extradition. Themselves safe from extradition in hospitable Taiwan, they can no longer arbitrate inter-Triad disputes – most of all in the heroin trade – and matters once settled peacefully by courier or telex from Hong Kong are dealt with locally by the boot and the gun.'

Unbelievable? Let us look at such pointers to the truth as are available. The following two extracts are from the 'Hong Kong Narcotics Report for 1977' prepared in 1978 by the Action Committee Against Narcotics, the government's sole advisory instrument on all policy matters relating to the eradication of drug trafficking and drug abuse:

During the year under review, the Narcotics Bureau continued to maintain its efforts against major syndicate heads and their organizations resulting in the smashing of Hong Kong's last major drug syndicate. By the end of 1977, Hong Kong could legitimately claim that it had neutralized all the established large drug syndicates within its territory. . . .

In August 1977, the Narcotics Bureau took action against the last remaining large narcotics syndicate. The success of breaking up this syndicate was the result of several years' investigation and preparation of evidence. This syndicate, which was one of the biggest drug distribution rings in Hong Kong between 1960 and early 1970 was believed to have sold multi-millions worth of opiate drugs to local users. Up until 1973, the syndicate was a major importer of bulk consignments of narcotics into Hong Kong. Police pressure then disrupted the syndicate's established operations. On the day when operations were mounted against this syndicate, the police raided over twenty-nine addresses in various parts of Hong Kong. In all nine persons, including two syndicate heads, and seven high ranking members were arrested. They were jointly charged with conspiracy to deal and traffic in dangerous drugs between 1969 and 1973. Committal proceedings against the defendants were completed in December 1977 and their case is currently pending trial in the Supreme Court.

This is a superb story of painstaking investigation and imaginative police work. But what has actually happened to the case 'currently pending trial in the Supreme Court'?

For a start, the No. 1 leader of this allegedly 'last major drug syndicate' was not even arrested. This man, Ma Sik Yu, had built himself into a multi-millionaire in just fifteen years. Introduced to the heroin business in the mid-1960s by a fellow *Chiu Chao*, he rapidly became a leading operator. In Thailand, where he organized massive shipments of heroin for delivery to Hong Kong, he was known as 'Bear Siku' and by thousands of junkies and small-time dealers as 'White Powder Ma'. He eventually used his enormous illegal profits to gain respectability through investment in legitimate enterprise and when he heard – *how?* – in February 1977 of police inquiries homing in on his syndicate, he slipped out of Hong Kong and sought shelter in Taiwan.

Taiwan has become notorious as a safe haven for criminals fleeing from justice in Hong Kong. 'The Isle of the Fugitives' was how the *Hong Kong Standard*'s chief crime reporter described it in a series of articles in October 1978. Taiwan, under its all-powerful president, Chiang Ching Kuo, son of the late Chiang Kai Shek, has no extradition treaty with Hong Kong; the KMT, the former Nationalist ruling party in pre-Communist mainland China, has always been the governing political party in what is still juridically the 'Republic of China', and seldom, if ever, does any major fugitive from justice in Hong Kong receive anything but token difficulties at the hands of the Taiwan authorities. Ma Sik Yu is reported to be enjoying life in his new home and there is not the slightest prospect of his being sent back to answer the warrant for his arrest that was issued only *after* his sudden departure.

Of the nine men who actually were arrested, the two most important were Ma Sik Chun, the syndicate's No. 2 leader and Ma Sik Yu's younger brother, and Ma Woon Yin, the third in command and the nephew of the first two. Ma Sik Chun is a flamboyant, highly popular character among the Chinese in the colony. With moneys earned through trafficking in heroin, he founded and ran Hong Kong's largest daily Chinese-language newspaper, *Oriental Daily News*.

A fifty-man police squad was deputed to keep 'strict surveillance' on all nine men. Their passports were taken, their names went on a stop-list at Kai Tak airport and at the seaports, but none of that prevented three of the major defendants jumping bail in July 1978 and getting away safely to Thailand. Then in September 1978, just one week before the trial was due to start in Hong Kong's Supreme Court, the two Mas themselves, uncle and nephew, released some nine months earlier by a magistrate on the somewhat inadequate (in their terms) bail of HK$1.5 million, followed suit and – despite police surveillance supposed to have been stepped up since the July escapes – managed to creep unnoticed out of their homes at around midnight. While a full moon shone over the harbour on what was appropriately the day Hong Kong celebrated its Moon Festival, they stepped aboard a Panamanian-registered vessel bound for Taiwan and headed to a joyful reunion with their older relation and leading partner in crime.

The chairman of the Hong Kong Bar Association protested: 'To suggest that an immensely wealthy man could be expected to stand trial for what could mean life imprisonment, simply because he is [unlikely] to forfeit HK$500,000 and two sureties of the same amount is an absurdity. . . . A case like this makes us out to be the laughing-stock of the world.' He called for a government inquiry into the Mas' arrest – a request which, in the words of the *Far Eastern Economic Review*, was 'flatly refused'.

That left four defendants actually available to go on trial. Of those four, the most important was a fifty-four-year-old Chinese businessman, said by prosecuting counsel to be the 'top executive responsible for making arrangements'. He was acquitted by a predominantly Chinese jury: 'Cheers as accused in drug case goes free,' reported the *South China Morning Post*. The only men to stand trial and be convicted were the three least important figures. Even the prosecuting counsel admitted in court that they were not top-level organizers but merely helped in the smuggling of the goods. And eleven months later even their convictions were quashed on appeal. So none ended up in custody at the end of the saga.

The situation becomes even more ironic, however, when one learns that in June 1979, some two years after the Ma syndicate had supposedly been smashed, the *South China Morning Post* reported in Hong Kong: 'A leading member of a drug syndicate allegedly headed by drug kingpin Ma Sik Chun has been arrested in Bangkok in connection with the smuggling of HK$1.5 million worth of heroin to Hong Kong.' The leading member was none other than fifty-one-year-old Cheng Ah Kai, one of the three major figures who jumped bail in July 1978 and got away successfully to Thailand where, clearly, he had continued in business. The newspaper report quoted the Thai police describing him as 'a strong-arm man [in this context, this usually means a Triad Society 'Red Pole' office-bearer, No. 426 in the hierarchy] of the Ma syndicate involved in arranging fishing junks to collect drugs', a revival of the old Thai trawler-traffic into the colony – Hong Kong policemen had assured me this was dead! Cheng had been picked up, in a joint DEA–Thai police operation, together with seven other ethnic Chinese, including three Taiwan crewmen, shortly before a Panamanian-registered freighter was due to set sail for Hong Kong.

The report confirmed what several people had already told me; that the Ma syndicate is alive and well and still operative, and that it has simply moved its power base to Taiwan.

And how does all this tie in with millionaire ex-police sergeants since none of the Ma family members and none of the seven non-family members arrested by the Hong Kong authorities were policemen or ex-policemen? The answer is simple: one of the charges against the syndicate's No. 2 leader, the young Ma brother, was that of conspiring with a man named Lui Lok, described tersely as 'not in custody', to deal in dangerous drugs between mid-June and 31 December 1968. At that date Lui Lok was a Chinese station sergeant, with a first-class official record and a Colonial Police Medal. He is now widely known to DEA special agents and other law enforcement officers throughout the world as perhaps the most notorious of all the Chinese ex-sergeant millionaires.

In January 1977 the magazine *Newsweek* called him 'the six-hundred-million-dollar man', for that is the staggering amount of his reputed wealth. In his later years in the Hong Kong police, the junior policemen called him 'Tai Lo' – the Chinese equivalent to the Mafia's 'Padrone', the 'Godfather'.

He fled from Hong Kong in November 1974, by then retired from the police, having received advance warning of the newly formed Independent Commission Against Corruption's increasing interest in his affairs. As with Ma Sik Yu, the warrant for his arrest was issued only after his departure. But unlike Ma Sik Yu, he fled not to Taiwan but to Canada, where he acquired substantial legitimate property holdings and, together with his four immediate associates, masterminded a fantastic escalation of the South-East Asian heroin traffic into Canada through the West Coast via Vancouver.

These four immediate associates, Choi Bing Lung, Chen Cheung You, Nam Kong and Hon Kwing Shum, were likewise millionaire ex-sergeants and collectively they were called 'the Five Dragons'. Canadian police activity eventually drove them out of Canada to seek ultimate refuge in the 'Isle of the Fugitives'. On 18 September 1978, two days after Ma Sik Chun and his nephew's successful flight from Hong Kong, Ma and his elder brother were reported to be seen dining in Taipeh, Taiwan's capital, with two ex-Hong Kong detectives, of whom one was Lui Lok. (This fascinating tit-bit of information comes from the *Far Eastern Economic Review* for 6 October 1978.)

The 'Five Dragons' are not the only ex-Hong Kong policemen to find a comfortable refuge and working base in Taiwan. In the mid-1970s, following the post-Godber anti-corruption purge, about forty senior Chinese detectives or ex-detectives sought sanctuary in that KMT outpost. Some jumped bail and were never convicted of anything; others were tried and found guilty and *then* fled.

How effective is the fight against corruption and criminal rackets in Hong Kong? After the furore of the Godber case, responsibility for investigating corruption was transferred from the anti-corruption branch within the police itself to an independent Commission answerable directly to the governor. In the Commission's Annual Report for 1978, Sir Donald Luddington stated: 'At the end of the year, there was still no evidence of the existence of any major corruption syndicate. However, this represents only a tactical victory for there is all too much evidence of small groups of officials, both in the police and in other departments of government, co-operating to extort money from people they should either be serving or dealing with in accordance with the law. It is rather as though after some set-piece, battles one side had decided to resort to guerilla warfare.'

Similarly, Police Commissioner Roy Henry told me during my visit: 'By about April 1977 we had reached the stage whereby we had broken up syndicated corruption, so far as the police were concerned, and we had created a new atmosphere of trust and accountability.'

These are the official versions of the situation. But there is also an unofficial version, given to me by two of Mr Henry's junior officers.

First, a young British detective inspector: 'The spirit of Peter Godber is alive and well. Corruption is still going on. It always will be. You can't put an end to it. The ICAC did a good job to start with but it's all fizzling out.

'The NB [Narcotics Bureau] have done some very good things in the last few years, there's no doubt about it; but they are wildly overstating things when they claim that they have smashed "the last of the big syndicates" and all that. The Fairy Queen has not come back to Fairyland. Only a few weeks ago, there was a seizure of twenty pounds weight of heroin. How can there be a twenty pounds weight seizure if the big days are over?

'Do the upper echelons know what is going on? Of course, they know but they won't tell you about what they know because they don't know what sort of a book you are going to write. I talk to you frankly because I don't want bullshit – plus the fact that I may well be out of the police force by the time your book appears. . . . I don't want a cover-up.

'If someone came up to you and said they'll give you $5000 to go and arrest someone, you'd tell him to fuck off but if he said, "I'll give you $25,000 if you don't arrest me," you do stop and think. Especially, when you're in a force where you know people with far more years' seniority than you have done exactly that. Besides, if you decide to say "No", who do you report it to? Do you report it to your senior officer, who may be on the take?

'It got to such a stage during the really bad days of corruption [that as] a young inspector just passed out of training school, you walk into your office, sit down, open your drawer and there is a brown envelope. You open it up and inside you'll find $1000.

'If you go to your [Chinese] station sergeant and you say, "What's this? I'm not having this. I'll make a report.", he will immediately say, "Right, this one goes out!" Next thing you know, you'll find yourself transferred to some bloody awful, one-eyed hole out on the Border.

'But if you say nothing about it and you take the brown envelope, next week, and every week after that, there'll be another brown envelope in your desk drawer. No questions. Nothing is ever said about it. You'll never find who bloody put it there in the first place anyway!

'Nowadays those little brown envelopes are beginning to come back.'

I asked how one knew which favours to give, what to do for one's money. He replied, 'It works like this. You're an inspector and I'm a detective sergeant: "Sir, we should release this man. We haven't got enough evidence on him." "Yes, sergeant," you say, without looking at any of the evidence against him.

'Or I come up to you and say, "Excuse me, sir. I've got an informant who has got some good information on a murder in Mong Kok [a district in Kowloon Town], can you get the whole squad together?" You agree and we all go racing down to Mong Kok, the whole lot of us. Then I say, "You stay here, sir, with the men and I'll just nip across to that grocery store and have a word with my informant."

'I dash across, see my informant, who is not really my informant but the man I am squeezing, and I say, "My DI [detective inspector] is across the road, see him!" – and I point to where you are standing amiably around with about fifty detective constables – and I say, "That's the full squad over there. My DI says he wants $5000 now. If you don't have $5000, they're coming straight in."

'Of course, I've chosen my place well: it's where there's some trading in DD [dangerous drugs] going on, or something like that, so the terrified storekeeper hands over $5000 in cash.

'I pocket it, walk back across the road to where you're standing and say, "I'm sorry, sir, the information was inaccurate. The man we're looking for was here yesterday. We may get him next time." You say, "Oh, fair enough, never mind. Let's call off the operation," and we all go back to the station.'

Second, another young detective inspector: 'Oh, sure, you'll read in the newspapers nowadays about policemen being arrested for corruption. But it's all small-scale. I've arrested "rank and file" members myself for soliciting a thirty-dollar bribe or being in possession of very small amounts of DD. Maybe it's confidential but rubbish confidential!

'Seventy-five per cent of the officer rank, apart from the Chinese officers and a precious few of the others, can hardly speak a word of Chinese. They never bother to communicate with the rank and file. They never get to know them. If only they did, they would get to know a great many more things about what's going on in Hong Kong.

'OK. I agree with you that some senior people in the force are so straight they just cannot think in terms of anyone else in the force not being straight. I accept that – but some of them don't *want* to know what's going on. It's a nine-to-five job or an eight-hour shift to them, and that's it. After that, they're out drinking and they don't want to know about the rank and file or what they're up to. They don't really care.

'I can tell you another thing too. ICAC were told to submit a report on all the established gambling places on Hong Kong island and TSB [Triad Society Bureau] were also asked to submit a report on the same thing. ICAC's list turned out to be far bigger than TSB's list, so they picked one of the ICAC's addresses, which TSB didn't have, to make a police raid on – and who did they arrest? Twenty or so police officers, including a station sergeant from Special Branch, DC's [detective constables] from various divisions and a sergeant from TSB itself!'

I do not believe that these are just the views of two biased young men. They struck me as sincere police officers with their feet very much on the ground. Indeed, the last incident had an intriguing echo some sixteen months later. In February 1980, the *South China Morning Post* carried a news item about a police raid on a restaurant in Kowloon where nine men 'suspected to be key members of the Sun Yee On Triad Society', who were trying to monopolize multi-million dollar design contracts in a large new housing complex, were arrested and taken to police headquarters for questioning – where 'it was then found out that three of them were police constables'.

In fact, the two young detectives' view of reality is supported for me by other 'straws in the wind'. For example, in May 1976 Superintendent Douglas Lau, then (at twenty-nine) the youngest serving superintendent in the Hong Kong Police Force and one of the highest-ranking Chinese officers, made a 'top secret' visit to London to see the head of the Metropolitan Police

Drugs Squad, Superintendent Fred Luff, who wanted to try and understand more of the nature of Triad involvement in London's blossoming trade in South-East Asian heroin. When Lau arrived at Heathrow, a British press photographer was already waiting for him – news of his departure had been leaked from within the Hong Kong Police to the local press. When I asked the likeable Douglas Lau in his Hong Kong office how news of such a highly confidential visit could have leaked from this building, all he could do was make a sad gesture with his hands and give me an even sadder smile.

Another 'straw in the wind' blew my way after my long session with a Triad 'Red Pole' in my hotel room in Hong Kong. He had been brought there by a detective inspector and a sergeant and I was due to have dinner alone with the inspector afterwards. However, it turned out that the sergeant and the Triad joined us and I asked the inspector if it would not blow the cover of the Triad (he doubled as an informant for the police) to be seen in public with two policemen. 'Quite the opposite. It will give him tremendous "face" – and you know how important that is out in the East – because they won't think that he is in *our* pocket, they'll think we are in *his*!'

The truth is that there are two police forces in Hong Kong within the one force. There are the young men as against the old men and there are the young men and the old men as against the Chinese. The Chinese 'rank and file' corrupt their officers and it is not necessarily restricted solely to Caucasian officers. Chinese sergeants and station sergeants have themselves been criminals of a major order, connected with the Triads and in some cases being outstanding Triad leaders. And it is the Triad ex-policemen of Hong Kong who are at the heart of some of the international activities of their criminal comrades. It is against this background that the following chapter on Triads in Hong Kong should be seen.

5 Hong Kong Triads Today

In 1956, serious political riots broke out in Hong Kong. They were particularly violent and, although the Triads did not start them off, they exploited them to the full. After the riots, Hong Kong police formed a specialist Triad Society Bureau within the Criminal Investigation Department, and shortly afterwards the back of the Triad movement was broken by arrests, imprisonment and deportation. Within two or three years, their organization was shattered and the formerly well-defined structure, chain of command, loyalty, secrecy and discipline all disappeared.

This quote is from an article written by Superintendent John Morris of the Royal Hong Kong Police when he was posted to Interpol as head of the drugs subdivision. Copies of the article were sent to many national police forces throughout the world – I received mine from Detective Chief Superintendent 'Algy' Hemmingway at New Scotland Yard, head of the British Central Drugs and Illegal Immigration Intelligence Unit.

Impressive figures of this 'success story' were quoted to me many times during my visit to Hong Kong in the autumn of 1978. In the five years following the 1956 riots, 10,500 suspected Triad Society members were arrested and 600 were deported.

However, this did not stop further 'Triad riots' breaking out in 1967. Like the earlier outburst, they were sparked off by political unrest but it was conceded officially that in the aftermath of the disturbances there was a fresh upsurge of Triad criminal activity, although that too, I was assured, was later successfully contained.

The supremely confident official line appeared in an article in *The Asia Magazine*, 29 December 1974, which reported that in July 1973, acting on orders to 'break the Triads once and for all', the entire 20,000-strong Hong Kong force participated in a long-range operation against them code-named 'Halam'. It was claimed that in the first two months alone, police swoops had picked up 500 persons accused of offences under the anti-Triad ordinance and 1200 persons were charged with other crimes. 'We can see this as a good thing,' Superintendent Norman Temple, then head of the Triad Society Bureau, was quoted as saying. 'One development we do not want is top Triad bosses getting together under any kind of monolithic leadership. We have them broken up now and we intend to keep them that way.'

These are strong words, impressive on the printed page. Alas, within two months of the article's publication, the first chink in the armour of official all-conquering rectitude appeared. Superintendent Temple – 'Nice chap, Norman. Bloody fool, that's all. He was tempted,' as one of his ex-colleagues put it – pleaded guilty in court to 'having control of assets disproportionate to his then present or past emoluments'. He was sentenced to one year's imprisonment, a comparatively lenient sentence that can be explained, at least in part, by him voluntarily returning assets totalling no less than £80,000 held in bank accounts outside Hong Kong. This was but another of the cases that revealed how far corruption had spread in official police circles in the late 1960s and early 1970s.

Whether one accepts or not the official claims that corruption, at least major syndicate corruption, has been eradicated, there has certainly been little change in the official line on Triad activity in Hong Kong. It continues to belittle the seriousness of Triad involvement in organized criminal activity and denies it completely on any international scale. The week that I arrived in the colony, Richard Quine, then Director of Criminal Investigations, admitted publicly at a dinner held by a local Lions Club that seventy per cent of all people sent to jail in Hong Kong during the previous year, 1977, had claimed a Triad affiliation and that as far as the police were concerned, Triads were Public Enemy No. 1. But he then added: 'Large cohesive and centrally controlled Triad Societies have gone, and now we have a multiplicity of small fluid criminal gangs which are potentially just as dangerous.'

On the narcotics scene, a similar picture was painted for me by Superintendent Leonard Hill, a former London policeman and second-in-command of the colony's Narcotics Bureau: 'There is no Triad control on drugs, as such. Where Triads are used in Hong Kong, they are at street level. The sellers look out for Triad fighters to protect them. There is a lot of hijacking that goes on in this business. The street seller with perhaps forty packets of heroin is quite likely to be knocked over the head and have his goods stolen by another seller. So to prevent this they all have their fighters with them.

'And always if you recruit fighters you must recruit the same Triad Society fighters. If you recruit from different Triads, you won't have an effective force. It's the same with look-outs. If you get a Sun Yee On fighter to protect you, then your look-outs will normally be Sun Yee On as well. That is as far as Triads' involvement in drugs extends – at a very low level. On the streets. There is no big crime organization behind anything.'

It was much the same story in Macao, the tiny Portuguese enclave sitting like a pimple on the face of mainland China, forty miles away across the delta of the River Pearl. I was met there by a stunningly pretty Eurasian police employee, Margharita, in tight blue jeans and pink denim shirt, whose boss turned out to be almost equally charming. Was this a deliberate public relations exercise to divert me from my research? The delightful senior Portuguese officer told me that in Macao, as in Hong Kong, Triads are now losing their ideological contacts and links. 'They try to be in legal businesses protected by their own members.' If it is a nightclub, a legal business, they will apply for a licence and everything will be running smoothly but, because they are afraid of another Triad asking them for protection money, they will get their own members to protect them. 'Sap Sie Kee [14K] was very big at one time in Macao – but now [it is] no problem. Ninety per cent of fights we have now are fights within the one Triad Society – between different groups of the same Triad Society.' They have lost all their power and all their contacts.

I had been told within the previous twenty-four hours by a Triad 'Red Pole' that because of increased police pressure in Hong Kong 'nearly all initiation ceremonies now take place in Macao because the Portuguese police do not know enough about Triads.' However according to the Portuguese police officer, there have been no reports of any initiation ceremonies or small meetings for a long time.

The *South China Morning Post* for 3 September 1978, some six weeks before I visited Macao, reported that one of the Chinese bosses of the vastly successful casino in the Lisboa Hotel, Macao, was seized by a 'mysterious bandit gang' and only released on HK$1,000,000 (about £100,000) being fetched from the casino in cash and handed over. It was 'believed that one of the gang is a former Hong Kong policeman who went to Macao and joined the casino in 1971. He lived in Sham Shui Po [a district of Kowloon] and has a criminal record.'

Back in Hong Kong, in the 1977 *Annual Review* of Hong Kong's Police Force, it was bluntly stated: 'During the latter part of the year an increasing number of reports appeared in the press regarding Triad activity in various countries. These gave the impression that Triad elements constitute a criminal syndicate of global proportions. This is sensationalism, and is simply not true.'

I was unable to speak directly to the Police Commissioner, then Mr Brian Slevin, about this, because he was in Panama attending Interpol's annual general assembly, but I was fortunate enough to see a copy of the official 'brief' he had taken with him, on the basis of which he was advising the free world's assembled police chiefs as to the allegedly true nature of Triad involvement in international criminality. This fascinating document, after re-stating the official viewpoint that Triad Societies in Hong Kong had degenerated into loose-knit groups of criminals, admits that, at the international level, ethnic Chinese out of Hong Kong and other areas of South-East Asia *had* become involved in criminal activity in Europe, the United States and Canada and, to a lesser extent, in Australia and other countries. Nevertheless, it maintains that it could not be accepted that any form of control, world-wide, existed over persons using the historical Triad name to assist their activities. Today's Hong Kong Triad gangs were too fragmented and insufficiently funded, it insists, to undertake operations on an international scale.

I was treated to more of the official line in my interview with the Chinese head of the Triad Society Bureau, Superintendent Peter So.

'Today, Triad Societies exist largely in name only. They have degenerated from strictly controlled, politically motivated organizations into loose-knit gangs of criminals which usurp the names of the Triad Societies of years past. The use of traditional rituals, to all intents and purposes, has disappeared. Most entrants come into the Triads today simply by "hanging the blue lantern", which is the name they give just to taking an oath – after the old idea that you hung a lantern outside a house when a death has occurred, to represent your being born again as a Triad.

'You must not think of a Triad gang as being something organized for a particular object – far from it!'

When I started to tell Mr So that, in Western Europe, the police authorities have found it absolutely impossible themselves to penetrate the overseas Chinese Triad communities, he twice interrupted me to say 'They don't have any!' and 'There is nothing to penetrate!'

This reaction is all the more surprising in view of the total evidence available and of what I myself discovered during my stay in Hong Kong.

At the very least, Mr So's statements seem to fly in the face of the 1963 Interpol circular and, indeed, the 1977 circular which warned of the outcrop of 'crimes of violence committed in various countries by offenders of Chinese origin (mainly from Hong Kong) against their compatriots. . . . In the murder cases, there was one case of vengeance involving two criminal organizations in Hong Kong (the 14K Triad and the Wo Li Kwan Triad Society).'

Furthermore, Commisaris Gerard Toorenaar of the Amsterdam police has written in *Communiqué*, the Drug Enforcement Officers' International Alumni Association's magazine: 'The recent growth of the Triads in the once peaceful and law-abiding Chinese community in Amsterdam has led to several murder cases and violent gang warfare believed to be related to gambling and drugs.'

What is going on? Who is kidding whom? I am not for one moment impugning the integrity of any of the Hong Kong police officers I have named but I can – and do – suggest that they are mistaken.

I do not question that seventy per cent of all crime in Hong Kong is committed by local Triad gangs or that, at the level of 'normal' everyday crime, they are a thorough and utter nuisance. I have been out myself round the resettlement estates and vast apartment blocks where scores of thousands of people live in circumstances so congested that they make the old-time Gorbals of Glasgow or New York's East Side seem holiday camps by contrast. I have heard tales from ordinary police officers 'on the beat' of resettlement blocks where young Triad gangs, still at school, fight literally 'border wars' to protect their territorial hold over one floor of a staircase. I have seen such gangs for myself, leaning over the staircase railings, staring defiantly at pólice patrols.

I have seen the Triad 'protectors' at work in ballrooms, gambling halls and massage parlours ('finger dancing' is how the massage in one darkened dive, supposed to be a ballroom, was called by one Chinese police sergeant with a sense of humour). I have seen the way in which, with easy arrogance, they keep watch like 'bouncers' in a Western discothèque – only they all wear sneakers instead of hard-soled shoes, because, as the Chinese sergeant told me, 'that is better for the martial arts'. I have seen street peddlers at work selling narcotics in doorways under the eyes of similar sneaker-footed youths as customers scurry past and make hurried, furtive purchases of tell-tale little packets.

I deny none of the pettiness of much of the crime committed by self-styled Triads in Hong Kong today, happy to cash in on the fear engendered among the local inhabitants by the very word 'Triad'. But is that the entire story? Is that all they are: 'fragmented gangs'? Or can they *also* be something else, something bigger, much more controlled, much better orga- nized – and having far-reaching consequences for the rest of us, thousands of miles away from that replica of Manhattan stuck on a rock just off mainland China?

Let us take the salient points of the official Hong Kong police's attitude and see how they stand up.

First, they claim that the traditional rituals, which enforced the secrecy and power of Triad Societies, have in effect disappeared. Even with the Hong Kong police, there are officers who do not necessarily go along with this 'party line'. I was given an account of a Triad initiation ceremony that took place on an off-shore lighter in May 1978 by Superintendent George Brooks at Kowloon Central Police Station on the mainland. He spoke with the approval and consent of his superior officer, Detective Chief Superintendent John Thorpe.

Two Chinese agents were infiltrated into a Triad Society,

after a suitable background had been built up for them in a poor class area – Triad Society ceremonies are extremely difficult for the police to detect and the Triad Society Bureau results have been almost non-existent for the last few years. The two men were told of the appointed day for the initiation ceremony and met at the location given, after which they were led to another, the off-shore lighter, where they and another four recruits were led inside by a man who acted as the Vanguard. A number of spectators were there, including some of the people who had introduced the men to the society. The Incense Master arrived to conduct the ceremony which in essentials differed little from the classic pattern described in Inspector Morgan's book.

A folded table was set up as an altar and a red piece of paper with writing on it – as a memorial tablet – pasted on the altar. A metal container with rice inside was placed before the altar and three flags – red paper with characters on them – were put in this.

'The three flags, translated literally, said: "Act on Orders"; the second: "Flag of the Army commander" and the name was given; the third flag was slightly more complicated: it signified the eighteen monks who escaped from the Siu Lam Monastery and a commemoration of the alleged day of the burning of the monastery on the first day of the sixth Moon. Another part of the characters on this flag signified the seventy days spent by the First Five Ancestors (the five monks that successfully fled the monastery) in fleeing from their Ch'ing pursuers and the last part related to the thirty-one battles fought by the First Five Ancestors against the Ch'ings.

'The initiation ceremony then commenced. The six new-comers were told to kneel on their left leg. The Vanguard then lit the joss sticks – a total of twenty-eight of them – and gave them to the Incense Master who, after citing some poems and words, put each joss stick into the metal container in front of the altar which contained the three flags: they call this the *Tau*. The Incense Master then told the recruits to follow, saying words to the effect that they went there voluntarily. After that, the recruits were given a joss stick to hold in both hands: four fingers left hand, five fingers right hand, with the lighted end pointing downwards. They were then told to dash the joss sticks onto the floor.

'The recruits then recited the thirty-six oaths – in much the same form as set out in Morgan's book – following the Incense Master. They were then each given another joss stick to dash the lightened end onto the floor as they had done before.

'The Incense Master then led them, and they followed him in saying words to the effect that, if brothers had difficulty, they should help them and not betray them. Then they were each given a joss stick again and told to do the same as before: the dashing of the joss sticks downwards, putting them out, signified that they would similarly be extinguished if they broke their oath.

'After that, the Incense Master tapped the back of the recruits with a kitchen chopper. It should have been a sword but they didn't have one! They were asked, "Which is harder, the sword or your neck?" and the recruits had to say, "My neck". This meant that even the threat of death would not cause them to reveal the society's secrets.

'After this came the pricking of the finger: the Incense Master pricked the left little finger of each recruit and told them to lick the blood and, after licking it, the recruits had to say, "It is sweet".

'A white piece of paper was then used with the words "Yellow gauze quilt" in Chinese characters on it. The six recruits crouched together and the Incense Master waved the piece of gauze above them saying some poems or words. He then taught the recruits to say:

(a) If they were asked whether they catch cold, they should answer "No, because they were covered by a blanket",

(b) If asked what blanket, they should answer "The three-cornered blanket",

(c) If asked why three corners, they should answer "One corner was burned when the Siu Lam Monastery was burned."

'The Incense Master then placed three pieces of red paper, each bearing one of the characters Ting, Hoi and Fau on the floor in a triangular shape. He then led the recruits to walk on these as if they were the stepping stones used by the First Five Ancestors to cross a river blocking their flight from the monastery.

'He then burned some paper on the floor and led the recruits to step over it, as if it were a fiery pit. They had to use their left leg first and he told them if someone told them that he would melt them or kill them, they should say that they could not be melted because they had stepped over "the fiery pit".

'He then gave a section of pear to each recruit to eat and gave them a bowl of water to drink. When they had done that, he drew a face symbolizing the traitor Ma Ning Yee on an egg – incidentally, they would normally have used a chicken but presumably they didn't have one in this case – and then the recruits put their right hand on top of the Incense Master's, who was holding the chopper, and he chopped up the egg, signifying that all traitors ought to die like that.

'Finally, he allotted each of them a number, which would be their number in the society. Each recruit had to give HK$10 to the Incense Master buying the number, they gave HK $1 to the *Tau* and HK$36 to their Triad protector. He was the person who had introduced them into the society and henceforth would be their protector, should they get into trouble. That would be his role: if, for example, they were out selling their wares as hawkers and somebody came up to them and demanded that they give him some money, they would mention the name of their protector and then the other party would go away or court a possible fight with this man.

'After that, everything was burned, including the paper and the flags and everything. But there was still one more thing to do. The Incense Master did not teach them any of the old Triad hand signals. That does not seem to happen any more. But he did give them to write down some of the Triad poems of that particular society so that they could in future use those poems as a method of identification with other Triad Society members.'

This account of a Triad initiation ceremony may seem like mumbo-jumbo to a Westerner, but there is no doubt that such a ceremony is still using the traditional rituals and is significant – and intimidating – to the Chinese recruit. 'I was scared,' a DEA informant undergoing a similar ritual in West Germany in 1979 told a DEA special agent, and a participant in a Triad initiation ceremony in a basement in London's Chinatown told Metropolitan Police Sergeant Bob Thomas in 1978, 'I felt very frightened by it'.

Second, the Hong Kong police claim that the 'hanging of the blue lantern' – the taking of an oath – is all that is required of most entrants to Triad Societies today. This is equally unconvincing. A 426 'Red Pole' introduced to me by a young detective inspector 'tired of all the bullshit' told me that 'hanging the lantern' simply means that a potential new Triad member is on probation. If he works out, there will always eventually be an initiation ceremony. 'And whenever you are promoted from being an ordinary member – more than just being a 49 – there will be a promotion ceremony as well, which is like an initiation ceremony all over again.'

Third, they claim that the two highest ranks, 489 and 438, in the Triad promotion ladder have fallen into disuse. Here again the evidence conflicts with this view. It was a 438, an Incense Master, who carried out the initiation ceremony just described, and the same detective inspector who did not like 'all the bullshit' told me on my visit in October 1978 that the 14K's new 489 had been elected two days previously. 'He's closely associated with loan shark operations, DD, gambling houses and massage parlours. The DD activity is selling: he's 14K remember. Importation is mostly done by the *Chiu Chao* groups.'

Fourth, they claim that 'Triads are just fragmented gangs'. The detective inspector thought that the 14K, the largest of all the local Triad Societies, *was* the most fragmented but he said that 'the others seem much more solid'. And I have seen confidential TSB and DEA memoranda which talk about over thirty active Triad Societies in Hong Kong.

But the fifth and perhaps most significant of all their claims is that there are no overseas Triad communities. That this is one of the greatest nonsenses of current policy mythology may be shown by just four instances:

1. In February 1977, the New York police raided the Flying Dragons' (a local Chinese youth gang's) clubhouse in Chinatown. They found a copy of the gang's initiation oath, which consisted of twelve points, including the following: 'I will obey the . . . Tong and if I do not, I will die under the condition of being shot'; 'The secret of the association must be kept and if I do not do this, I will be stabbed a thousand times'; and 'If the Tong comes into difficulty and I do not come to his aid, I will die by the electric shock or be burned by fire.' Changing the word 'Tong' for 'Triad', in what significant way do these oaths differ from those in Morgan's book – or those sworn by the Hong Kong Police Force's courageous undercover Chinese officers on that lighter in May 1978?

2. In September 1977, two London Metropolitan Police

Drugs Squad sergeants, staking out a Chinese-owned restaurant in Manchester in northern England in connection with enquiries into a Triad gangland knives-and-cleavers battle in a London Chinese restaurant the month before, stopped a van because an informant with them said he recognized one of the four Chinese males in the van as a man involved in the affray. The van was searched and it contained two large knives and large bits of iron bars. The man wanted in connection with the London job was taken off down to London but the other three were charged in Manchester with being in possession of offensive weapons in a public place.

On being searched, two of them, who were Chinese waiters working in Manchester and had nothing whatsoever to do with the London affair, were found to have betting slips in their pockets – on the back of which lines of Chinese characters were set out in a formalized way. One of the sergeants from London, a keen young police officer, had read Morgan's book. He thought he recognized the look of those writings on the back of the English betting slips. He asked the police interpreter to look at them – and they were Triad poems! Those two men were subsequently convicted of the offensive weapons charge and sentenced to three months in jail apiece.

·3. In October 1978, in Vancouver, Canada, local Police Inspector Ray Peterson told me about a strange incident that had occurred two years earlier when a person who had newly rented a house reported that he had found a little box buried in the garden. It contained a small coffin with a Bible on top and inside was a cloth wrapped round deteriorating flesh, a perfume bottle, a toy watch and a few other odds and ends. 'We thought it might be a foetus and so we ran an identification on it . . . . The guy gently unwraps the cloth and has a look at it and he turns to us and says, "It's a chicken!"' It was a chicken with no head on it. The people who had lived in the house before were Chinese – Vancouver has the largest Chinese community in Canada.

4. In Los Angeles in the autumn of 1978 I talked to Ross Arai, a Japanese-American who is the team leader of the only police Asian Task Force, comprised solely of men of Asian origin, in the whole of the United States, about local Chinese youth gangs and their appalling record of violence and murder. He was sure that they took some kind of oath but did not know what. He had attended the funeral of a Chinese waiter who had been

assassinated and 'there were a lot of Chinese "scriptures" written on paper put on his coffin and he was buried with them on top. I asked what they were and I was told they were letters from his "brothers" promising to avenge his death at the cost of their life.'

At first he said, 'It sounds like Triads, I know, but it's not. And you know why? Because what is happening is that they are *patterning* themselves after the Triads system. . . . There are no connections that we have seen yet that put them back with any Triad organization or society back in Hong Kong.'

But then, as we talked, he began to change his line. He conceded that the local youth gangs were very well organized and that there *was* a national network of some kind – for example, one of his officers visiting Chinatown, New York, on a case walked into two of the local Los Angeles youths. He said, 'You have a national leader who . . . moves from city to city in the United States to make sure everything is running all right.' This leader is the equivalent of a 489 or *Shan Chu*. 'The groups we are dealing with do not pattern themselves after any gangs here in the United States. Their mode of operation is that of the gangs that are running in the streets of Hong Kong.'

When I commented that the situation reminded me of the successful film, *Lassie,* which, when the original collie dog of that name died, was followed by a sequel with another dog called *Laddie, Son of Lassie,* he said 'OK. I'll buy that. That makes sense to me. When you come to think about it, it's the same with Japanese criminals in this country too. In Japan, we have the Yakuza organization, meaning the gangsters, and anybody coming from Japan in the criminal area of activity patterns himself directly after the Yakuza organization back in Japan. It's the same with the Italians. If a guy comes from Italy to here and he's going to be a criminal within an organization, he will pattern himself after the *mafiosi.*'

It is a cultural phenomenon. Organized Chinese criminals today, both in Hong Kong and the Western world, will follow the old method of operation, and use the same structure and organization pattern as is traditional for them – and that is a Triad pattern.

But is there more to it? On the international narcotics scene, how does one explain the 'connections' between points of supply and demand that are thousands of miles apart? Or the hit men sent to commit murder from one side of the world to another? Or ethnic groups working in harmony on a basis of complete trust when at any given moment their organization might be uncovered or their merchandise purloined?

When it comes to drugs, is not the Royal Hong Kong Police Force's official view of Triad activity as fragmented and 'petty' crime somewhat less than adequate? To answer this question, we must examine the structure of international trafficking in South-East Asian heroin.

6　The Golden 'Triangle'

The Golden Triangle – 150,000 square miles of forest-covered highlands where field after field of yellow opium poppies glow in the bright mountain sunlight – is made up of the western fringe of Laos, the four northern provinces of Thailand and the north-eastern reaches of Burma, including the semi-autonomous Shan States. This great area is the officially acknowledged source of South-East Asian heroin but, like so much in this whole story, there is another, unofficial, view of it. The Golden Triangle is really a Golden Quadrangle – its fourth side made up of the mountainous extreme southern province of Yunnan in Communist China, the only part of the country where the Chinese government has not yet succeeded in abolishing opium growing.

I first heard of this 'fourth dimension', which may come as a surprise even to those informed on the subject, from Superintendent Leonard Hill, second-in-command of the Royal Hong Kong Police Force's Narcotics Bureau. 'Yunnan province probably produces more opium than anywhere else in the world. They get their opium through into the Golden Triangle and down into Bangkok and then it follows the normal export pattern to wherever it is in the world.' Now that the Thais have stepped up border control on their northernmost frontier with Laos (where Thailand comes nearest to southern China), the drug comes down through Laos to round about level with central Thailand and then diagonally across to Bangkok.

This non-official version was confirmed for me by, among others, an unusually outspoken DEA special agent in New York who pointed out that in the 1950s, when it was CIA policy to present Communist China as blackly as possible, heroin activity in the southern tip of China was an openly accepted reality. Since President Nixon's visit to Peking in 1972 and a subsequent change in the United States' stand towards China, it has become equally accepted to deny the reality of this fourth side.

Utter political cynicism abounds in the long, sordid history of greed, ruthlessness and corruption connected with the Golden Triangle. Alfred W.McCoy in his *The Politics of Heroin in South-East Asia* in 1972 disclosed how United States foreign policy and CIA money supported and encouraged the burgeoning trade in heroin – even though it led to thousands of young Americans in Vietnam being corrupted and eventually spread the contagion over to Western Europe and back home to North America – in order, in the name of 'containing Communism', to shore up sordid totalitarian regimes simply because they were 'anti-Communist'.

In a 'good' year, the Golden Triangle produces over a thousand tons of raw opium – about seventy per cent of the world's total illicit opium supply, according to an official estimate quoted by McCoy. Before World War Two it produced only about forty tons a year and most of that was smoked legally in various parts of Asia. However, in the 1950s and 1960s one Asian country after another yielded to United Nations pressure and proscribed the centuries-old panacea for misery. As Satharn Pairaoh wrote in the *Bangkok Post,* 'Opium was banned throughout South-East Asia in order to protect the heroin addicts of Europe and America. This did not stop heroin reaching Europe and America, but it had the effect of driving Asian addicts off opium – which is relatively harmless – and on to heroin which is much more dangerous but easier to smuggle.'

The ban coincided with Chiang Kai Shek's defeat in mainland China and the flight of his supporters. Two of his armies, the 3rd and the 5th, stationed in the remote, isolated southern province of Yunnan, took the only possible escape route – south over the mountainous frontier into the Shan States of northern Burma, the part of the country that forms the Burmese sector of the Golden Triangle.

Burma had only recently, in 1948, acquired its independence from British rule and the central government in Rangoon had not – and still has not in 1980 – fully established its sovereignty over the Shan people who continue to claim to have been promised independence under the 1948 Constitution. Shan chieftans had been encouraged to introduce the opium poppy to their fiefdoms by the British as far back as 1866 and opium shops had been opened throughout Burma to retail the narcotics to licensed addicts. The British thus succeeded in making large profits for themselves while blunting resistance to alien rule by spreading the opium habit among the native peoples.

The Rangoon central government passed a special law prohibiting opium growing and trafficking within two years of independence but its writ did not run to the rugged terrain of the Shan States, where opium poppies continued to be grown. When Chiang Kai Shek's two tattered armies arrived, they were not slow to see the potential. This is an area where man-made borders mean little and the most numerous of the local hill people, who actually grow and harvest the opium crop, are an ethnic Chinese group, the *Meo*, whose roots go back well over three thousand years into the mountain fastnesses of southern China.

However, for the first few years after the Nationalist armies' arrival, patriotism triumphed over private greed. They were occupied in the attempt to re-take mainland China, a task backed by the Truman administration in Washington who had been shocked by the sudden final collapse of Chiang Kai Shek and ruled by the 'domino theory' – if urgent aid was not given to the existing regimes in South-East Asia, they would all collapse like a row of upturned dominoes nudged from one end by pressure from Communist China. It was decided to re-arm and re-supply the remnants of the Nationalist armies in Burma and recruit the hill tribes to fight with them. In April 1951, the assembled force, accompanied by CIA advisers, crossed back into China – and were ignominiously routed. A second invasion in August 1952 proved equally a failure and the Nationalist generals gave up hope of military victory. Their attention was free to turn to the much more potentially successful prospects offered by the fields of opium poppies.

With the Burmese Army preoccupied with its battle against Shan insurgents, the Nationalist armies virtually took over the north-eastern reaches of the country. Many of the Chinese troops married into the local hill tribes, villages were forced to pay an exorbitant annual opium tax and, under ruthless pressure from the Nationalist generals, opium production in the area doubled and then quadrupled. An outlet for their wares was needed. Burma was too shut off from the outside world, underdeveloped and concerned with sorting out its many internal problems to fulfil this role, but its neighbour and fellow-member of the Golden Triangle, Thailand, was ideally suited for the part, with Bangkok, as one of the world's great ports, a superb jumping-off point for exportation to the outside world.

Thailand was then governed by an inordinately corrupt military dictatorship and the Nationalist Army bosses found an ideal partner in General Phao Sriyanonda, then Director-General of Thailand's para-military police force of 45,000 men, complete with its own air force, armoured division and paratroops, largely equipped with the help of the CIA's Sea Supply Corporation. As Alfred McCoy wrote: 'The CIA had promoted the Phao-KMT [Nationalist armies] partnership in order to provide a secure rear area for the KMT, but this alliance soon became a critical factor in the growth of South-East Asia's narcotics traffic.'

With CIA support, the KMT remained in Burma – which has always produced by far the greater part (eighty per cent) of the Golden Triangle's opium crop – until 1961, when, in the words of my DEA informant in Bangkok, 'the Chinese Communists came over into Burma at the request of the Burmese government and kicked the remnants of the KMT armies out of Burma and into Thailand. They still operate today in the border area but they do not any more operate deep into Burma.' In the same year of 1961, with US State Department backing, there was a massive airlift to Taiwan out of northern Thailand of over 4000 KMT troops who opted to be 'repatriated' to their so-called homeland of 'China', as that island ninety-odd miles off the mainland considered itself.

Thereafter, there was only a token attempt to provide a legitimate military pretext for the continuing presence of an estimated 20,000 ex-Nationalist soldiers in the area. As General Tuan Shih Wen, commanding the rump of the 5th KMT Army at its base at Mae Salong just within the Burmese-Thai border, told an intrepid British journalist, the late Peter Duval Smith, in a rare interview in the winter of 1966/7 for a British magazine: 'Necessity knows no law. That is why we deal with opium. We have to continue to fight the evil of Communism, and to fight you must have an army, and any army must have guns, and to buy guns you must have money. In these mountains, the only money is opium.'*

But the military realities became ever grimmer against the increasingly more isolated troops. In 1969, there was a second and final 'repatriation' to Taiwan. All official contacts with Chiang Kai Shek's administration were now cut off: the remaining troops, estimated at some 4000, lost their title of an army. They were henceforth known as 'Chinese Irregular Forces' (CIF). The US State Department had by then other anti-Communist fish to fry: in the cruelly escalating war in Vietnam in which US troops were now openly involved. CIA aid was virtually cut off to the ex-Nationalist soldiers and their generals, its main thrust now transferred to the Vietnam sphere of operations.

At about this period, a Communist organization known as the Red Meos began subversive operations in northern Thailand and the hard-pressed Thai Army, unable to stamp out the insurrection on its own, appealed to the resident 'Chinese Irregular Forces' for help. Assistance was readily given, for the ex-Nationalist generals now had a new military pretext for staying in the region, as an acceptable 'cover' for the true reason for some of them to do so.

That situation still obtains today. 'The Thais see them as a viable buffer against the Communist insurgents up there,' says my DEA informant in Bangkok. 'This is kind of sensitive stuff – but there are tacit agreements between the Thai government and the CIF and they allow certain things to happen because of these relationships.'

Those 'certain things' are a massive involvement by the 'Chinese Irregular Forces' in the vital early stages of the transportation of opium from the poppy fields of the Golden Quadrangle to the exit points of Bangkok and, increasingly, via Haadyai in southern Thailand to the international airports of Penang and Kuala Lumpur in northern Malaysia.

The process begins with the hill tribesmen of the Quadrangle, whose subsistence-level existence relies on rice as the food crop and on opium for cash or barter. The opium is gathered from the end of December to the beginning of March each year, when the poppy loses its flowers. A series of small cuts are made around

* In June 1980, General Tuan Shih Wen, then seventy-two, died of lung cancer – not in a mountain armed camp, but in a Bangkok hospital.

the green pod that is left on the stem, white liquid oozes out and by the next morning it has coagulated into small drops of brown opium. In an average harvest each family can expect to collect between ten and fifteen kilograms of opium, some of which they will keep for their own use but most of which they sell – either to middlemen, mainly ethnic Chinese tribesmen, or direct to the Yunnanese Chinese from the CIF who visit the villages and pay the farmers either in cash or, more often, in goods such as clothing, blankets, tea, sugar, salt, candles, etc. In Burma, the insurgent forces of the Shan United Army (SUA), the Shan United Revolutionary Army (SURA) and the Shan State Revolutionary Army (SSRA) will also be involved.

In the Golden Triangle itself, the poppy is sold either through middlemen or direct, and it is the Shan insurgents or the commanders of the nearest CIF garrisons in Thailand who are responsible for the crop's transmission out of the growing region. As for how it gets out of the Yunnan province of Red China, I simply have drawn a blank: all that I have been able to discover is that it *does* get out. From whichever source, the opium, packed in crates, is loaded on to mules and the long journey is made in caravans down to the ramshackle temporary refineries set up in jungle clearings where the opium is converted not usually into its final heroin form but into morphine, the first, uncomplicated, stage in the conversion process. This is enough to reduce its bulk to one-tenth of the original and make onward transmission that much easier.

Where are those first-stage refineries? They used to be in northern Thailand but because of recent law enforcement efforts with the increased DEA commitment in the area and a stronger, if still ambivalent, attitude by the Thais themselves, they have been pushed westwards into Burma. The DEA special agent in Bangkok told me: 'The refineries now are always in the Thai-Burmese border area – *but always in Burma*. Just inside the Burmese border. . . . The CIF *now* is a sort of protective group for that border area against the Burmese as well as against the local Communist insurgents.'

As long as the refineries exist on the other side of the border, the Thai authorities do not cause the CIF too much trouble. There is no real control in that part of Burma. 'The Burmese Army can come in at any time and kick the CIF out of those areas but then they'll have to go back to re-fit, re-arm and re-supply themselves before they can come back and make further strikes.' Some of the refined morphine from Burmese poppy fields filters through Burma (where there are an estimated 60,000 heroin addicts) but most is taken, under trading arrangements between the Shan insurgents and the CIF, into Thailand with the rest of the refineries' products and enters the mainstream of Golden Quadrangle narcotics distribution.

The deals that regulate the flow from the Quadrangle to the outside world are made in Chiang Mai – 'Flower of the North' – Thailand's second-largest city and capital of its northern provinces. Situated almost within spitting distance of the foothills of the Golden Triangle, this ancient and beautiful city attracts more than tourists. Every spring, the drug traders and financiers gather here to negotiate the export of morphine and sometimes finished heroin to the world market; automatic weapons and Japanese transistors will find their way in and fortunes will be made or increased even further. It is also to the Chiang Mai region that the leading traffickers, based in Bangkok, flee when police pressure gets too great in the capital.

The multi-billion dollar trade – the value of the hundred tons of heroin or morphine-base pouring out of Thailand in a good year would make Croesus seem a pauper – is divided between the syndicates and the independents. The syndicates themselves are of two kinds. There are the Yunnanese Army bosses – the CIF – who control the border areas and the *Chiu Chao* merchants who mastermind the rest. These are the men who meet every spring after the opium poppy harvest in the fashionable hotels and restaurants of Chiang Mai to make their deals for the coming year. As my DEA informant in Bangkok said: 'There is no question about it: the facilitation of the vast quantity of illegal narcotics going out of here to the eventual consumer is done by the *Chiu Chao* Chinese operating principally out of Bangkok with their financial contacts among their fellow *Chiu Chaos* in Hong Kong, Singapore and Amsterdam. . . . The relationship between the Yunnanese in the border areas and the *Chiu Chao* down here in Bangkok is a relationship consistent with two corporate conglomerates that find it profitable for both to deal with the other. They don't have to *like* each other – and traditionally the *Chiu Chaos* are among the most clannish of all Chinese.'

Even the insurgent armies from the Shan States in Burma are

involved in this syndicate dealing. As Melinda Liu wrote in the *Far Eastern Economic Review* in August 1979:

The Shan United Army is a title which seems grossly misleading. Its members are not Shans, informed observers in Burma say, but mostly ethnic Chinese. Numbering less than 1000, it is not united and is not an army but a modern-day feudal following under notorious drug war-lord Chan Shee Fu, known also as Khun Sa. Another group is dubbed the Shan United Revolutionary Army, composed of KMT 3rd Army remnants and headed by millionaire General Li Wen Huan, who lives in a remote fiefdom in Thailand's Chiang Mai province near Burma's border.

It was General Li Wen Huan who was allegedly responsible for a one-million dollar rip-off of the US government in 1972, when the Nixon administration agreed to pay this sum for twenty-six tons of opium, supposedly Li's entire supply for the year, so that it could be destroyed. After the transactions were completed, Li offered a twenty-seventh ton for an additional pay-off, the American negotiators declined the offer and the General kept his extra ton – and, one suspects, several more tons – for his usual business dealings over the jasmine tea in Chiang Mai.

These syndicates are responsible for bringing the drug down to the Bangkok area and for getting it converted in the laboratories near Bangkok from morphine-base to the final heroin product or sometimes, especially for the Hong Kong trade, to the 'ester of morphine' stage, which is one of the last phases in the chemical process before final distillation into heroin. Having done all this, the syndicates have then to find their customers.

There are an estimated 600,000 addicts in Thailand but the ethnic Chinese syndicates do not sell direct to them. 'There is a stockpile here in Bangkok,' my DEA informant told me. 'You've got to have it on steady supply because otherwise your customers will go elsewhere. They have to keep the pipeline continually flowing with stuff so that, bearing in mind the tremendous job the Thai police have done relatively over the last years, even if they take a big hit, it doesn't impact on the availability at street level.' Heroin for local consumption usually passes into the mid-level distribution stage – half-way between the syndicates and the street pedlars – which is mostly in the hands of native Thais. The 'home team' takes over from the ethnic Chinese.

However, it is the ethnic Chinese who are very much involved in the transportation of heroin to addicts outside the country and this is where the trade divides between the syndicates and the independents. International syndicates linked to the outside world plan and plot their deals not in Chiang Mai but in Bangkok and Hong Kong and they form one part of the trade. The other part is formed by the independents who come in to Bangkok and find the source there with whom to deal.

The major export deals for both the European and the American markets are done in Bangkok itself, however the distribution pattern thereafter may differ. In Europe, the ethnic Chinese do their own distribution, allied to the importation, but in the United States the Chinese importers do business largely with non-Chinese distributing organizations. They have yet to get their own distributing network, although the Chinese youth gangs in the States may possibly emerge as future distributors.

Several DEA special agents in various countries of the world have told me that they know of frequent trips made by their own host country's leading traffickers to Bangkok to make deals – and to Hong Kong to arrange finance. ('Host country' is the standard way of referring to the country where DEA personnel are stationed: the Agency's role is limited to intelligence gathering and back-up for the local police, it has no rights of arrest and is very conscious of its guest status in any country where it is operating.)

I used to think that because of the swelling Chinatown populations of North America after the liberalization of the immigration laws in the 1960s, the pattern of distribution would be through the new immigrants from South-East Asia who would use their access to friends and relatives back home to bring in the heroin and then, when it was safely in the country, look around for their customers. But it does not work like that. 'The connection is not here,' a DEA special agent in New York told me. 'It's in Thailand, in Bangkok. . . . The Hong Kong people are now mainly the financiers. But if you want the dope, the dope isn't in Hong Kong. The dope comes from Thailand. .`. . In Bangkok, you can buy a kilo of heroin, if you've got really good connections, for US$3000. In Hong Kong, you'll have to pay US$10,000 for a kilo of exactly the same quality. So, of course, you'll go to Bangkok to buy your stuff!'

One of the many DEA stories that show the situation in

operation was told me by Lionel Stewart, a DEA special agent
working undercover in Los Angeles and a rare example of an
agent who actually gave evidence in court under his name. In
1976 an investigation was being made in southern California
into three individuals and their suspected involvement in
importing very high purity South-East Asian No.4 heroin. A
phone call had been traced to Thailand to the residence of a man
named Preechar Leeyaruk, who, on checking the records,
turned out to have been very active in the drug scene from
1968/9 to 1972. 'In that year the Thai police made a case on him
and lost the evidence – the Thai police lost the evidence! – so he
was turned loose in about 1973.' He had dropped out of sight for
the next three years but in 1976 his name came up again and not
only in connection with the southern California investigation.
Lionel Stewart had been called in after the arrest of a Vietnam
'vet' caught with about seven ounces of white heroin brought in
from Thailand and who talked about going back to Bangkok to
buy more dope – from a man named Preechar Leeyaruk.

The Vietnam veteran agreed to co-operate with the DEA in
return for a lesser sentence and in September 1976 he
introduced Stewart, as a potential buyer for the US market, to
Preechar Leeyaruk, a Thai Chinese, in Bangkok. The transaction was US$6000 for one kilo.

What were the terms? 'It was money up front. That is usual
when the Chinese are not dealing with their own kind. The
Atkinson organizations, for instance.' (This is a reference to a
notorious organization, based in Bangkok, of black Vietnam
veterans under ex-army sergeant Leslie (Ike) Atkinson, who
masterminded the use of military aircraft and other service
means of communication to bring an estimated 300 million
dollars' worth of No.4 heroin into the Baltimore region of the
United States. They were finally cracked in June 1976 when
Atkinson and five associates were jailed for up to twenty-five
years.) 'Everything is in advance with the Chinese – that is if
you're not Chinese yourself. If you don't trust them, you don't
get to do anything. . . . He won't welsh on the deal. He will give
you the best stuff he's got and that usually will run to ninety-two,
ninety-eight, per cent purity. But you've got to go to Bangkok to
make the deal. You couldn't make the deal with his representative here in the United States – he hasn't got one!'

Having made this first purchase to put Preechar Leeyaruk at

his ease, Stewart, still in Bangkok, then negotiated the purchase of another kilo of No.4 heroin. The deal was in order to nail the trafficker. Stewart managed to lure Preechar to Hong Kong on the basis that he had arranged for his own courier to pick up the stuff from there. The price was US$18,000, a substantial increase on the original kilo, because as Preechar explained, he would have to lay out, apart from various 'handling expenses', US$10,000 for his courier to get the heroin to Hong Kong.

Stewart and Preechar flew to Hong Kong, booked into a hotel on Causeway Bay, a select tourist area, and awaited the arrival of the courier. Not one man but two arrived in the hotel, with a suitcase in which heroin was concealed within the sides of the frame. Officers of the Royal Hong Kong Police Narcotics Bureau, who had been waiting in another room, arrested the three surprised Thais. 'Only then did we discover that the two courier guys were members of the God-damned Thai parliament! They were Thai MPs!'

The three were put on trial and convicted. As Stewart said, it was a story of good international and national co-operation. In that case Stewart had been posing as an independent with his own line of business but something else should be mentioned. Stewart is black and traditionally ethnic Chinese narcotics traffickers are supposed to dislike dealing with representatives of any other ethnic group. 'They would prefer to deal with their own kind but, of course, that's not always possible,' says Peter Fong, a Chinese-American and a DEA supervisor in New York after being special agent in charge at the Hong Kong office. 'They have had some bad experiences in the past: at one time, it seemed to them that practically every time a black man was arrested, he would turn around and inform on who his source was. So they shut down for a while. But of late they've started opening up again.'

And what about the Italian Mafia, the most powerful organized crime institution in the United States? Peter Fong told me a revealing story of one of his own undercover transactions when he had succeeded in enticing a *Chiu Chao* Chinese to come from Bangkok to New York to collect money for a heroin shipment that had been made. He had taken an Italian-American agent with him to one of the discussions, explaining that he was grooming him because he belonged to the Italian 'family' and, without a distribution point, what could he do with the heroin he was given?

'How did he take it? No problem. He was happy to see this Italian guy. Look, they understand perfectly: they've seen the movies, they've read the books overseas, they've never been to the United States but they know what the "Godfather" is and that type of situation.'

In that case, the Chinese operator was arrested but it does not always end as happily for the forces of the law. Peter Law, Assistant Police Commissioner in Hong Kong, told me of a syndicate-to-syndicate transaction in Bangkok when he was narcotics attaché there. A Thai Chinese member of the production syndicate from the north, a financier from Hong Kong, the boss of a courier team from Singapore and an importer from Amsterdam – 'the big boys' – were meeting in a hotel room in Bangkok. The Thais heard about the meeting and rushed the hotel room, seizing sixteen kilos of heroin and arresting the four men who were there. But these four were only representatives – the big boys had all gone home by then. They did not, however, like losing sixteen kilos of heroin and it was heard that they had scheduled another meeting in Singapore.

'So we phone up Mike Hannam in Singapore. He was the head of the Narcotics Bureau there then. "You've got those four buggers there. All away planning. They're in room such-and-such at the such-and-such hotel," I say, and he says, "What the fuck do you expect me to do? Rush in and bash the living daylights out of them? What kind of evidence have I got? They're sitting in a hotel room talking. What kind of evidence have I got to go in there and do them? There is nothing there that I can touch. No documents, no nothing."'

They knew that an arrangement was being made for an export but could do nothing about it, nor could they find out which way it would go. 'Sometimes stuff for New Zealand will go to Switzerland so that the origin of the thing is Switzerland, and nobody will unbutton a suitcase of someone coming from Switzerland in a way they will unbutton it coming from Thailand.' It is, after all, coming from the opposite direction.

But where in all this story of the Golden Quadrangle, with Bangkok as the centre of all the major export deals, do the

Triads fit in? Clearly, many of the members of the Nationalist armies who fled into Burma after Chiang Kai Shek's defeat were likely to be Triads simply because these secret societies existed all over China. It is the remnants of those armies, the Yunnanese – the CIF – who control the heroin trade in the border areas; the *Chiu Chaos* control the rest. And do the *Chiu Chaos* in Thailand and their contacts elsewhere, particularly in Hong Kong, Singapore and Amsterdam, have a stronger unifying bond than just their renowned clannishness and shared racial origin?

Again, there is an official view and a non-official view in South-East Asia. General Pow Sarasin, Secretary-General of the Thai Narcotics Control Board in Bangkok, gave me the official line – they do not have much of a problem with Triads in Bangkok. 'There are Triad problems concerning Singapore' [problems, incidentally, denied by the police there!] 'and Hong Kong and Amsterdam. They try and fight who is to be boss in Amsterdam – but they are Chinese from Singapore not from Thailand. A lot of the Chinese in Amsterdam were sent back to Hong Kong and Singapore – and this was because some of them were traffickers, some of them Triads. But none of them was sent to Thailand.'

As for the skilled Chinese chemists who come from abroad to work in the opium-to-morphine laboratories in the Burmese hill forests or in the morphine-to-heroin laboratories near Bangkok – 'Most chemists in Bangkok here whom we arrest come from Hong Kong but I don't think they are Triads. It is possible that men financing the drug – in Hong Kong, Singapore or Amsterdam – are Triads, but we do not yet have any Triads here in Bangkok.'

The official view among the Hong Kong police is, again, that Triads only operate in the colony at a very low level: muscle men protecting the street pedlars. But according to Superintendent Leonard Hill; 'Undoubtedly there are Triads in Thailand. A lot of people engaged in drugs in Thailand are Triads.'

Like civil servants passing the buck, few officials wish to admit that they might have Triads operating on their own home ground. Over in someone else's field, yes. Even my DEA informant in Bangkok supported General Pow's official stance: 'If you are relating to the drug traffic and the ethnic Chinese, the Yunnanese and the *Chiu Chao* Chinese who control the traffic here in Thailand, you are not dealing with the Triads at all.

Triads operate relative to the drug traffic very strongly in Hong Kong and in Singapore in this part of the world. But they have not become any kind of a force in Thailand.'

I repeated this remark to Peter Law, who served for five years in Bangkok as drugs attaché for the British and Hong Kong governments and is a personal friend of my DEA informant. 'I'm surprised he told you that. I wonder if he was being absolutely straight with you. I don't think he was. I wonder if he was because he's in a different position from myself. He's American, he's DEA and he's got to operate in the atmosphere of Thailand. I have a high respect for him but maybe he is toeing the party line for the Thais in that respect.'

I also asked Peter Law whether the four men, 'the big boys', who met in the hotel in Bangkok and later in Singapore were likely to have been Triads. 'I have an argument with my Thai colleagues over this,' he replied. 'They say that they haven't got any Triads operating. But, having been a police officer in this part of the world for very many years, I know, and a number of us know, that when you get two Englishmen together you've got a club, when you've got two Irishmen together you've got a fight and when you've got two Chinese together, you've got a Triad Society – you've got a secret society anyway. For the Thais to say to the contrary is just completely against the run of the play, the nature of the animal itself.'

What I believe to be the real answer is contained in the speech made in the United States Congress on 17 May 1977 by Congressman Lester Wolff, Chairman of the Select Committee on Narcotics Abuse and Control, and considered by DEA agents I have spoken to as the most knowledgeable United States politician in the narcotics field. The following is an extract from that speech which I consider should be required reading for every drugs enforcement police or customs officer in the free world:

The Select Committee studies indicate there is cause for real concern with respect to the appearance of larger amounts of South-East Asian heroin in the United States, as our joint eradication programs with Mexico begin to produce substantive results in eliminating poppy fields and thus reducing the availability of Mexican heroin.

I have learned the names and identities of some major ethnic Chinese residing in Thailand who are primarily responsible for the purchase, shipment and support of the large volume of heroin that is distributed from Thailand into the western countries of Europe and the United States.

Before describing the activities of one major group of these individuals and naming them, which I intend to do in a few moments, I would like to present my colleagues with some background on what appears to be one of the recent developments in international heroin trafficking.

The Chinese Triad Societies which began their existence centuries ago as self-help organizations, have largely become criminal syndicates in recent years. Because of loose banking regulations and practices in the Far East and the close connection these ethnic Chinese have with relatives and friends scattered all over the globe, they have been able to assume a major role in the distribution, receipt, and dissemination of heroin. They work in mysterious ways, their business transactions clothed in coded language. Much business is transacted by word of mouth and the trust that is extended by one Triad member to a blood brother is inviolate. They have their own code of silence not unfamiliar to law enforcement officers around the world who once dealt with organized gangs of criminals that transported Turkish heroin to the United States.

The secret societies known as the Triad were formed in Mainland China during the eighteenth century. Their original purpose was self-protection and opposition to the various Chinese dynasties. The names of the various secret societies are taken from the areas in China from which the original members emigrated. The headquarters of the secret societies are in Hong Kong. As members of the secret societies scattered throughout South-East Asia and Europe, smaller branches were formed. Right up through the 1960s the secret societies were importing No.3 heroin and opium for use in the countries where they were located. In the early 1970s the secret societies began to import No.4 heroin along with No.3 heroin which is used for smoking purposes. These groups, located in the various European countries are connected with the base operation, and families of Hong Kong. It is believed that they are largely responsible for the upsurge in heroin trafficking coming from South-East Asia to Western Europe. The increase in level of heroin smuggling is reflected in the increase of heroin seizures in Western Europe from a level of 15 to 20 kilograms in the 1960s to over 600 kilograms last year. The primary secret society in Western Europe as far as heroin trafficking is concerned was the 14K group which has recently been pushed out by a rival based in Malaysia and Singapore. In most countries, including Hong Kong, it is illegal to belong to a secret society. However, because of the ethnic ties which all members of secret societies have, it is very hard to infiltrate these organizations.

The Triads use the trafficking in narcotics to support their other legitimate and illegitimate activities.

Many of these individuals reside in Bangkok, living in baronial splendor, adopting Thai names, and represent the primary reason why South-East Asian heroin has become an overwhelming threat to the national security of our country.

Yet still so many allegedly well-informed police officers say, in effect: 'The Triads – who, or what, are they?'

7 Thailand and Heroin Trafficking

Entering Bangkok for the first time is an unforgettable experience for anyone from the Western world. None of the books I had read and none of the people familiar with the Far East whom I had spoken to had prepared me for the totally different world in which I found myself. I now believe that it is only by seeing at first-hand such places as Bangkok, Kuala Lumpur, Singapore and Hong Kong that the reality of existence there – and the workings of the Chinese criminal mind and the capacity for ruthless cruelty that I have come to believe is synonymous with the word 'Triad' – can be properly understood.

It seems appropriate that Bangkok should be the capital of the country that is at the very heart of the murderous trade in one of the world's most lethal drugs. Just below the surface of the dozen or so splendid modern hotels in the centre of Bangkok, with doormen literally bending low in smiling deference before Western tourists, is rank poverty and, alongside it, cold indifference to suffering. The Thais are the Spaniards of the East: friendly, open and warm but with a cruel streak to their character that makes cock-fighting, like bull-fighting for the Spaniards, one of their favourite sports.

Beneath an all-pervading heat that, even on an evening in October in the 'cool' season, hits you with the force of a steam-wrapped sledgehammer when you leave the air-conditioned coolness of your hotel, Bangkok is a city where contrasts in wealth strike you with an intensity that is almost obscene. A shanty town of rotting, rat-infested dwellings with the smell of human excrement high upon the warm air is only round the corner from the lush green lawns and imposing entrances of the foreign embassies and expensive apartment blocks that line Wireless Road.

On the streets of the notorious vice district around **Patpong Road** in the heart of the tourist area, young girls – and boys – are sold for casual sex. 'You don't like her?' said one tout, as I pushed away a proffered photograph of a girl who looked about eight years old. 'What about boy?' and he produced a sheaf of photographs of boys of about the same age. A city that hawks in the streets the bodies of its children for exploitation is surely a suitable starting point for the world-wide distribution of a drug that corrodes and eventually destroys the bodies of many young people.

Money means everything here: the only city I have visited where a high-ranking police official apologized to me for not warning me never to hail a taxi in the street. I had done this one night and found myself driven in the wrong direction through ever narrower and darker streets towards the outskirts of Bangkok. I only escaped robbery or perhaps worse by threatening (unrealistically, if they had but known it) extreme personal violence. As I later learnt from Police-Colonel Damrong Vaivong, the only safe way is to take a taxi from the hotel, which has a list of taxis attached to it and payment is made through the hotel. What an admission!

'You must forget your Western moralistic attitudes,' I was told. 'The people here are too poor to be honest.' Small children will squeeze detergent on the windscreen of your car, stuck in the customary Bangkok traffic jams, in order to beg for money to wipe it off. A girl will kneel before Buddha to ask forgiveness before she starts a day of the most degrading forms of prostituted sex.

In such a place, life is cheap and money is power. And with money comes corruption. 'You can hire a killer here for four hundred Baht. That is a hundred English pounds or two hundred US dollars,' a foreign narcotics attaché said. 'No one knows for sure but it is generally said that over 10,000 people are murdered in Thailand each year. Everyone believes that many officers in the police are corrupt and that if you have money, you virtually make your own laws.'

Bangkok was not the most reassuring place to have started my research in the Far East. On my second evening in the city, after a day spent visiting Thai police officers, foreign embassies, DEA special agents, I had retired to my hotel room to relax and take a shower before dinner. Just as I was about to step into the shower I heard a slight noise from the door to the adjoining room and saw the handle begin to turn. As with the incident in the taxi, I shouted aggressively and banged on the door. There was silence. But remembering all the spy films I had seen, I wedged the door handle with a chair which I left there for the rest of my stay.

Certainly, it could have been a newly arrived tourist trying the door from his side to see where it led but the next morning that room was open and unoccupied. Whoever had been there the previous evening had departed. Strange for a hotel that catered almost exclusively for foreign businessmen and tourists who are most unlikely to make only a one-night stay. And the only people who knew where I was staying were the Thai police. I am definitely not suggesting that it could have been a Thai policeman on the other side of the door but leaks of information within the force are notorious. I had been told only that morning by a foreign narcotics attaché of an incident in which he was personally involved where a seizure of a considerable amount of heroin in a Bangkok hotel (incidentally, the same as mine) had been foiled through a police leak. Am I only imagining that it could perhaps have been a member of the city's Triads who tried to gain entry to my room to scare me off or search through my papers?

Whatever the truth, Bangkok is a city where violence and corruption provide the background for its role as a major heroin trafficking base in the world today. There are four main strands in this trade to be considered.

The first is the role of the ethnic Chinese. We have already seen how the Yunnanese in the north, the remnants of Chiang Kai Shek's armies and their descendants, control the heroin trade in the border areas, while the *Chiu Chao* merchants in the central area mastermind the rest. The *Chiu Chaos* first came to Thailand in substantial numbers from their home region on the coast of mainland China in the 1920s and 1930s, shrewd enough to realize early that the troubles in China were likely to escalate with time. They came with little money but their nimble business minds and natural astuteness soon made them the leaders of the commercial community as Thailand (then Siam) struggled to bring itself into the second quarter of the twentieth century.

They gradually merged into native Thai society and changed their names into the Thai language. Today, there is one foolproof way of knowing an ethnic Chinese from a true Thai, Police-Colonel Damrong Vaivong told me, and that is the length of their name. The *Chiu Chaos* made straight translations of their long names, like 'Son of the Golden Moon', into one long Thai word, but Thais themselves all have short names.

As a DEA agent in Bangkok pointed out, people with money, regardless of their background, are particularly accepted in underdeveloped countries and the major *Chiu Chao* traffickers in Thailand are also property owners. They own shipping companies and export companies and banks. 'You must remember that they can be legitimate millionaires anyway, completely apart from heroin. To them, they regard their business affairs as a diversified commercial operation in which heroin is merely one of the principal money-makers.' Hence, a major drugs violator could have his photograph in the *Bangkok Post* attending a highly respectable trade dinner as a leading member of the *Chiu Chao* business community.

The second main strand also has its origins outside Thailand itself, but this time in the Western world and particularly the United States. In the 1970s, American policy in Thailand changed dramatically from the cynical, CIA-mounted support for the drug-running ex-KMT Nationalist armies during the late 1960s. In June 1971, at the height of the US Army's heroin problem in Vietnam – ironically, the direct result of CIA support – President Nixon sent his historic message to Congress: 'Heroin, this deadly poison in the American lifestream, is a foreign export. No serious attack on our national drug problem can ignore the international implications of such an effort, nor can the domestic effort succeed without attacking the problem on an international plane.'

Almost overnight, US policy in the area was transformed. The Bureau of Narcotics and Dangerous Drugs, the forerunner of the DEA, increased its contingent of special agents in South-East Asia from three to twenty-one by mid-1972. By late 1974 the figure had risen to thirty-one and although public expenditure cuts have led to cut-backs in DEA offices in other parts of the world, the DEA operation in Thailand has continued to expand.

'What we have been trying to do ever since the re-evaluation,' a DEA special agent in the US Embassy in Bangkok explained to me, 'has been to gather the type of intelligence that identifies the trafficking organizations involved and to "make cases" and to help the Thai police to "make cases" that can be qualified in terms of their significance in disrupting the traffic.'

Although the DEA is the only anti-narcotics organization operating on a world-wide basis, other countries in the Western world, increasingly affected by the heroin explosion, have also sent representatives out to Bangkok to liaise for intelligence purposes with the local law enforcement forces. This practical involvement amounts to one person at the embassies of France, Holland, West Germany, Sweden and the United Kingdom (who for five years shared their one representative with Hong Kong) – almost ludicrously inadequate in the fight against traffickers at their home base. Australia, too, has a representative and the United Nations has also been involved, although with minimal effect to date.

The UN task is indeed prodigious: to wean the hill tribesmen of the Golden Triangle from their dependence on the opium crop by substituting coffee and other innocuous products of the soil. Money is scarce, the prospects daunting and so far only thirty villages out of an estimated 1000 in the Thai sector of the Triangle have even taken part in a pilot scheme. You cannot drag a semi-primitive group of people into the last years of the twentieth century overnight or even in a decade of effort, even if the financial support was available from other countries of the world – which it isn't. Only the United States is prepared to put its hand in its pocket to fight the scourge of heroin at source and even American wealth is not forthcoming for anything but token assistance to this particular project. As for the United Kingdom: 'Nothing! I am sorry to say,' Police-General Pow Sarasin told me.

The third strand in the pattern of Thai involvement in the heroin trade today is woven out of the country's tenuous security. Thailand is surrounded by threats on all its borders. On its southern border with Malaysia, Communist insurgents and Muslim nationalists tie down thousands of troops. In the east, the border with Kampuchea (formerly Cambodia) is plagued with a constant series of bloody 'incidents'. In the north-east, the Thai Communist party is most active and holds effective sway over some regions. And in the north and west, the

Bangkok central government feels compelled to let the Chinese Irregular Forces assist in guarding the frontiers.

Against such a background, it is understandable that the Thais consider that they have more important things to worry about than heroin trafficking, even allowing for their own 600,000 or so heroin addicts. 'We help you people in the West. We stop the drug going out, and what happens? It stays here. It gives us our own addict problem,' says Police-General Pow Sarasin.

Even in the minutely small crop-substitution scheme in the Golden Triangle itself, the Thai authorities are reluctant to press too hard for fear that the hill tribesmen, who are by very definition wanderers anyway, will move on to an area controlled by Communist insurgents. And in the south, there are ominous signs of strong links developing between the drug-runners from the north getting their goods down into Malaysia and the Communist guerillas operating in the jungles of southern Thailand.

Politics, as such, mean nothing in this context. In November 1978, for instance, army troops and police sweeping the Thai-Malaysian border district of Sadao uncovered heroin-conversion factories run by the guerillas in clearings hacked in the jungle to process morphine consignments brought down by drug syndicates from northern Thailand. Both the syndicates and the guerillas were ethnic Chinese: it made no difference whatsoever that the northern part of the syndicate was led by Yunnanese ex-soldiers of Chiang Kai Shek's bitterly anti-Communist Nationalist armies and that the guerillas were daily risking their lives fighting for the Communist cause.

The fourth and final strand in the intricate tapestry of Thailand today is that comprised by the central government itself. There too in recent years there has been a change almost as dramatic as the volte-face of US involvement after President Nixon's June 1971 'declaration of war' on heroin.

For, although to the outside world Thailand may still be what it has seemed for decades: a nationalist, capitalist military dictatorship with varying degrees of surface 'democracy', under the titular rule of a king, that is a considerable oversimplification. The recent government under Prime Minister General Kriangsak Chamanand, was deeply conscious of the need to strike at least a posture of concern about the problem in front of the outside world and there is every reason to suppose that his successor in March 1980, General Prem Tinsulanonda, will continue to follow this line.

'Drug suppression cannot be solved by any nation in isolation,' General Kriangsak told a five-day conference of narcotics police from Asian and Pacific countries in Bangkok in November 1977. 'The problem of the Golden Triangle cannot be solved by one country, or by the three countries immediately concerned. It needs international participation that is unified and well organized. The international community must co-operate to make the entire narcotics programme more effective. Thailand, on its part, is fully committed to drug control and is willing to shoulder its burden squarely.'

In late January 1979, on the eve of an official visit to the United States (to ask for greater arms aid to protect his threatened borders), watched by foreign drug agents, diplomats and a cluster of Thai officials and policemen gathered at the firing range of the Royal Thai Army's 11th Infantry Division in Bangkok, General Kriangsak Chamanand ceremonially set alight what was probably the most expensive bonfire in history. The fuel was 6.5 tons of illicit narcotics seized over ten years, including more than 1.6 tons of heroin worth up to US$650,000,000 at international street prices. He claimed the destruction was proof of his country's determination to fight the narcotics trade but, as some of the pearly white No.4 heroin trickled through his fingers, he could not help saying with a wry smile: 'Imagine all the tanks we could buy with that!'*

Given all this as the general picture of Thailand today, what are the practical realities of the fight against heroin trafficking? A DEA special agent in Bangkok claimed that in recent years the Thais had done 'a tremendous job' in disrupting the drug-running organizations operating out of their country, and it would be churlish to deny that there have been arrests, long terms of imprisonment and even executions of those engaged in the heroin trade. But what is the real success of the Thai police authorities and, indeed, the DEA itself in attacking the ethnic Chinese – and Triad – connection? 'You don't need to have to ask me to tell you the result,' says Police-General Pow Sarasin.

---

* An even more cynical point of view was uttered by a DEA agent, who said to me: 'I wonder how much of that stuff really was heroin. I wouldn't put it past that bunch to cheat their own Prime Minister and sell off the real stuff to their friends in the business.'

'You've read the newspapers.' And if one looks in the newspapers, whether in Thailand or elsewhere, there will be items like these:

San Francisco Chronicle, 1 March 1977: A Thai court sentenced a forty-two-year-old American to thirty years' imprisonment yesterday for trying to smuggle 2.2 pounds of heroin from Thailand to the United States last year. The American, identified as Thomas Kiley of Hawaii, was arrested at the Bangkok airport in November.

South China Morning Post (Hong Kong), 21 November 1977: Well-synchronized raids by narcotic agents in New York and Bangkok this weekend led to the arrest of nine drug traffickers heading a vast ring which supplied the American market, Bangkok police said yesterday.

Seven suspects – two Thais, two Americans, and three Italians – were arrested in New York with two kilos (4.4 lb) of heroin, while two Thais were arrested in a hotel in Bangkok with 700 grams (over 24 ounces) of heroin in their possession. A police spokesman in Bangkok said one of the Thais held there had agreed to co-operate by giving the authorities full details about the ring's operation.

Detroit News, 5 July 1978: The Thai supreme court ordered life prison sentences yesterday for a Tacoma, Wash., man and a German woman convicted of drug trafficking. William Ward, forty-six, and Sylvia Bailey, thirty-six, were arrested 2 February 1974 in a downtown Bangkok hotel room where the police said they found thirteen ounces of heroin, worth about $550 on the Bangkok market. The police claimed that the pair sent twenty-eight ounces of heroin to the United States in airmail letters before their arrest.

South China Morning Post (Hong Kong), 18 June 1978: Concerted police action has led to major drug seizures in London, Bangkok and Hong Kong since Friday. Their network of exchanged intelligence reports and tip-offs have won police and customs men three major victories in the war against narcotics:

At London's Heathrow airport, customs men uncovered the biggest haul of heroin ever found in Britain.

In Bangkok, police grabbed their biggest haul of morphine, opium and heroin in recent years.

In Hong Kong, a customs swoop has uncovered a new *Chiu Chao* syndicate trying to cash in on a market left wide open by police successes in recent years.

. . . In the Bangkok swoop, a Hong Kong resident was arrested after police found 213 lb of No. 3 heroin, 128 lb of morphine base and 73 lb of raw and prepared opium. The drugs, valued at about HK$42,700,000, were about to be loaded on to a trawler bound for Hong Kong. A Thai narcotics expert said the heroin and opium were probably intended for Hong Kong consumption, but the morphine base was probably scheduled for shipment to the United States after being converted to No.4 heroin in Hong Kong. Two Thais, one of whom owned the trawler, were also arrested.

Bangkok Post, 27 October 1978: Heavy prison terms were summarily imposed last night on six men for possession of morphine blocks. They were arrested on 8 July in Bangkok with the drug hidden in a secret compartment of a Land Rover. Police said the morphine was due to be smuggled to Haadyai the same day.

South China Morning Post (Hong Kong), 1 December 1978: Thai and American police believe they have smashed a heroin smuggling ring with the arrest of eight Thais in New York, Los Angeles and Bangkok. Seven suspects have been arrested in separate raids in the two American cities by US narcotics agents. One of the men arrested in New York was a lieutenant-colonel attached to the Supreme Command of the Thai Army. Members of the alleged ring have been under surveillance for two years. Police made their eight arrests in a swoop last night in Bangkok.

Since my departure from Bangkok, Police-Colonel Damrong Vaivong has also supplied me with details of two further cases:

23 January 1979: Mr Ma Ching-ling alias Lee Ming, Chinese-Haw [an ethnic Chinese hill-tribe] heroin maker – death sentence (still at large). Mr Chusak Tansiri – life imprisonment. Mr Pulor Wangluengsan, a hill-tribesman – life imprisonment. All were charged with attempting to sell 144.48 kilograms of 'White Dragon Pearl' heroin and No.3 brown sugar heroin to two Malaysian undercovers for two million Baht. The heroin was made by Ching-ling and delivered by the two others.

14 February 1979: Pol. Lt. Boonsuab Arpasat – forty years' imprisonment. Pol. Mst-Sgt. Sa -ard Srinoon – forty years' imprisonment. A civilian identified as Louis – thirty years' imprisonment (in absentia). They were charged with trying to sell 2.04 kilograms of heroin chloride to undercover agents for 165,000 Baht. The two police officers attached to Ayutthaya District Police Station, Ayutthaya Province [in central Thailand north of Bangkok]. A heavy jail term on two policemen is to set an example to other policemen and because they were law enforcers, but broke the law themselves.

Such achievements may seem not unimpressive – but what do they mean in real terms? Says a senior DEA special agent in Bangkok: 'What is required is a vigorous enforcement effort, not only in seizures, but in identifying the people that facilitate the traffic, in disrupting their organizations and in making key arrests – not just arrests, but key arrests, *significant* arrests.' I would add: 'And in keeping them in jail once you have arrested them.'

For did you notice those two little phrases in Police-Colonel Damrong Vaivong's letter to me: about the Chinese heroin maker sentenced to death '(*still at large*)' and the civilian known only as Louis sentenced to thirty years' imprisonment '(*in absentia*)'? The reality is that there is to date no major heroin trafficker captured in Thailand who has not subsequently managed to escape the authorities. My guess is that the police lieutenant sentenced to forty years' imprisonment in February 1979 need not worry about serving anything but a short sentence. And if this sounds cynical, consider the following five cases of major Thai traffickers or their principal aides:

Poonsiri Chanyasak, alias Chou Chao Chung: a married man with four children, arrested in March 1974, who, although he was alleged to have heroin in his possession, had the case against him dropped by the Thai Prosecution Department and was unilaterally set free. Some police officers claimed that he was the central figure in a multi-million dollar narcotics ring with connections in Laos, South Vietnam, the Philippines, Hong Kong and the United States. He fled after his release and was reported, in the *Far Eastern Economic Review* in June 1979 to be in Vientiane and still involved in the heroin trade.

Police-Lt. Colonel Sawai Phuttaraksa: arrested in July 1974 after Thai and DEA agents uncovered a heroin laboratory in his orchard on the outskirts of Chiang Mai. He first escaped from police custody by jumping out of a second-floor window of his house but, when recaptured and waiting to make a subsequent court appearance in March 1975, he asked his police guards to remove his handcuffs so he could go to the lavatory. He then simply walked out of a side door and stepped into a waiting limousine. He has never been seen again but is now said to be in charge of a morphine-conversion laboratory on the Thai-Burmese border close to the Thai northern provinces where he had previously spent the greater part of his twenty-six years in the Thai police.

Sukree Sukreepirom: Thai-Chinese businessman arrested in March 1975 in an underground car park in downtown Bangkok by Thai police with DEA special agents in attendance. An on-the-spot search revealed twenty-five kilos of heroin and, under threat of having his wife indicted as an accomplice, he signed a full confession of his role in the trade. Police then raided a local hotel where they arrested a visiting Chinese businessman from Malaysia named Hoi Se Wan, and seized a suitcase containing several hundred thousand United States dollars in Thai currency.

Police-General Chavalit Yodmani, head of the National Narcotics Suppression Centre, promptly called a press conference to announce the arrests of 'top international drug traffickers'. US President Gerald Ford sent letters of commendation to the two DEA special agents responsible for the months of undercover work that led to the arrests. The summer 1975 issue of *Drug Enforcement*, the DEA official journal, hailed the arrests as the culmination of two years of careful fieldwork and the two suspects were described as men who had 'controlled a transcontinental heroin pipeline for more than two decades'.

And what happened? In June 1975, the Thai Public Prosecutions Department decided not to file charges on obscure procedural grounds and, eighty-four days after his dramatic arrest at gun point, Sukree walked out of prison, a free man. High-ranking Thai police officers protested to the Prime Minister, demanding a full investigation of the Public Prosecutions Department, and angry police narcotics agents leaked to the local press that Sukree was only one of six international traffickers who had been released by the Department in recent months on similarly spurious grounds.

The investigations ordered by the Prime Minister homed in on the Director-General of Public Prosecutions himself as the official allegedly chiefly responsible for Sukree's release. Nothing was ever proved against him but, despite his denials of any complicity in the affair, he was found guilty of a 'serious violation of discipline' and sacked from his post. Sukree has never been seen since and has variously been reported in northern Thailand, Burma and Malaysia.

Siri Sirikul: Thai-Chinese trafficker arrested in October 1976 while handing over heroin in a suitcase to an undercover buyer in another Bangkok underground car park. He was sentenced to life imprisonment in April 1977 and duly appealed against his sentence. Subsequently, he was three times summoned from Bangkok's Bang Kwang maximum security prison to hear the verdict on his appeal but three times he failed to appear. Court officials put it down to confusion, but when in May 1979 he still did not turn up for the fourth time they finally checked back with the prison – and found that he had been freed twenty-three months before at the end of June 1977, on the strength of an apparently badly forged release warrant letting him out on temporary bail!

The prison had made no effort to check the authenticity of the warrant, which carried a forged court seal, despite the fact that it purported to be signed by a judge who did not even exist.

Police-General Pow Sarasin exploded in rage to the Bangkok press: 'Before a major trafficker like Siri is arrested, the police have to spend a lot of time, money and effort and put their lives at risk. It is utterly discouraging for them when someone like Siri is allowed to go free.'

Lao Su: a Yunnanese Chinese and ex-KMT Nationalist Army soldier, known to the Thai police under at least five aliases, arrested in a police raid in August 1977 in possession of a revolver and a plastic bag containing traces of heroin powder. Because Thailand, like Holland, has no conspiracy laws, the police cannot arrest a trafficker, however major his role, unless they can find him with some heroin actually on him. Merely being a ringleader is not enough. That was why Police-General Pow Sarasin's National Narcotics Control Board was so delighted with the traces of heroin in the bag found on Lao Su. They had waited years for that moment: he was – at last – charged with trafficking in drugs to Europe and the United States. His arrest was hailed in the Bangkok press as a great coup.

Less than a month later, he was free. Transferred 'under close supervision' from jail to Bangkok's Central Hospital because of 'serious headache and earache', he took a leaf out of Police-Lieutenant Colonel Sawai Phuttaraksa's book and simply walked out of the hospital after being given permission to go to the lavatory.

He was later sentenced to death 'in absentia' and is still at large, believed to be somewhere in the Golden Triangle in the

Thai-Burmese border area. In January 1980, the *Far Eastern Economic Review* reported him to be operating in Burma under the protection of the Shan State Revolutionary Army.

The above list of heroin Houdinis is very depressing but the situation is even worse than this. Those five men were at least arrested. They had the discomfort and disgrace – and in the Far East loss of 'face' is almost a punishment in itself – of being apprehended by police officers, guns pointed at them, being bundled into police cars or vans and spending some time, however little, in a Thai jail which, even with special treatment, is definitely not an ideal location. But the real villains, the No. 1 men, the top traffickers, have not even been arrested or charged, despite the expanded DEA programme and intensified Thai police activity.

Congressman Lester Wolff in his remarkable speech on 17 May 1977, from which I have already quoted, actually named twelve major traffickers – 'ethnic Chinese residing in Thailand who are primarily responsible for the purchase, shipment and support of the large volume of heroin that is distributed from Thailand into the western countries of Europe and the United States'. This was his fascinating exposé*:

[Mr A] left Yunnan Province in China in 1949 and took refuge in Burma to escape the Communist take-over. He then married and has eight children, some of whom study in Singapore, Taiwan, and the United States. He moved to Chiang Mai, Thailand, in 1965 and began his narcotics operation. Within five years, he had become and remains a most prominent figure in the Thai narcotics community.

Mr [A] has residences in Bangkok, Chiang Mai, and Mae Sai, Thailand. *He is the head of the largest heroin distribution ring in that country.* His list of associates is a 'Who's Who' of Chinese ethnics in the Bangkok narcotics market. He has investments and is the co-owner of many businesses in Bangkok and Chiang Mai, Thailand. . . . Mr [A's] operations in northern Thailand are conducted by confederates who purchase most of his narcotics from the hill tribes with financial support provided by Mr [A]. Originally, Mr [A's] narcotic business was located on the northern frontier of Thailand and northern Burma where he produced '999' brand of morphine.

* Much as I would have liked to give the names made public by Congressman Woolf, I cannot do so – for sound legal reasons. If the speech had been made in the British Parliament by a British MP, British libel laws would protect their republication here – but British law does not confer equal immunity upon a speech in a foreign legislature. The important thing, however, is that Congressman Woolf openly categorizes these notorious traffickers as Triads.

After moving to Chiang Mai because of pressure from the Burmese government, he went to Laos and set up a mining company which was a front for a heroin factory at Gold Delta, Laos. In 1976, the heroin refinery was moved to Tachilek, Burma, at the edge of the northern border of Thailand, under protection from certain of the opium warlords in that area. Mr [A's] confederate, [Mr B], is the superintendent of the refinery and Mr [A] remains in Bangkok distributing his poison to regular customers. *Mr [A] has excellent narcotics connections in Holland, Singapore, Malaysia, Hong Kong, and the United States.* His 'bag man' is Mr [C], who also lives in Bangkok and who has contacts with many government officials. Mr [A] has Thai citizenship, resides at [an address in] Bangkok; he also owns a house in Mae Sai, Thailand. As of this date, Mr [A] roams about the globe frequently and can be said to be one of the most important figures in the spreading of Asian poison to the youth of the world.

There are more such persons. *Mr [D]* was born in Thailand with an ancestral home in Teachow, China. He lives in Bangkok in a beautiful modern home which has an underground room used for gambling and smoking opium. He is close to Mr [A], whom I have already described, and the various other ethnic Chinese who live in Bangkok who are in the narcotics business. He owns the [—] Hotel in Bangkok and a jewelry store at the rear of the hotel. . . . About ten years ago, he went to the Thai-Laotian border and stayed there for some time before returning to Bangkok. He began to make considerable amounts of money in 1968 when Thailand's armed forces participated in the Vietnam war. This effort gave him the opportunity *to smuggle large quantities of heroin to Saigon for sale to American soldiers, in collusion with some Thai Army officers.* Intelligence sources reveal that between 1970 and 1971 [he] *smuggled 100 kilograms of No. 4 heroin and several tons of processed opium to Saigon where* [a] *fellow Triad member . . . distributed the narcotics.* [He] has a knack for making friends in Thai government circles. He has close connections with the Thai Army and the Thai police as well as officials of the former government. [He] also owns two export-import firms . . . in Bangkok. He has recently purchased a sumptuous villa in the area of Suthisan, Thailand, where Mr [A] and his associates often visit to conduct business and to gamble.

Another significant piece of intelligence relates to a *Mr [B]* . . . a Yunnanese Chinese who resides in Thailand. [He] moved to Thailand from Burma in 1961 and now occupies the first important position of principal assistant to Mr [A]. In 1966, when Mr [A] established a heroin factory in the jungle area of Hui Hse, Laos, Mr [B] was made superintendent of this factory. The chief pharmacist was a well-known heroin refiner. . . . At a later time this refinery was moved to Tachilek, Burma, under the protection of two Chinese opium warlord leaders. . . . Mr [B] built a large laboratory at this site where he purchased raw opium while Mr [A] supervised sales in Bangkok. In 1971, as the result of the loss of protection of the local armies and a change in Burmese government policies, Mr [B's] heroin refinery lost its armed protection and the result was the scattering of the refinery equipment to several mobile factories in the mountainous Golden Triangle area. At the present time, Mr [B] is actively operating a comparatively large heroin refinery near Chiang Mai, Thailand.

Another associate of Mr [A] is [Mr E], also a Yunnanese Chinese who came to Burma from China in 1949 and joined Mr [A] as a partner in the opium business. Mr [E] is an extremely wealthy man, having made fortunes in the opium smuggling operation that he conducted from 1961 to the present time in Hong Lo, Burma. In 1964, Mr [E] and his family moved to Bangkok. He and Mr [A], his partner and fellow Triad member, invested in the [—] Tea Co. in Bangkok and used the company as a front for the trans-shipment of large quantities of heroin into international markets. He owns interests in [a] hotel and [a tea company], both of Bangkok, and is closely associated with *General [F]*, a notorious opium exporter and Mr [A].

Mr [G], another Yunnanese Chinese, who came to Thailand when he was very young, lives in a Western-style ranch house with a large garden adjacent to it. He also owns a house in Chiang Mai, Thailand. Between 1969 and 1971 he worked for a number of refinery operators, including the gentlemen I have already named. He is mainly responsible for supplying the precursors necessary for the manufacture of heroin. He is a major distributor of narcotics in Bangkok and has recently earned the equivalent of $1 million with part of which he purchased two houses . . . in Bangkok. Mr [G] moves around from house to house in order to confuse law enforcement efforts and is known to be well connected in government circles.

I wish also to call attention to the following three narcotics financiers and power brokers: *Mr [H]*, a Yunnanese Chinese, *Mr [I]* who is also Yunnanese, and *Mr [J]*. These three gentlemen reside in Thailand and are *principal distributors of N.3 heroin* with connections in the Golden Triangle as solid as those they have in the United States. They own houses, hotels, export-import companies, and other fronts for their nefarious businesses.

It must be realized that these individuals supply the vast amount of money necessary to guarantee a continuous large flow of opium. They finance the refineries which produce No.3 and No.4 heroin. They provide support for the smuggling operations after the merchandise arrives in Bangkok, and also the front money for the costs of distribution. *Fortunes are collected in exchange for a nod, a handshake or an understood password from their Triad brethren all over the world.* Their wealth is reminiscent of the legendary rulers of ancient days.

Mr Speaker, to my knowledge, this burgeoning and extremely

dangerous situation has never been made public before. I am doing so now because it is necessary for the American people to identify their enemies. Together with the corrupt officials without whose connivance this traffic would be impossible, they are princely purveyors of universal misery.

What has happened to those 'princely purveyors of universal misery?' I asked Police-General Pow Sarasin in Bangkok. 'One has been executed. The rest go outside the country. They are afraid to stay here.' The following is a list, supplied by a member of the General's staff, of all persons executed in Thailand for narcotics offences to the date of my visit since April 1977, when the death penalty was first brought back for this category of offence by the then Prime Minister, Thanin Kraivichien.

Thavorn Sae Khoh, a Laotian Chinese executed on 14 April 1977.
Charn 'Siewsan' Sriphadungkul (alias Lao San) and *Lao Fan* (alias Fan Tsu Hsiang and Lao Fen Sae Yang), executed on 3 November 1977.
Meesiam Sae Heng and *Sung Hong Hwak,* a Hong Kong chemist, executed on 2 August 1978.
Ung Pang Chong (alias Panchong Sae Ung), executed on 4 October 1978.

I have checked and re-checked the names and aliases of those five men, and not one of them is to be found in Congressman Wolff's list of major traffickers. Furthermore, I am assured in Bangkok and Hong Kong that what happened to *all* twelve men named by Congressman Wolff was that they were not arrested but merely went into comfortable exile in the northern provinces of the country. Says a DEA special agent: 'Once in a while they sneak back into Bangkok – but there still has been no arrest.'

I have asked Congressman Wolff why he took the un-precedented step of naming those men in the debating chamber of a legislative congress thousands of miles away from their base of operations. His reply: 'Because nobody else was doing so.'

Executions in Thailand are a grisly business by any humane standard. The prisoner is strapped, blindfolded, to a wooden, cross-shaped support embedded in the floor of the execution room at Bang Kwang prison in Bangkok. He is placed facing a sandbagged wall and with his back to his executioner. A movable board is positioned between him and Police-Corporal

Pratom Kruapeng, Thailand's chief executioner, standing behind his Blackmann machine-gun which rests on a four-legged stand facing the board. Corporal Pratom does not aim at his victims. 'As a good Buddhist,' explains a DEA special agent in The Hague who has served in Bangkok, 'his religion would forbid him to kill any defenceless being, even an animal. So when the order to fire comes, he is not told to shoot at the man – but only at the board!'

What was the offence that the Thais considered so heinous that they put these five men through that last gruesome ordeal when many others have gone free?

Thavorn Sae Khoh, the first man to die, was not even charged with international trafficking. He was arrested in Bangkok in March 1977 when found with 30 lb of heroin in his car, which only brought a 'possessing drugs for sale' charge. Yet he was executed suddenly and without prior warning a bare three hours before the opening in the Thai capital of the United States Far East Asia Narcotics Conference, set for 15 April 1977.

The *Washington Post* reported the next day that Thavorn did not seem to know that he was to be executed until he received a blessing from a Buddhist monk and his two young children only learned of their father's death when they arrived at his jail cell with food for him. The newspaper's Bangkok correspondent reported that the execution 'struck several observers here as an international ploy to impress the Americans'. The then Prime Minister, Thanin Kraivichien, who ordered the execution had only come to power the previous October following a coup d'état, and from the start had made a crackdown on narcotics a major plank of his policy.

Charn 'Siewsan' Sriphadungkul and Lao Fan, executed in November 1977 following an order signed by a Thai admiral, chairman of the Revolutionary Party in the brief interregnum between Prime Ministers Thanin and Kriangsak, were both ethnic Chinese. Charn, a Chinese-Haw, with origins in the hill tribes of the Golden Triangle, was a member of the syndicate run by Mr [A] (named in Congressman Wolff's list of 'twelve major traffickers') but, according to the *Bangkok Post*, his job was merely to control a drugs storehouse in Bangkok. Lao Fan was a Yunnanese ex-KMT Nationalist soldier assigned by syndicate leader Mr [A] to co-operate with Lao Su, the gentle-man with the earache who after his arrest walked out of

Bangkok's Central Hospital while 'under close supervision'. The *Bangkok Post* does not specify the nature of Lao Fan's supposed 'co-operation' with Lao Su, a palpably powerful figure; but, if he was in the same league, is it not possible he too might have been able to develop a useful malady?

Meesiam Sae Heng and Sung Hong Hwak, the two men executed in August 1978, were both arrested when, acting on information supplied to the Thai police by the DEA 'in back of some arrests in New York', as it was described to me, the police raided a heroin-conversion laboratory and Sung was the chemist working there. Police-General Pow Sarasin has denied to me that Sung was a Triad – even though he *was* ethnic Chinese and had been brought over to Thailand specifically because of his expertise as a heroin chemist. 'Most chemists for the drug here come from Hong Kong. All we arrest come from Hong Kong. But I don't think they are Triads.'

Ung Pang Chong, the last to be executed, in October 1978, was also an ethnic Chinese from Hong Kong. He was the 'Hong Kong resident', cited in the colony's *South China Morning Post* newspaper's report early in this chapter as having been arrested in June 1978 with over 400 lb of heroin, morphine base and opium in his possession about to be loaded on to a trawler bound for Hong Kong. In fact, the drugs were not on him personally but hidden in sacks in a van parked near to where the waiting trawler was moored off Samut Prakan, nearest seaport to Bangkok on the Gulf of Thailand. The *Bangkok Post*, announcing his execution, described him as a 'major heroin trafficker' and related how Thai police had kept him under surveillance while he talked to two Thai accomplices, the trawler owner and his nephew, in a coffee shop at Samut Prakan near the harbour.

But would a man who was really a 'major heroin trafficker', setting up deals to be calculated in hundreds of thousands, perhaps even millions, of United States dollars, be involved in dockside discussions or get himself anywhere near so massive a consignment? The *Bangkok Post* claimed that he 'pleaded guilty to the police and admitted that he was the financier for the planned narcotics smuggling to Hong Kong'. But was it his *own* money that he was putting into the deal or was he merely the bag-carrier for his Triad bosses higher up in the hierarchy? Was he truly a 'major heroin trafficker' or rather a cog in a wheel?

I can only pose the questions. I cannot supply the answers –

but a senior police official of another country, who has had many dealings with the Thai police authorities, has told me: 'Of course, they have honourable men among them – Pow Sarasin and a few other really first-class men like him are absolutely incorruptible, I'm sure – but they don't always have the last say. The Thais have executed people because they didn't want them to talk. One person said he would talk and name names – and I am not at liberty to tell you who he was – and they took him out and shot him.'

The five executions all took place under the summary powers of the Prime Minister or his surrogate to order an execution of those who threaten national security, the economy, natural resources, public order or morals. Under the new 1979 Constitution (allegedly part of Kriangsak's 'window-dressing' to get more American aid), the Prime Minister lost those summary powers. Since February 1979, the death sentence in drug cases can only be imposed by the ordinary courts after a full hearing and upon considering all the evidence brought against the accused. To date, there has been no such case. Is it mere coincidence that, once the Thai police have had to prove the precise nature of the accused's activities so as to justify the death sentence, there have been no executions?

As a DEA special agent said to me in West Germany as our car sped along the rain-scudded *autobahn* to Wiesbaden police headquarters, 'We're all pissing in the wind unless the source-of-supply countries that produce the heroin get on the bandwagon and really start to do something about their problem and ours!' I must apologize for the vulgarity of that assessment, but I do not find it totally unfair.

8 Triads in Malaysia

If the narcotics situation in Thailand is depressing, it is worse still in Malaysia. Heroin was being sold openly on the roadside, with no attempt at concealment, when I drove through the streets of Johor Bahru in the southern tip of the country. In Kuala Lumpur, the nation's capital, in the north, it is possible to wander into almost any bar catering for the young, hippy-type foreigner and 'make your score', as Western addicts and independent small-time dealers call it. The number of young foreigners in Kuala Lumpur is very noticeable, many of them wearing stout shoes and ankle socks and clearly having travelled many miles on foot. They include all nationalities but Americans and Australians seem to predominate.

'The attraction is the easy availability of heroin up there,' the DEA special agent in charge of the Singapore office told me. 'And it's not only for the kids. What we see is a second Golden Triangle, if you will, in Malaysia, with European cities – and Australasia – being supplied from Malaysia more often, at least of late, than from Thailand. The American market is still being supplied primarily out of Thailand itself with some coming on as well by way of onward shipment from Hong Kong. But for Europe and Australia and New Zealand, more and more stuff is going out by air by couriers from the airports at Penang and Kuala Lumpur.'

The Thai police and DEA agents in Bangkok claim that this is due to increased activity by the law enforcement forces in Thailand but as a police officer in the Singapore Narcotics Bureau said, 'It may simply be that it is much easier to get the stuff out through Malaysia. So far as heroin is concerned, it is "open house" over there.'

Certainly, Malaysia faces severe problems over law enforcement. Some inkling of the situation had been given me back in London when I received a reply to my introductory letter to Jerry Lieuw Wing Lin, then Deputy Director of Criminal Intelligence at Kuala Lumpur's police headquarters. This arrived in an ordinary registered airmail envelope, within which was another envelope marked 'Confidential' and sealed with wax marked 'Polis di Raja Malaysia'. I later learned that this elaborate procedure was to prevent anyone reading the letter – surely remarkable when it was coming from within the police force itself. Jerry Lieuw was candid about Malaysia's enormous narcotics law enforcement task. 'The demand is there, supply is there and for any law enforcement agency to be able to tackle that problem manpower is the biggest setback in terms of quantity as well as in terms of quality.'

The enormity of the task can only be appreciated against the background to modern Malaysia. This underdeveloped and poor country, where, as in most other nations of South-East Asia, corruption is endemic, dates only from September 1963 when the Federation of Malaysia was founded as an independent member of the British Commonwealth. It comprised the eleven states of spindle-shaped Peninsular Malaysia (the old-style Malaya), Singapore and the two distant states of Sabah (formerly British North Borneo) and Sarawak away on the large island of Borneo off to the east across the waters of the South China Sea. Singapore seceded as an independent island republic two years later in August 1965, depriving the new state of its vast commercial resources.

Apart from its economic problems, the new Federation – and the old Federation of Malaya – has been plagued with Communist insurgency both on its borders and within the country itself. A state of emergency against the Communists was declared in June 1948 and lasted for twelve years until formally declared at an end in 1960, but in 1975 the Malaysian Communist party began a renewed offensive. Dozens of policemen have since been killed and in June 1978 64,000 troops were put on war alert against a possible upsurge of Communist terrorism. In November 1978, the nation's Prime Minister, Datuk Hussein Onn, admitted at a press conference that China had refused to give up its support of Communist guerillas in his country.

Police headquarters at Kuala Lumpur are like a military encampment, with armed guards and strict security. The military-style Royal Malaysian Police have enough problems, even of survival, without having to worry unduly about the effect of the heroin that goes through their territory upon the lives of people thousands of miles away, of different race and different nationality – although according to David Khoo, one of Jerry Lieuw's most trusted officers, Malaysia's own heroin addicts are now 'something between 60,000 and 100,000 people.'

But perhaps the most important factor in the emergence of Malaysia as 'a second Golden Triangle' is the openly admitted presence of powerful Triad Societies operating in the new nation. For once, no one seeks to deny that ever since the first Chinese immigrants – as always mainly from southern China – came down into Penang in the late eighteenth century and then, in greater numbers, to work in the newly opened tin mines around Kuala Lumpur, Ipoh and Taiping in the mid-nineteenth century, Triad Societies have flourished on the peninsula.

'The Chinese imported into Malaya their beneficent district and clan associations and also their secret societies,' wrote Dr Victor Purcell, former Principal Adviser on Chinese Affairs to the British Military Administration, in his classic study *The Chinese in Malaya*. 'As early as 1799 in Penang the latter set the administration in defiance and strong measures were necessary to reduce them to obedience. The ends of justice they often defeated by bribery and false swearing, and sometimes by open violence.' His book, written thirteen years before Hong Kong Police Inspector W.P.Morgan's *Triad Societies in Hong Kong*, contains an account of a Triad initiation ceremony and the thirty-six oaths which reads like an advance trailer for the later work. If Morgan had not read Dr Purcell's book, which seems highly likely – he never refers to it in his text – it would again show how universal the Triad ethos is.

The names of the various historical Malayan Triad Societies cited by Purcell – Ghee Hin, Ho Seng, Toh Peh Kong, for example – and their modern counterparts, such as Ang Boon Huey and Wah Kee, are different from the former Chinese mainland and present-day Hong Kong societies but their structure, hierarchy and the direct descent claimed from the original Triad monastery near Foochow in Fukien province are exactly the same. So is the story of their degeneracy into criminal associations. Writing in Kuala Lumpur in 1975, Mr N.J.Ryan, formerly of the Malaysian Education Service, states in his *A History of Malaysia and Singapore*:

Perhaps the most important aspect of the Chinese way of life introduced into the region with the immigrants was the secret society. Today the secret society is an illegal organization of criminals, who control sections of the underworld in Singapore and in the larger towns of the peninsula, and who extort, assault or murder for a price. Today the secret societies operate on a large scale, forcing protection on shopkeepers and controlling gambling, prostitution and drugs in their own areas. They have become a vicious menace, *but they have not always been as bad as they are today* [my italics].

Against that background, it was inevitable that, as South-East Asian heroin's vast potential for money-making became clear in the early 1970s, the Triad criminal elements among the Chinese population of the country (forty per cent of Malaysia's estimated twelve million people are ethnic Chinese, ten per cent Indian and only fifty per cent Malay) were going to get their greedy fingers into that very remunerative pie. As we have already seen in Thailand, the borderline between legitimate and illegitimate business can become very blurred.

As long ago as 1827, Dr T.M.Ward, a British doctor stationed in north Malaya, was writing in an official report (quoted by Purcell), 'The Chinese here are the most enterprising, the most opulent, the most industrious and the most determined in pursuit of wealth.' Habits scarcely change over the years. When asked by a foreign visitor the times kept by Kuala Lumpur shops, a local chauffeur replied in October 1978 (as quoted in the magazine *Asia World*): 'It depends. If it is a shop run by a Malay, it will open at 10 am and close at 5 pm. If it is a shop run by an Indian, it will be open from 7 am to 7 pm. If it is a Chinese shop, it will be open from 7 am to 7 am.'

The heroin trade through Malaysia, which, as in its northern neighbour of Thailand, is controlled exclusively at the higher levels by the ethnic Chinese is 'open from 7 am to 7 am'. And it is a very successful trade indeed, run hand-in-glove with fellow Chinese on the other side of the border. 'The police can arrest a man on suspicion and, provided they can prove their case to the Law Minister, they can get him put in detention on a small island between Penang and the mainland for two years followed by a further two years' restriction without having to get sufficient evidence to prove a case in court to put him in jail,' Jerry Lieuw has told me in London. 'I arrested one major drugs trafficker once for detention and his brother came down to see me from southern Thailand with one million Malaysian dollars in cash to offer me as a bribe! This is the difficulty we are faced with and I don't mind saying it again: unless you are fanatically honest you cannot be in drug enforcement. You have to be a fanatic – and there are not many of them around!'

'There is no such thing as an overall Triad organization,' Stanley S. Bedlington, US State Department Foreign Affairs political analyst for the area and author of *Malaysia and Singapore: The Building of New States*, told me in Washington DC: 'There is a multiplicity of organizations which co-operate (or fight) with each other. The societies tend to focus on clan and dialect groupings. For instance, the Wah Kee is very strong in Kuala Lumpur, as in other inland cities, but the Ang Boon Huey is very strong in Penang and in other seaports. The Ang Boon Huey will co-operate with the Ang Boon Huey in Singapore for the onward distribution of drugs, but it is highly unlikely that they would co-operate with the Wah Kee in Kuala Lumpur in terms of distribution. They are more likely to compete with them for it!'

In his book, Mr Bedlington relates how, as a Chinese-language student in Malaya, he learned a polite Chinese phrase that involved asking a new acquaintance: 'Where is your ancestral village?' The majority of respondents knew exactly where this was, even though their family may have lived in Malaya for several generations. As elsewhere in the world, Malaysian Triad Societies are rooted in these ancestral origins.

As elsewhere too, modern Triad activities in Malaysia follow the 'normal' pattern. Says Mr Bedlington: 'They are very much into gambling, the numbers racket, prostitution – and, since the heroin trade first took off in the early 1970s, the drugs traffic.' But also, unique in the last quarter of the twentieth century, Malaysia has seen its local Triads playing a *political* role: it has almost been, for once, a return to their legitimate origins as a valiant resistance group on behalf of their own people against alien oppressors.

Malay–Chinese racial antagonism is always simmering below the surface in modern Malaysia. The Malays, on the whole less intelligent than the Chinese, less commercially oriented and without their business acumen, resourcefulness or capacity for genuine hard work, have always resented Chinese financial success. It seems to me, as an English Jew, that the Malays feel to the Chinese in their midst rather like over the centuries so many Europeans have felt to the Jewish people in *their* midst. It matters not that, as with the Jews, the Chinese reputation for being possessed of vast wealth is a factual absurdity. As Stanley S. Bedlington writes in his book: 'Far from all being wealthy capitalists and exploiters, many poor Chinese make up an urban proletariat and are rural farmers and smallholders. Many of the Chinese urban proletariat earn only about US$30 per month when they can find work: they are poor and often embittered, and from their ranks the secret society criminals and the Communists recruit their members.'

The Prime Minister and most of the government heads are Malay but, so I was told, the really effective force in most government departments (and even in the police) is not the Malay chief but his Chinese deputy. (Jerry Lieuw was the Deputy Director of Criminal Intelligence: his Director was a Malay, or 'Son of the Soil', a term that the Malays use about themselves with pride but the Chinese, and Chinese policemen, repeat with disdain.)

Racial tensions exploded into violence in May 1969, following the re-election of the middle-of-the-road Alliance Party. In N.J. Ryan's measured terms, 'There was the feeling of many urban Chinese that the Malays had been given too many political privileges and more importantly the knowledge of many rural Malays that, despite the growing prosperity of the country, very little of this prosperity was being passed on directly to them.'

On 13 May 1969, Kuala Lumpur was torn apart by bloodshed and rioting. Writes Ryan: 'In the enforcement of law and order by the military which followed the declaration of a state of emergency, the heavier casualties were suffered by the Chinese community and it was a week before the curfew was lifted.' But Stanley S. Bedlington says that it went considerably further than that: 'There were shootings. Hundreds of people – mainly Chinese – were killed or injured. The police, who were reasonably impartial, could not control the situation. They called in the army, and the Malay troops caused some very ugly scenes. The Chinese community in the capital – the riots never spread out of Kuala Lumpur – felt themselves in great danger, so they called in their own, the Triads!' Once again, Triads fought in defence of their people.

The political disturbances continued for nearly two years. Then in February 1971 the country was considered to be back to normal. The National Operations Council was changed into the National Security Council and parliamentary government returned with, however, certain restrictions on what N.J.Ryan calls 'sensitive issues'. It is impossible to determine the exact nature, if any, of continuing Triad involvement in the politics of this troubled new state. Mr Bedlington says, 'I haven't gotten very far in trying to persuade people in the State Department of the political importance of the secret societies in Kuala Lumpur.' My own hunch is that, once having become involved, I cannot see the Triads very easily becoming un-involved: not so long as racial prejudices and hatreds still flare in the country. It was, after all, not a Chinese but a Malay minister who threatened to shoot ethnic Chinese boat refugees from Vietnam if they still persisted in trying to set foot on Malaysian soil.

It is perhaps this racial ill-ease that caused the reluctance of both Jerry Lieuw and his aid, David Khoo, to identify positively any named Chinese traffickers in Malaysia as Triads or not. It was continually, 'We have no evidence that he is a Triad' or 'We do not believe that he is a Triad' or 'So far as we know, he is not a Triad.'

By contrast, thousands of miles away from these homeland difficulties, at the Old Bailey in London, there have been several major cases in the late 1970s when the British police authorities have had no trouble at all in naming important Chinese–Malaysian traffickers as Triads.

For instance, the Kok Lian 'Jason' Ng conspiracy trial from April to June 1977 revealed an astonishing story in which twenty-five-year-old Jason, the son of a millionaire Chinese tin-mine-owner in his native Malaysia, was convicted along with six others for operating a drugs ring that the Crown alleged had brought into Britain a total of 26 lb of Chinese No. 3 heroin with a street-level price of £10 million. Originally bought in Malaysia from traffickers bringing it over the southern Thai border at £700 a pound, when 'cut' and diluted to ten per cent purity, it was selling at £472,500 a pound!

Jason's capture and the crushing of his syndicate was one of the successes of 'Operation Templar', a beautifully planned and executed operation against Chinese heroin traffickers mounted in the summer of 1976 by the Metropolitan Police Drugs Squad when under the command of Superintendent Fred Luff, a dedicated police officer and one of the few senior 'Met' men properly to appreciate the menace of the Triads.

It was Luff who suggested to the jury how Jason had got a twenty-two-year-old Chinese–Malayan student, Toh How 'David' Lim, to 'co-operate' with him: 'We have heard in this trial about the Triad organization and we have had instances in this country of serious assault on persons who do not follow the doctrine of that organization, and I can only think that this is what influenced David Lim.'

It was a classic story of undercover 'cat and mouse' tactics in which Jason organized his deliveries so that no member of his ring could be caught in physical possession of drugs. The seller would collect payment and tell the buyer where to collect – buried under a tree in Hyde Park or taped under the shelf of a telephone kiosk. A former photographer for a well-known pop group told the court that he had spent £800 a week on Jason's drugs in this way. The police evidence had been slowly built up to the point of arrest, with a final car chase that was just like a scene from an American television cops-and-robbers series – startled London shoppers witnessed a car screech past them leaving a trail of small packets behind – the heroin cargo that Jason's passenger and main courier, Abu Syed Bakar, was desperately trying to jettison before the police cars caught up with them. A search of Jason's house produced sixty-eight packets of heroin in a drawer. Two pounds of heroin, worth about a million pounds, were found buried in a garden in Ilford, Essex, which had been used by the syndicate as a convenient underground warehouse.

The syndicate was said to have maintained links with Amsterdam and Rome and two men found guilty came from Hong Kong. It was an international conspiracy. 'We have heard about the Triad,' Judge Edward Clarke, QC, told the jury in his summing up. 'It is an organization, as far as we know, that deals with the importation and supplying of heroin in this country. There is no doubt that heroin is imported from Malaysia and the Far East. One of the main centres of distribution for contacts for supplying heroin in London is Gerrard Street in illegal gaming houses. It may be mysterious but it is not attractive. You are not dealing with a minor offence, but with something that is a real scourge of civilization in the world.'

Another major trial at the Old Bailey in which the British were content to dub as Triads heroin traffickers operating out of Malaysia was the May Wong trial, December 1976 to January 1977. Sentencing the diminutive twenty-nine-year-old Malaysian girl, May Wong, to fourteen years in prison (later reduced to twelve), Judge Michael Argyle, QC, told her, in classic British judicial style: 'When your tiny shadow fell on Gerrard Street, the whole street was dark and you and your confederates walked through the valley of the shadow of death.'

According to the story reported in the British newspapers, the source of supply was Ricky Chan, a Chinese trafficker living in and operating out of Ipoh in northern Malaysia, near the Thai frontier, where May Wong herself was born. His representative in Britain handling the drug's distribution was a Hong Kong Chinese 'student' named Anthony Mann who had come to London in 1971. He was already at that time a member of the Wo Shing Wo, a Triad Society originating in the colony's New Territories with a home-based contingent of about 5000 members. The working link was profitable and Mann lived like a wealthy playboy, collecting a stable of attractive white-skinned girl-friends – 'par for the course' for young Oriental successful traffickers – many of whom he introduced to heroin and also got to work for him as couriers.

However, Mann himself became an addict and functioned increasingly less efficiently as a distributor for Ricky Chan until the latter sent over a Chinese–Malaysian 'student', Chin Keong 'Mervyn' Yong, to replace him. Tony Mann was relegated to the position of 'runner' to his new boss but then Yong himself was 'bitten by the big elephant'. Moreover, he was an excessive gambler – in March 1975 he lost £13,000 of Ricky Chan's money in one night. Increasingly desperate to pay the large debts to Chan, Yong and his fellow addict Mann carried out a series of wild and ever more reckless robberies, culminating in a raid on the home of the Thai military attaché in London which led to their arrest. Mann turned Queen's Evidence and received a five-year sentence, Yong was given ten years, but according to

9 Triads in Singapore

The city of Singapore was founded by Sir Stamford Raffles in 1819 but the independent Republic of Singapore has existed only since 1965. This island state in the middle of a Malay sea, with an area of 232 square miles and an estimated population of 2,300,000 people of whom seventy-six per cent are ethnic Chinese, has been ruled by the People's Action Party led by Lee Kwan Yew ever since 1959, when Singapore first achieved partial independence within the British Commonwealth.

The long-serving Prime Minister Lee is a London-trained Chinese barrister, a member of the same Inn of Court as me, and it was directly to him that I wrote for assistance with my research. As a result I was put into contact with the Assistant Police Commissioner, Director of the Criminal Investigation Department, Mr Chai, who was very helpful and generous with the time he and his colleagues allotted me.

Yet I was left with the same feeling that I had in Hong Kong. The official version of current local Triad activities does not tally with the non-official view. It was fully accepted by everyone, including Mr Chai himself and Mr Lim Soo Gee, officer-in-charge of the Secret Societies Investigation Branch, that, as with Peninsular Malaysia from which their country so recently seceded, there is a long history of Triad criminal activity. But all *serious* activity is put firmly in the past.

'In the old days, before the Second World War, there were very active Triad Societies,' Mr Chai told me. 'But now they have degenerated into very loosely-knit street gangs: young hooligans calling themselves secret societies but only using the old names.' He gave the example of the Lo Kwan, an old Triad Society group, whose name is now being used by bands of young boys who call themselves 'the new Lo Kwan'. These 'very loosely-knit street gangs' are active in fighting for street territory, within which they try to operate protection and prostitution rackets. 'If there is a housing estate within their territory, they may perhaps try to get the subcontractors doing work on the estate to pay them protection money to be allowed to carry on with their work. . . . They also try and get protection money from newsvendors selling newspapers on the housing estates.' Their average age is between fifteen and twenty-two.

As for secret society activity in drug trafficking: 'We have had individuals arrested for drug abuse, arrested for pushing, who were secret society members but they were just individuals who were secret society members and drug users who, because they required money to sustain their habit, push drugs at the same time but not on an organized basis.'

How does this square with the stories told in Europe about the activities of Singaporean Triads operating in the heroin trade in Holland, Scandinavia and West Germany? And how does it tie in with May Wong's activities and her flights back to Singapore? (Mr Chai told me that the first that they had heard of the May Wong case was when it was reported in the British newspapers and in the *Straits Times*.) Clearly, as in Hong Kong, the official view does not reveal the whole picture.

Nor is that all. Michael Chai told me that initiation ceremonies no longer took place, partly because of fear of detection and partly because present-day gangs are very loosely organized, and that the tattoo marks Triads used to have on their arms are no longer used. Yet in the copy of *Police Life Annual* 1977, given to me by Mr Chai, there was an article written by him and a Singapore University lecturer called 'Crime Patterns and Socio-legal Responsibility' which included two photographs. One showed the bare arms of a prisoner and was captioned 'Tattoos used as identification marks by Triad members'; the other showed a covered table-top on which stood various bowls, knick-knacks and candlesticks and was captioned 'The altar used by a Triad during its initiation ritual for new members'.

What is going on? I do not question the statement in Stanley S. Bedlington's book on Malaysia and Singapore published in 1978 – 'Any person who has lived in Singapore cannot but be impressed with the efficiency of the state. . . . The state bureaucracy is one of the least corruptible in the world and is staffed by dedicated officials.' – but I do feel that, for whatever reasons of 'good public relations' with the outside world or of sheer complacency, I was not told the full story by the Singapore police.

This impression was heightened by my own observations and by my discussions with Mr Poh Geok Ek, generally known as Tony Poh, the Deputy Director of the Central Narcotics Bureau, and with DEA special agents in Singapore.

Having seen for myself how heroin is sold openly on the streets of Johor Bahru on the Malaysian mainland – reached from Singapore by a mile-long causeway – I could but totally agree with Tony Poh's scornful remark, 'Malaysia is an open market for heroin'. The Singaporeans have immense difficulties in adequately policing the causeway, across which commuters swarm daily to and from the island republic and where the Customs check must inevitably be quick.

'Operation Ferret' was launched on 1 April 1977 'with the objective of identifying and arresting as many drug traffickers, pushers and abusers as possible and containing them', Mr Poh has written in an article in *Police Life Annual* 1978. 'This has been achieved with considerable success – 1686 drug offenders were prosecuted and 6647 sent to the Drug Rehabilitation Centres. In addition, the arrest of 297 traffickers and pushers disrupted the distribution network of heroin trafficking and pushing in Singapore.'

Mr Poh proudly claimed: 'The spread of heroin abuse in Singapore was effectively contained by the end of 1977.' He also told me about a change in the law in 1975 whereby anyone found guilty of trafficking in more than fifteen grams of heroin (about half an ounce) or thirty grams of morphine now faces a mandatory death sentence. Such sentences have indeed been carried out: in April 1978 two Chinese Malaysians were hanged and in 1979 two more were executed. But all four were merely couriers, one of them found with less than two ounces of diamorphine wrapped in newspaper hidden in his underpants. No major trafficker has yet been hanged in Singapore, despite Prime Minister Lee Kwan Yew's proclaimed determination to rid the country of its own internal spiralling heroin addiction problem.

It goes even further than that. On the very day that the

second execution took place in Changi Jail, a Malaysian Chinese businessman held on drug charges and facing the death penalty if convicted was dramatically released from the same jail. The police said that he may have been framed. 'Such melodramatic gestures,' wrote Ian Ward, the highly respected London *Daily Telegraph* Singapore correspondent, 'have tended to heighten outside criticism of Singapore's tough measures and penalties to counter the drug problem. Critics point out that, despite these measures, the instances of drug abuse have continued to rise.'

I turned for information to the two DEA special agents based in the US Embassy building in Singapore. They certainly seemed to like playing up the CIA 'cloak and dagger' image: when I went to deliver my introductory message at a locked and barred Embassy on a steaming hot Sunday afternoon, I was faced by two large mirror doors that I am sure were two-way facing, and an unidentified voice on the other side instructed me to push my envelope under the door – whereupon I stood there on the almost empty street and saw it disappear before my eyes as the (undoubtedly) armed guard pulled it under the door. And when I met the two DEA men a couple of days later, they insisted on talking to me – and my tape-recorder – against a loud musical background from a radio or cassette player in a corner of their office. They politely declined to turn the sound down – as a precaution, so I gained the impression, against some possible bugging device in the room. Most of the talking was done by the younger of the two agents who was due to go off (as he told me) on an undercover mission to Indonesia on the following day.

Whatever the image, the account that they gave me of the nature and extent of Singaporean Triad involvement in both the internal and world-wide trafficking in South-East Asian heroin seemed both factual and well balanced. The following is a summary of what the young agent had to say:

When the Chinese first settled in Malaya, they settled around the tin mines in the north and brought with them their own Triad Societies, the original Triads. These societies acted as self-defence groups, community and welfare groups, and were based on dialect and clan groupings – a Cantonese would belong to one Triad Society, a Hokkienese to another. They evolved to a point when, just before the Second World War and especially

Heroin factory seized in Hong Kong

Preparing heroin for smoking, Hong Kong style. This is the method known as 'playing the mouth organ' in which smoke from the heated drug is inhaled through a matchbox cover

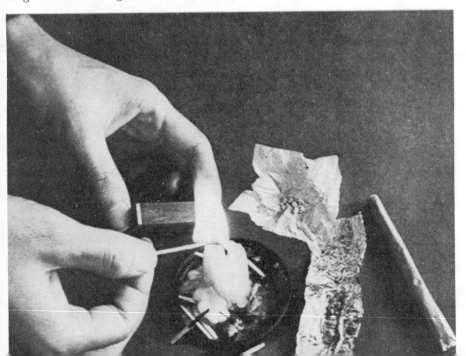

ABOVE Tattoos used as identification marks by Triad members in Singapore   BELOW The altar used by a Triad during the initiation ritual for new members. These captions are taken from *Police Life Annual 77* published by the Singapore Police Force referred to in the text

General Tuan Shih Wen, one of the ex-KMT drug warlords, photographed in 1967

Part of General Tuan's force of 2000 men on parade in north Thailand

LEFT The basis of General Tuan's army – an opium poppy. The ring round the neck of the Yao girl holding it is solid silver – from the proceeds of selling opium

BELOW General Kriangsak Chamanand, then Thai Prime Minister, at the ceremonial burning of R120 million of heroin seized by the Thai authorities in January 1979 – or was it merely white powder?

RIGHT Georgie Pai,
born in Hong Kong's
New Territories, who,
as 'Red Pole' became
the scourge of
London's Chinatown

BELOW May Wong
and her lover, Li
Mah, jailed at
the Old Bailey for
heroin trafficking in
January 1977 despite
a cock-and-bull
story about joining the
triads to seek out her
murdered father's
assassins

Chung Mon, first 'Godfather' of Amsterdam, in the days of his glory –
and on his last day, gunned down in the streets of his adopted city

...ta Nightingale jubilant on her release from jail in Thailand, freed
... Amnesty after serving just over two years of a twenty-year
...ntence for heroin trafficking

...argharita photographed on the steps of Police Headquarters,
...acao, by the author

The author *(2nd left)* at the start of an evening with an Anti-Triad Action Squad of the Royal Hong Kong Police, Kowloon, October 1978

M.B. Lee *(3rd from right)*, former 'uncrowned Mayor' of New York's Chinatown, a year after the attempt on his life, relaxes with US and Canadian police officers (and the author) at the dinner to close the New York City Police 'Triad Societies' conference, September 1978. Detective Neil Mauriello is the man with the moustache in the middle

after it, the old traditional part of the Triad Society, the benevolent part, became the *Chiu Chao* clan association and the criminal element separated off and formed the now familiar street gangs.

The latter kept a lot of the ancient Triad initiation system but watered down – instead of cutting off a chicken's head and drinking the blood, they might just drink water. These young Triads or Tongs, as they called themselves, became extortionists, each group with its own territory – coffee shops, prostitutes, etc. They became totally out of hand – street gang clashes using hatchets were common even in broad daylight – and the Singapore government had to clamp down. It brought in two emergency ordinances, one against the Communists and the other against the Triads, which enabled it to detain people without trial or appeal just for belonging to a secret society.

In about 1947 'Operation Dagger' came into effect and throughout the last part of the 1940s, through the 1950s and into the 1960s, the Triads were almost totally wiped out here in Singapore. Nowadays young uneducated Chinese who have failed to make the grade in school and who have practically no job opportunities will be attracted by the street gangs and the money to be made from crime. These gangs take their names from the old classic Chinese Triad stories, for example Hai Lok San, which means 'Sea, Land, Mountain'.

There was no 'Dr Fu Manchu' or 'Dr No' figure operating in Singapore and pulling strings that stretched over to Europe and the other side of the world. But there were three groups who were 'going over to the other side', as going to Europe is called, most of which had a common genesis in their youth – seven out of every ten people in these groups were Triads before they left Singapore.

The first group the DEA called 'the sailors'. For uneducated seventeen-, eighteen-, nineteen-year-olds, the only way out of Singapore was to get a job on a ship. Malaysian and Singaporean Chinese youths in the 1960s would leave the street gangs, get a job on a ship and go back and forth to Europe for two or three years. They would work extremely hard and save money. When they had enough, they would stay in Europe, particularly Scandinavia which appreciated their industriousness, and probably get jobs in factories. Once they had saved enough from this work, they would nearly always open a restaurant. Three of them would usually work together, one as cook, one on the counter and one as waiter, and once the business was a going concern, they would get one or two more kids to join them from Singapore.

By the time this first group, hard-working and law-abiding, were well established in Europe, the last of the gang clashes were happening in Singapore. The last major clash was on 24 October 1969 in broad daylight outside the Odeon Theatre in Singapore, when the See Tong, or the Skeleton Tong, fought the White Gold Dragon Tong. Two kids were killed and ten arrest warrants went out for those responsible, but they were able to get on a ship to Europe. These were the nucleus of the second group – 'the fugitives' – who, once arrived in Europe, had a bond with the first group: they were Singaporean Chinese against other overseas Chinese. It did not matter that they might come from rival Triad groups back home. They were from Singapore and that made them non-Hong Kong – whereas Hong Kong secret societies, especially the 14K, as far as the DEA is concerned, control Chinese criminal activity in almost every overseas Chinese city.

In about 1970/71, after the original group had been joined by 'the fugitives', another and very important group arrived on the scene – the 'ex-soldiers'. The youths that stayed in Singapore had been drafted in to the two years of military service that are compulsory in Singapore for males at the age of eighteen. Well trained in commando tactics but with hardly any education at all, they came out of the army at the age of twenty with no job prospects and were naturally attracted by the stories of their ex-colleagues prospering in Europe. They joined them and by 1972/3 the three separate groups became knitted together. They saw that the Hong Kong Chinese were smuggling heroin into Europe and the ex-soldiers were very confident, after their military training and with their knowledge of modern weapons, that they were tougher than the Hong Kong Chinese in Europe.

In Singapore and Malaysia a lot of families belong to the same family groups. These young Singaporeans had connections in Malaysia and had seen for themselves how easily available heroin was. They realized that if they could get the heroin into Europe, to Amsterdam – the heroin capital of Europe – they might be able to muscle in on the Hong Kong Chinese territory.

At about this time, the 14K in Amsterdam was having its own

problems. In March 1975, Chung Mon, the 14K 'Godfather of Amsterdam' was killed and a replacement, Chan Yuen Muk, was sent over from Hong Kong, the traditional seat of the 14K. Chan Yuen Muk made the mistake of throwing his weight around too much, demanding tribute that the 14K did not have the muscle to back up. People had been prepared to go along with the demands of Chung Mon as long as they were not too harsh but now some of the casino owners and others being hit hard by 'Mao Tse Tung', as Chan Yuen Muk had become known, were no longer willing to accept the treatment.

They turned to the young Singaporeans, one of whom had recently fought – and thoroughly beaten – a 14K Kung Fu expert in a bloody brawl in one of Amsterdam's casinos. And in broad daylight on the open street in front of the Yowlee Casino, with all his bodyguards in attendance, 'Mao Tse Tung' was assassinated.*

The murder gave the young Singaporeans their stature and they were quick to put their power into effect. They went to the people on whom 'Mao Tse Tung' had been putting pressure, told them that, unlike the Hong Kong people, they did not demand payment *but* from now on they would distribute all the heroin coming into Amsterdam! This meant in effect that anyone who did bring in heroin and distribute it would have to report to them, pay them *and* put it through their distribution service. The penalty was torture or death and they kept their threat – people who did not comply were burned with cigars and stabbed to death.

In addition to getting their stake in the heroin brought in to Holland from other sources, they formed their own syndicate to bring in heroin themselves. This syndicate is called Ah Kong, which means 'The Company', and so far there has been little in the newspapers about it. Investigations are going on at the moment and it will be several years before the results are known publicly. A case presently going on in Germany is unlikely to finish its way through the courts until at least the end of 1980 so no names can be given at the moment. But this is 'the largest

* According to the Hong Kong 'Red Pole' to whom I talked previously, the killing was in fact done by an expert 'hit man' sent over from Singapore at the request of the young overseas Singaporeans, who realized the importance of the murder and wished to ensure that it would be accomplished with optimum efficiency. However, this could be the story circulated among the Triads at home base in Hong Kong to save 14K face for a perfectly executed killing by overseas Singaporeans.

Chinese conspiracy that we know about in the world. We are talking about over a hundred principals with, I would say, easily 200 hangers-on. Right now they are in Malaysia, Singapore, Scandinavia, Germany and Holland. Britain? Not that we know of, at least not yet.'*

At this point in the DEA special agent's account, I showed him a cutting of a Reuters report headed 'Major Drug Ring Reported Broken' which I had culled from the *Washington Post* a couple of months earlier: 'Police said yesterday they had smashed an international drug ring involving Chinese gangsters with the arrest of more than forty people here and abroad. Heroin worth about $4.5 million was also seized in the operation mounted by Singapore, Malaysian, American and European narcotics agents, they said.'

He confirmed that this indeed referred to Ah Kong and was the summation of six months of enforcement effort in many different countries. The release had been given out by the Singaporeans, not them, and the forty people arrested were forty of the 100 principals mentioned before. This was, however, only the first swoop; more would be coming.

The agent went on to explain how the young Singaporean traffickers' shared origins in the Triad Societies or Tongs of their native island related to their banding together in the Ah Kong conspiracy.

Originally, there were five major leaders based in Amsterdam, Hamburg, Copenhagen and here in Singapore. They put lieutenants into Penang, Kuala Lumpur, etc., and had two or three major financial controllers. The banking system is almost incredible – the controllers sometimes carried as much as 700,000–800,000 Dutch guilders in a shoulder bag and would sit in a casino, armed to the teeth with two or three bodyguards, distributing the money.

Of the original five founders, two came from the original 'sailors' group, two were 'fugitives' and one was an 'ex-soldier'. They were later joined by a man known as 'the Brains of Ah

---

* This ties up with what another DEA special agent told me in New York: that as part of the deal eventually reached between the Ah Kong and the 14K in Amsterdam, the Dutch traffic was left squarely under Ah Kong control and supervision but the 14K were given a free hand in Britain. A typical delineation of territory between two Triad groupings!

Kong – a Singaporean graduate from an Australian university – and by two other men, called 'the computer' and 'the Lawyer'.

They diversified. Some went into the movie industry – buying Kung Fu films cheaply in Hong Kong and making a lot of money showing them in Europe. Others went into diamonds. They started putting their money into legitimate businesses. Some of them came back to Singapore and opened stores.

That is another difference between the Singaporean and the Hong Kong Chinese. If the latter is arrested in Europe and deported home, there are no possibilities there for him and he will be forced back on the streets. The young Singaporean can rent a flat for a reasonable sum, invest in a company; he has opportunities.

The street gangs in Singapore today, the Tongs, are very similar to the Chinese youth gangs in the United States. They have a similar organization and a similar discipline; there is a chief, a treasurer, an adviser, a 'Red Rod' – the enforcer, five fighters and ten, twenty, thirty ordinary members. When working against the Ah Kong, they can be similarly classified – a good fighter; good with figures, very trustworthy – therefore he must be working for the treasurer; particularly bright, therefore working for the adviser – just as they would be for a standard Triad Society. The Ah Kong is a modern adapted form of Triad Society.

That is the substance of what the DEA man had to tell me; and it was backed up by confidential reports to agents in the field in Europe that he showed me and by my own subsequent enquiries in West Germany about the Ah Kong arrests in that country. There can be little doubt to my mind that the version of Triad reality that I heard from the DEA in Singapore is to be preferred to that given me by the local police. In the classic phrase frequently used by British judges when expressing their preference for one witness's word against another in court: 'I accept wholeheartedly the evidence of the former but I am only able to give credence to the testimony of the latter except insofar as it agrees with it.'

Why have the Singapore police so grievously misread the situation, as I believe them to have done? I would rather not express an opinion. All I can report is that to my mind they are looking at the drugs problem centred on their country through blinkers: tunnel-vision, you might call it. And, as we have seen, this official attitude is much the same throughout the countries of the Far East. Yet the effect of criminal activity in the South-East Asian heroin trade is reaching out across the world to corrode the lives of people in countries thousands of miles apart, of different cultures and history, between whom one would have thought there was not the slightest link. I am firmly convinced that it is the ethnic Chinese secret criminal societies – Triads, whether in a new, adapted form – which *are* that link.

PART III

Triads on the International Scene

10 Overseas Triads in Operation

'Wherever you have a Chinese community, on the Continent, Germany, the Netherlands, France, abroad, the Far East, in a way it is almost incidental to the community where they live because as yet there is much to be done in terms of integration.' This statement was made by Detective Superintendent Fred Luff of the London Metropolitan Police when giving evidence in the Kam Tong restaurant case in June 1978. This case centred on a territorial dispute between two rival London branches of Hong Kong-based Triad Societies (the Wo Shing Wo and the Shui Fong) which had erupted into cleaver-slashing violence, just as a dispute would have been sorted out back home in Kowloon or a township in the New Territories.

The ethnic Chinese, wherever they may be in the world, take their home environment with them. I have visited unlawful Chinese gambling houses in back streets in Kowloon, in basements in London and in New York and, once you are past the 'look see' boy on duty outside, there is absolutely no difference between them whatever the language or the cut of the police uniform outside.

This was confirmed by a Triad senior official whom I met in somewhat scary circumstances in a hotel room in Toronto, Canada.*

*I had been given a telephone number on which to contact this man by a DEA special agent in New York and had duly arranged an appointment with him for the next evening. However, when I arrived in Canada, I found that the local police knew about my prearranged rendezvous and because I had been seen talking to them in the hotel lobby, they suggested that I telephone this man and arrange for him to come straight up to my room – 'We don't want you being seen with him in the hall downstairs.' I was thus left on my own in my eleventh-floor room to await the arrival of an unknown Triad. On the dot of six o'clock there was a knock on the door and with some trepidation I opened the door to a stocky Chinese man in plain black trousers and black patterned silk shirt.

As he told me:

'[The Chinese] go to gamble because there is no other entertainment for them. There is no other way for them to let out. They don't want to mix with white guys. They don't want to play, to have sport. They are worse off than the Negroes. They stick together.

'A gambling house is not only a gambling house. It is a gathering place. You don't have to go there to gamble; you talk to people, have tea and coffee free. Sure, you gamble as well, if you've got the money, and the guys running it make a hell of a lot of money out of it. But if you have a problem, you go there and say, "I need twenty dollars" and the house will give it to you.

'I was in Amsterdam last year in July and August, and in Rotterdam I spent two to three months. Then I was in Paris. I saw guys come to the places there and say, "Look, I'm busted. I need a plane ticket to go home to Hong Kong." When they have found out who the guy is, they say "OK. Give him a ticket!"'

And if in the great Oriental diaspora there is no gambling house easily to hand, there will always be a Chinese restaurant where much the same facility obtains. The explosion of Chinese restaurants in Britain in the late 1960s, with substantial immigration from Hong Kong to staff them, has been the pattern all over the world in countries to which the ethnic Chinese have migrated. In the north of England the Chinese have even taken over nearly the entire traditional 'fish and chips' business.

John Warner, DEA European and Middle-Eastern regional head in Paris, says: 'We have seen over the last perhaps ten years a tremendous influx of ethnic Chinese in Western Europe. You go to the smallest hamlet in England and you'll find a Chinese restaurant or take-away, and the same thing applies throughout Western Europe. You find your Chinese restaurants all over.

'We have found that ninety-five per cent of those restaurants are .perfectly legitimate, are owned by very honest, hard-working Chinese; but five per cent perhaps are used as meeting places, as communication centres and as depots of narcotics that are being smuggled.'

Jan van Straten, Head of the Dutch Police Central Intelligence Division at The Hague, told me: 'In the last years before the Second World War, the original Chinese restaurants came to the Netherlands. Even today, they are mostly called "Chinese-Indonesian" but they are really all only ethnic Chinese. In the last ten years or so, there have been more and more of them: not so long ago, I spoke to an ex-president of the Chinese Restaurants' Organization in the Netherlands and he told me that there are now about 2500 in the whole country: 400 in Amsterdam alone, 150 to 200 in Rotterdam, 100 to 150 in The Hague. There is no small place in the Netherlands without at least one Chinese restaurant. Many of them you will go into, both at lunch and at dinner time, and you'll find them almost empty. They *must* have some other way of earning a living!'

One Chinese restaurant opened up in a suburb of Paris near the home of M. François Lemouel, head of the French Centre of Suppression of Drugs. He visited it one Sunday, liked it and took its card for future reference. At his office the next morning, he was told of the arrest of two Hong Kong Chinese men on suspicion of drugs. Among their possessions was a note with a telephone number which seemed familiar to M. Lemouel – he checked it against the restaurant card he had acquired the previous day and it was exactly the same!

The identical pattern of ethnic Chinese communities throughout the world means that contacts with fellow Chinese can always be easily made. Such contacts can be mutually beneficial and perfectly legitimate. They can also be criminal. And any ethnic Chinese criminal coming from the overcrowded and often appalling conditions of life in Hong Kong and other parts of the Far East in the last quarter of the twentieth century must, almost inevitably, have been a member of a Triad Society in the sense of one of the local street gangs that have adapted Triad mythology, Triad terminology and Triad tactics. There is always someone – a fellow Triad 'university' graduate, a co-alumnus – with whom he can make contact as a blood brother who has also, at one stage in his life, taken the solemn thirty-six oaths. Some put their past behind them and never indulge in criminal activity again. Others grow deeper into it and because of their past, they have a built-in link with all the other graduates of their criminal 'university'.

I firmly believe that there is an international criminal network operating on this level. It does not necessarily mean that crime is a planned Triad operation with orders coming down the line from a senior Triad but simply that by being, or having been, a member of a Triad Society, the ethnic Chinese criminal automatically has a globe-straddling network available to him that can be used to seek help in his activities.

Most, if not all, the narcotics law enforcement agents – both 'injuns and chiefs' – that I have spoken to have agreed with this view. Even Roy Henry, Commissioner of the Royal Hong Kong Police, accepted it in effect when I asked him why he thought a Hong Kong 'hit man' should have been hired to carry out the vicious stabbing attack in September 1977 on Mr M.B.Lee, the uncrowned king of New York's Chinatown:

'I think there could be several reasons. Probably the most likely one is that they wanted a strange face, an unknown face, who could get access to the victim without the victim taking normal precautions. If it was a well-known local hit man, he wouldn't begin to have access – so they introduce a new face, a stranger. And it would be on the basis of: "I've got a cousin in Hong Kong who I know is a tough thug and he would be prepared to do it for so many dollars."'

And would he be a Triad?

'Yes, of course, he would be! That's why his cousin would know him because they were probably initiated into the local gang in Mong Kok [a central district of Kowloon] five years before. If one wanted to be pedantic about it, we could say there are no Triad organizations in Hong Kong now at all – if one said that the Triad Society is the one that existed in China before the Communists took over, when it was well organized, well controlled, well disciplined and all worked to a common end. But, if we take your definition – i.e. local gangs of thugs adapting Triad mythology, Triad terminology, Triad tactics – then of course there are Triads.'

And Triad methods of exacting revenge are universal in nature, exercises in the macabre at whichever end of the world they take place. In Hong Kong, a detective known as the 'Kojak of Hong Kong', told me the following story:

'We had one body found floating in the Tai Tam Reservoir. It was decomposed, stab wounds all over him, his eyes had been cut out and acid poured on his face so that he couldn't be identified, and they'd cut off all his fingers as well so that we couldn't even get any fingerprints.

'Then I did another one found floating in Lai Chi Kok Bay to the west of Kowloon about a couple of years later. This one was in a sack and he had been sawn in half at the third vertebra with an electric saw. Not only that. They had disarticulated his ankles. So not only did he have no head, no finger or footprints but the thing was that in the first case, in the Reservoir, the press had said – wrongly as it happens – that, even though the culprit had cut off the fingers, the clever police had identified him by his footprints. In actual fact, we never did – probably because his footprints weren't on record – but, because of this, in the second case they had taken steps to destroy his footprints.'

Narcotics were suspected as the reason behind both murders: 'If you make a bad delivery, the 426 or whatever will go after you!'

An equally grisly story from another side of the world came from Lieutenant Martin Kennedy at New York City police headquarters, who told me of a nineteen-year-old Vietnamese of Chinese background who was supplying information to the police. He had been warned to stay clear of the Chinese community for his own safety but 'the next we heard of him, he was found with a bullet in each eye, in each ear and one slightly below the nose where apparently it had missed the mouth. They wanted to tell us as policemen that they knew he was seeing, hearing and saying things he shouldn't!'

He added that the police there are very, very protective of any and all of their sources of information. 'We protect their identity to the nth degree. We will even lose a law case, a heavy case, to protect the identity of an informant. We won't surrender his identity in any manner. We are dealing with very vicious people who would kill anyone.'

They will also, as a universal working method, deliberately maim rather than kill in certain circumstances. Detective Sergeant Derek Boone, a local Lancashire policeman with extensive experience of the community of 3600 Chinese inhabitants of Greater Manchester, told me:

'I'm convinced that the Triad movement is bigger and crueller and better organized, more sinister actually, than the Mafia has ever dreamed about. It certainly has been going on for a lot longer. They don't set out to kill when they go out with these choppers (in a gangland war), they cut from the shoulders down here in the front across the back – and that's to cripple the man so that his back muscles are all destroyed and he walks around with his arms hanging down. He can't do anything with them. He'll live, but every day that he lives he is a walking symbol of the powers of the Triads, you see, because he's a cripple.'

Detective Sergeant Ken Beever told me a similar story at New Scotland Yard in London concerning a dispute over a heroin delivery: 'Someone had delivered the goods but not handed over the money to his bosses. So what happened? On a Monday night, in front of about 600 people – all Chinese – going to one of the regular late-night, twice-a-week showings of Chinese films at the Odeon Cinema, Leicester Square, some young fellows come in and slash this man within an ace of death – and then disappear.

'And they're all so scared – all those 600 people – that the police don't even hear about it until about an hour later when we get a call from the casualty department at University College Hospital to say that this Chinese guy has been brought in with these awful injuries to his back.

'He discharged himself after seven days, although clearly he should have stayed in hospital much longer. I went to see him a month later at his home and he was still hardly able to move. He just lay there on the sofa. They had cut practically every muscle in his back. But he still wouldn't give me any information about his attackers, although I'm sure he knew who they were. He was just too scared.'

The bad delivery that sparked the London Odeon Cinema case in February 1977 did not even happen in Britain but in the Netherlands, as a British detective inspector (whom I cannot name) explained. 'We got information that the personal organizer was living in Jersey, a so-called respectable citizen. So we had him out of there very quickly through the Amsterdam police who work in very close contact with us.'

Is there more to such an ethnic Chinese criminal link between countries than just the ethnic relationship and the Triad 'old boy' network? Can it go further and form an international criminal network operating on an 'organized crime' basis, in the American Mafia-type sense, with syndicates operating within a hierarchical control that ultimately, however great the autonomy allowed in the field, goes back to central headquarters – in this case in the Orient?

An experienced investigator in the US Immigration Service in

New York, whom I asked about the nature of Triad involvement in Chinese criminal activities in New York, made this reply:

'I would say that the Triads are involved. Now, perhaps they're not as formalized as they were in the past or as they may be in Europe still today, maybe the ritual isn't there as it used to be, but the association between a criminal group in New York and a criminal group in Hong Kong is still there.

'I back this up with this: when we used to hit the gambling houses, when we went in, we used to search everything. We always came up with toll receipts and in a typical toll receipt in these gambling houses you had calls to Londonderry in Northern Ireland, you had calls to London, England, you had calls to Amsterdam, to Hong Kong, to Singapore, to the Philippines, to California, to Dallas, Texas.

'Now why should a gambling house here in New York City be concerned with such a variety of different cities throughout the world? Why? Why should they call Londonderry? At the time, there was a big business in guns going between Northern Ireland and the rest of the world and we had heard from rumours at the time that some of the money from the Chinese, some of the profits from the gambling houses, was being used to buy weapons which, in turn, were being sold to either the IRA or whatever group was involved at the time in Northern Ireland.*

'Why call up Dallas, Texas? What was the connection there? It was a port of entry through the international airport there. Why call up California? The upper northern part of California is near Vancouver, and that's another – major – port of entry. Why call up Amsterdam? That's where the narcotics are distributed from. That's where they come into Europe from the Orient on their way to the United States.

'So you say, "All right. You found this at one gambling house, but it was only one!" But I tell you that if I hit *forty* gambling

---

*If it seems too far-fetched to suggest that Triads are involved in gun-running operations to the Provisional IRA fighting the British Army in Northern Ireland, I can only counter that a well-known feature of the Triads is their quick involvement in any lucrative activity. And is it entirely coincidence that when Scotland Yard were seeking the killers in the only known Triad murder in Britain, that of a middle-aged Chinese restaurant owner called Wong Kam in a basement gambling house in London's Gerrard Street, February 1976, they discovered that one of them had sought refuge for a time with 'friends' in Belfast, the capital of Northern Ireland?

houses I'd find the same toll receipts every time. Now to me that shows an international conspiracy, that shows an organization. You try and run these telephone numbers down and you'll find an international conspiracy among the Chinese criminal element.'

'International conspiracy' is an emotive phrase and, please note, not one that I personally introduced. But this investigator's view was reiterated by other law enforcement officers I spoke to, most of whom were admittedly 'injuns' rather than 'chiefs'. But not all – a former special agent in charge at the DEA office at The Hague, interviewed at DEA headquarters in Washington DC in connection with the role of the Triads in the international trafficking of heroin, replied: 'I think there is most definitely a conspiracy and it is controlled by ex-Hong Kong officials. Some of these people are still very much alive and well. They are ex-Customs people, ex-detective staff sergeants in the Hong Kong police.'

It was a DEA special agent in London who suggested I meet one particular British detective inspector 'because he's the only guy in the police force in all of Britain who seems to understand what is really going on'. This was that police officer's view of the Triad role in Britain today:

'At one stage everything was controlled from Hong Kong, but due to the political embarrassment and the loss of status of these people, there is more control locally now than as from a central body. These people, thank God, have now split up into much smaller groups and basically what they are now, instead of being a recognized "black society" [his alternative name for Triad Society] as we know it, or as they know it, the Hong Kong Chinese, it has now developed into a gangster system in a very much smaller way. And thank goodness!

'If they ever got their heads together, these different groups, the police force or the enforcement agencies in the United Kingdom would never cope with the problem at all because they don't understand the problem: they don't want to understand the problem.'

Back on the other side of the Atlantic another police officer – Lieutenant Martin Kennedy in New York, who does not know the British policeman and is hardly ever likely to meet him, told me about Triad control over New York's Chinatown, and in particular about a suspected 14K member who is 'the father of the criminal element within the Chinese community down there. He's a very firm disciplinarian and he is looked upon as the man who controls everything in Chinatown. He would be tantamount to the "Godfather" in Italian Mafia terms. . . . He is known as the Big Brother. Yes, he is Hong Kong born. He has already gone to prison for a substantial length of time just to keep someone else who had a higher echelon position within the criminal structure at that time from going to jail.

'He is one of the nicest men you would want to meet. He's very intelligent, speaks good English and he must be . . . in his late sixties. We've never been able to substantiate that he is 14K but we know that he has been involved in this kind of activity practically all his life. I would assume he didn't start this thing over here. He must have been involved before back in Hong Kong when he was a young man. . . .

'We know that his legitimate business is controlled by relatives and we know from informants that he had a part-interest in several on-going restaurants and places of theatrical entertainment. He had at one time a hundred per cent interest in several gambling houses. Right now he is running one gambling house from a distance because he knows that I would love to catch him in this place. If I caught him, he would be violating his parole and he would go back to prison.'

But how is such Triad control first put into practice and how does it then operate? The Triad informant I met in Canada told me:

'Each specific organization operating within its own territory has its own flag. If I want to become a new Triad head, I have to ask the original guy [this is as much description as I could obtain – whatever the conditions of anonymity under which we were talking, the Triad member is still bound by the code of silence in the thirty-six oaths] back in Hong Kong or Taiwan to give me a flag which means I can bring it over here and that means this is my territory. The flag is a triangular flag. It authorizes me to go to the new town and organize my branch.

'Theoretically, there is no control over me from the original base. Once I have my own flag, I become independent. I am a 489. But really I am only semi-independent. Spiritually, I am linked with the old country.'

It is only the most powerful Triad Societies that still operate in this strictly regulated fashion. And it is the 14K that is the most powerful of all Triad Societies operating overseas. The less important societies are always fragmenting and re-forming in ever shifting patterns of small groups, which even fight among themselves.

Says the former DEA special agent in charge at The Hague: 'The "Five Dragons" and many of the other ex-Hong Kong police sergeants are high-ranking members of the 14K.' Says a DEA special agent in New York: 'The 14K is the only Triad Society I know of operating in New York City.' Says the British detective inspector: 'Gerrard Street [the centre of London's Chinatown] is controlled by three Triad Societies, of which the 14K is the most important.'

But in no country has the 14K been more important, at least in the early days of modern heroin trafficking, than Holland and if there is an international ethnic Chinese conspiracy in the trafficking and supply of South-East Asian heroin to the rest of the world, then it is Holland where it would first manifest itself.

11 Triads in Holland

Amsterdam has the dubious honour of being called the heroin capital of Europe, a title she looks well set to maintain in the 1980s. The second-largest city and seaport in the Netherlands, Amsterdam has the largest Chinese community in Europe. By early 1976, the numbers had swollen from about 1500 people made up of about 500 families in the early 1970s to about 7000, of whom an estimated 5000 were without passports: these figures were given by Amsterdam's Police Commisaris Gerard Toorenaar to the DEA International Alumni Association's first working regional conference held in Bangkok in February 1976. At the same conference, Toorenaar stated: 'The recent growth of the Triads in the once peaceful and law-abiding Chinese community in Amsterdam has led to several murder cases and violent gang warfare, believed to be related to gambling and drugs.'

The Dutch police, unlike many other police forces, do admit to major Triad involvement in their drugs problem. The following frank statement by Hr Jan van Straten, head of the Dutch police Central Intelligence Division at The Hague (to whom I am grateful for permission to quote this extract from his speech to a conference of international narcotics law enforcement officers in October 1977) is a model that might well be copied by other high-ranking officials. He explained how Amsterdam had been chosen as the European centre for illicit heroin trafficking:

'In the first place, there was already a rather big Chinese colony in Holland, mainly in Amsterdam and Rotterdam, two seaport towns. These Chinese were there because of the old relationship of Holland and the former Dutch East Indies and because of the fact that in the early thirties, during the world's economic crisis, many Chinese stayed in Holland when they were fired as crew members on Dutch ships. This colony formed an ideal area to settle for the Chinese criminals.

'In the second place, it could be expected that United States soldiers in West Germany would turn out to be good clients for the heroin to be imported, since the Vietnam war was (so far as the American troops were concerned) over.

'Third, Holland was situated well, geographically speaking, with a long and uncontrollable coastline in the north and the west, an uncontrolled southern border with Belgium and with a big victim country in the East, the Federal Republic of Germany.

'And finally, there was a lenient legislation on drugs in the Netherlands: a maximum penalty of four years on each drug crime. Besides, one knew that the maximum was seldom given and that the criminal was to serve only two-thirds of his time, provided he behaved well.

'Europe was, at that time, the time of decision for the big organizers, totally unaware of the danger that would come to this part of the world, the heroin danger. And when it came, it took us by surprise. We were hardly prepared; our law enforcement agencies were not, or almost not, specialized in combating illicit heroin trafficking; international police-co-operation in this field was new or was to be established. And not only the police were unprepared, our governments were too.'

He was indeed speaking the truth. The first heroin seizure of any size in Amsterdam was not until 1971 when the police found about fifty grams, slightly less than two ounces, in the pocket of a man arrested in the back room of a Chinese gambling house in Amsterdam's Chinatown. There had been two earlier small seizures, in 1970, each one only enough for an addict's personal dose. The DEA special agent at The Hague said, 'I don't think it was a sudden explosion of the stuff into Holland. I think they just began to notice it more. It was there for a while before the Dutch police knew anything about it.' Even after these early seizures, some of them did not really know what was going on. Detective Chief Superintendent Michael Huins, a British police officer involved in narcotics law enforcement from 1972 to 1978, recalled a visit to colleagues in the Amsterdam drugs squad at Easter 1972. They told him they had not yet seen any Chinese heroin nor made any seizure of it. Yet this was a full year after the fifty-grams seizure had been made in Amsterdam.

In March 1973, only two years after that first fifty grams seizure, US narcotics officials first identified Amsterdam as the main distribution point for Asian heroin in Western Europe. As a result of a case started in New York, two DEA undercover agents travelled to Holland and successfully negotiated for the delivery to them of 30 lb of Chinese heroin, whereupon the goods were at once seized and three Chinese traffickers arrested. 'One of those two undercover guys is a friend of mine,' a present-day DEA special agent in Holland informed me. 'He told me that he only got 30 lb because he only had enough money to show for 30 lb. If he had had enough for 100 lb, they could have bought 100!'

'Practically throughout the entire seventies,' the DEA special agent in charge at The Hague told me in 1978, 'Amsterdam has been the clearing house and distribution centre for South-East Asian heroin in Western Europe.' As Commisaris Toorenaar remarked in a *Time* magazine interview in early 1976, 'It is raining heroin in Holland!'

Hr Jan van Straten committed himself to a significant statement on the whole problem in an article entitled 'For Export: Chinese Triad Societies' in the February 1977 issue of Interpol's official publication *International Criminal Police Review*: 'The Chinese nationals' connections in Hong Kong are a basis for suspecting that *some instructions come from Asia*' (my italics).

Let us look at those connections and the story of heroin in Holland.

Until the Singaporeans took over control of the heroin trade in Amsterdam in the spring of 1976 – when Chan Yuen Muk or 'Mao Tse Tung' was assassinated – the 14K had dominated all of Holland's heroin trafficking. Since then, the Singaporeans have remained the masters in Amsterdam itself while the 14K has been driven into the rest of the country: The Hague, Groningen in the north and the world's largest seaport, Rotterdam, where in any event it has always been powerful.

Another version of events put forward as a possibility by some DEA men is that in the realignment after Chan Yuen Muk's murder it was mutually agreed between the 14K and the Singaporeans that there should be a 'Balance of Power' type of arrangement, with the 14K ceding supreme 'sphere of influence' status to the Singaporeans in Amsterdam on the basis of a reciprocal concession of like status to the 14K in London. 'I wouldn't be at all surprised,' was the comment by one British police officer when I put the suggestion to him.

The DEA office in The Hague knows exactly where the 14K masterminds its operations in that city, which is the seat of the Dutch government. It is in a restaurant and when I went to look at it from the outside with a Chinese-American DEA agent from the US Embassy, he insisted on our watching the place and the people going into and coming out of it from across the road, rather than go up close to it. 'I've become sort of paranoid,' he explained, 'ever since it appeared in a Dutch newspaper that the DEA over here now have a Chinese guy on their staff.'

'Since both you and the Dutch police know about this place, why on earth don't the police go in and make some arrests?' I asked the DEA special agent in charge on my return to the Embassy. 'We haven't yet got the evidence that would stand up in a Dutch court,' he said. 'There is still no law of conspiracy in this country and, unless the police can be 100 per cent sure that at the specific moment in time when they go in there they will find someone in actual possession of heroin, they cannot make an arrest.

'It's not even enough to find a guy there with a key to a left-luggage box at the local railway station with heroin in the box. That is only "constructive" possession of the stuff. It has got to be physically on him. Practically the only tool the Dutch police have today is still only wire-taps – and these guys are not going to say over the phone when a delivery is going to be made!'

The Dutch authorities have made tremendous strides in the last few years. 1976 marks the date when they came of age so far as fighting the Triads in their midst is concerned. In that year, parliament upped the maximum sentence for trafficking from a laughable four years to (a still amazingly low) twelve years; a national drugs intelligence unit was set up under Jan van Straten within the Central Criminal Information Department at The Hague to centralize intelligence for the splintered police units in a country where 135 municipalities each has its own police force for a total population of only 13,770,000; and the drugs squads in twelve major cities were increased in size. The DEA started training Dutch police personnel, the government sent a senior police officer to be stationed permanently at its

Bangkok Embassy and the Amsterdam City Police began massive deportations of illegally arrived or criminal Chinese, with a police officer accompanying them on the plane to make sure they did not get off at intermediate airports. (In the first two years of these deportations, 1200 Chinese were escorted back to the Far East: 930 to Hong Kong and the rest to Kuala Lumpur. But such is the nature of the problem that most of them, I am told, turned up later in London and some even got back illegally into Holland!) In addition, Customs control at Amsterdam's Schipol airport was tightened to such a pitch that today it is one of the most effectively anti-heroin monitored airports in the world.

'We are now containing the problem,' claims Hr Jan van Straten. However true that claim may be, up to the mid-1970s the Triads operating in the Netherlands had it all their own way. And that was due largely to the efforts of one man – Chung Mon, the 14K 'Godfather' of Amsterdam. This major Triad criminal figure was a fascinating character. According to Dutch journalist Cees Koring, writing in *De Telegraaf* in November 1978, three-and-a-half years after Chung Mon's murder: 'At the Amsterdam police headquarters he is still a day by day subject of discussion, just as in the early seventies.'

The following 'profile' on him was specially provided for me by the DEA regional office in Paris:

CHUNG Mon
(aka: CHEN Hsen; FO Ki Lun (nickname meaning unicorn); also given as: FOR Lei Lun and HUA Chi-Lun)
    Described as: Hakka Chinese male, born 10 September 1920 at Po On, Kwantung, China. 5 ft 6 in tall, black hair, dark brown eyes, weight unknown, but he was described as being fat. High forehead with receding hair.
    Murdered in Amsterdam, Netherlands, 3 March 1975.

Held Malaysian Passport No. A–0197758 issued at Kuala Lumpur in name CHEN Hsen; and Malaysian Identity Card No. 1836729. Also in possession of Taiwan (Republic of China) Passport No. BRH 56229 (possibly DRH 56229) in name of CHUNG Mon. RC Passport issued in Brussels in 1968 and subsequently renewed.
Home address: Ilpervelde Straat 139, 2nd Floor, Amsterdam, Netherlands.
Business address: Sze Hoi (or Si Hoi) Restaurant at 106 Prinshendrikade, Amsterdam, Netherlands.

Occupation: restaurant owner.

Permanent resident of Holland.

Wife: reportedly married to Dutch female Ann HESS for about 20 years. They had one daughter who was born *circa* 1948. Some reporting give wife's name as WONG Mo Kwan, aka WONG Yin Kwan, aka WONG Yeung Kwan. (This may be Chinese name given to Dutch wife.)

Also located at the 106 Prinshendrikade address in Amsterdam were: WAH Kiew Chinese Casino, travel agency which also went by the name Si Hoi or Four Seasons, and offices supporting CHUNG's role as Chairman of the Overseas Chinese Association in Holland.

Sometime about 1973, early 1974, Chung Mon became generally labelled as head of the narcotics business in Holland. Chung was described as a multi-millionaire who employed a large group of bodyguards and travelled in a bullet-proof Mercedes automobile. Chung's business interests included his restaurant, travel agencies and casinos. He was reportedly head of the 14-K Triad in Amsterdam, a 'Godfather' figure in his community.

DEA Europe became interested in Chung Mon's role in heroin trafficking between South-East Asians in Europe in 1973. DEA's attention was drawn to the frequent use of the address 106 Prinshendrikade, Amsterdam, as a destination for couriers, or in possession of couriers, arrested at European airports. The primary airports used by these couriers were in Brussels and Paris. Also Chung's Mercedes appeared at airports at the time when flights arrived from South-East Asia with couriers. It was possible that Chung's car was sent to pick up the couriers and the heroin. Some arrested couriers had worked for Chung at the time of arrest or prior to arrest.

Chung Mon was Chairman of the Overseas Chinese Association in Holland. In this role he would be sought out by newcomers to the Chinese community who would go to him for advice, employment, and to stand for sureties for their stay in Holland. For his welfare work rendered to the Chinese community, Chung was decorated by the Dutch government. At the same time, his power and influence engendered rivalry.

Chung explained the appearance of his business enterprises among documents seized from couriers as a result of his activities as Chairman of the Overseas Chinese Association, and the prominence of his restaurant and casino as meeting places for Chinese travellers and residents in Holland.

Anonymous information received by the Hong Kong Narcotics Bureau over a period of time identified Chung Mon as the organizer and boss of the heroin traffic between Hong Kong and Europe.

Although reportedly Chung Mon dealt in large quantities of narcotics, all information was circumstantial and based on hearsay and allegation.

Despite that cautionary note about all information being 'circumstantial and based on hearsay and allegation', there is no doubt that Chung Mon, more than any other single person, was responsible for introducing the organized trafficking of South-East Asian heroin into Europe. 'He was never found in possession of even one-tenth of a gram of heroin,' says Jan van Straten; but 'he was one of their big bosses sent by the 14K to organize this trade,' says Dutch journalist Nico Polak confidently – and I am convinced that that is right.

Although born in China, Chung Mon was already living in Holland in the years before the World War Two and by the late sixties he had moved to West Germany, where he owned a restaurant in Dusseldorf, one of the few German cities which at that time had anything like a sizeable Chinese community. The restaurant was none too successful. Chung Mon gave no appearance of considerable wealth.

Yet suddenly in 1969 or 1970 (the exact date is not clear) he left Dusseldorf and turned up in Amsterdam – his pockets, metaphorically speaking, bulging with cash. He appeared on the Amsterdam scene as a financier, a man of substance, and had no difficulty within a very short time of becoming the most respected member – in Dutch as well as Chinese eyes – of the Chinese Amsterdam community. Where did the money come from? Who sent him? There is only one logical answer: the 14K central authority which, at that stage, before the mass exodus of the 'Five Dragons' and the other millionaire ex-police sergeants from the colony, was based in Hong Kong. 'The money itself came from Taiwan,' maintains Nico Polak, but my view is that the actual decision was taken in Hong Kong, where the ultimate heads of the 14K (which I believe to be a Mafia-type council authority) were then still living.

Chung Mon made frequent visits to the Far East, both to Hong Kong and to Taiwan where, according to Cees Koring's article in November 1978 in *De Telegraaf,* Holland's leading national newspaper, 'he was always given a hero's welcome and was received by the Vice-President and government officials, even just before his death.' The same article contains this remarkably revealing item: 'Kim Djan Tjong, an Indonesian and once secretary of his Wah Kiew Casino, says: "In Hong Kong, Chung Mon was questioned by the police on a number of occasions, because of his role in the heroin world. He was once released because a friend with the police, a certain Ma, had some influence there." '

I am prepared to take a sizeable bet that 'a certain Ma' was one of the two millionaire brothers, Ma Sik Yu or Ma Sik Chun, the two main leaders of the Hong Kong Narcotics Report's much-vaunted 'smashed last major drugs syndicate', who got clean away from the British colony to Taiwan, where they were soon seen in convivial company with ex-police sergeant Lui Lok, one of the famous 'Five Dragons'. He in turn, it will be remembered, was reported to be a member of the 14K.

In June 1978, Commisaris Gerard Toorenaar told me in his office in Room 126 on the first floor at Amsterdam police headquarters that Chung Mon was called 'Mr Five Per Cent' – 'He never touched the heroin himself, but they say he had five per cent of every heroin deal in Europe.' But before Toorenaar realized the truth about Chung Mon, he treated him as a trusted informant and leader of his community. According to detectives to whom Cees Koring has spoken, in the early seventies he was considered to be an important informer for Toorenaar. They still remember how he 'was forever at Toorenaar's door' after a neighbour of another police commisaris had put him in contact with him. Toorenaar even intervened personally to recover Chung Mon's Mercedes from Belgium, where the Belgian police had seized the car in a heroin case. That is the same bullet-proof Mercedes that the DEA's 'profile' mentions as 'possibly' being used to pick up couriers with their heroin at airports when flights arrived from South-East Asia!

The quality of at least some of the information that Chung Mon gave Toorenaar can perhaps be gauged from what Nico Polak has to say: 'In the early seventies, there was a sudden outbreak of murders and woundings among the Chinese community in Amsterdam. They had always been so law-abiding before that the police could not understand it. So they went to the bosses of the gambling houses, the leaders of the community – people like Chung Mon and his associates – and asked them who had done it. They told them – but it was sometimes false information. They got rid of their enemies that way.

'When the police then went to the person and accused him, acting as they thought on reliable information, the man confessed his guilt – even when he had not done it. Why was that? Because here in Holland, if you kill anyone you get perhaps four or five years, six at the most, in prison. So a man would rather spend five or six years in a nice comfortable Dutch prison than face certain death at the hands of the Triads, if he denied his guilt.'

In January 1979, Toorenaar, despite his insistence that there was nothing improper or mistaken in his relationship with Chung Mon in the years before his true role was known, found that his early reliance on the 14K leader may well have been a factor in his losing his post. He was transferred to be head of another division of the Amsterdam police after disclosures in *De Telegraaf* of his help in getting Chung Mon's Mercedes released from the Belgian police and of a letter, referred to in Chung Mon's diary, in which he was said to have confirmed that the Chinese man had nothing to do with the heroin trade. Chung Mon was stated to have shown that letter to the Hong Kong narcotics squad to obtain his release from custody when they arrested him on his last visit to the colony in February 1974.

Toorenaar commented to Cees Koring on the alleged contents of that letter – 'You don't believe I'm that stupid' – but the Dutch journalist also told his readers that Superintendent R.A. Williamson, then head of the Hong Kong Narcotics Bureau, had not denied the existence of *a* letter: 'We cannot reveal its contents as it was secret and confidential.' Koring also claimed that 'it was generally known in the Chinese community' that Chung Mon had the letter. He 'showed it proudly to everyone who wanted to see it. A number of detectives also knew about it.'

Whatever the truth of the letter may be, there is no doubt that as other lesser Triad organizations from Hong Kong – in particular, the indigenous Wo group of Triad Societies dating back to the New Territories in the early 1900s – poured into Amsterdam (mostly illegally) scenting the heady perfume of easy money, Chung Mon's position became steadily more and more challenged. There were also 'young Turks' from within his own 14K *and* the brooding, intensely dangerous 'let's get rich quick' young men from Singapore now beginning to appear. As the mid-seventies approached, it was a classic tale of 'the old moustache piece' in Mafia terms at bay. Godfather No. 1 could not much longer survive.

He went everywhere surrounded by a massive bodyguard, he always carried a Beretta revolver for his own protection, and in 1974 he made 'a kind of will' telling his wife that she would have half a million guilders and their son would 'get all the business'. His whole world seemed to be falling in on him. In early 1975 he discovered that the Amsterdam police were beginning to change their view of him and now suspected him of major involvement in the heroin trade. On a tip-off from Hong Kong, the police checked a food shipment for him arriving on a vessel from the Far East at Rotterdam, but nothing was found.

Even so, time was running out for the ageing criminal. On the night of 3 March 1975, as he left the old Dutch building on a canal waterfront that housed the central headquarters of the business that he hoped his son would inherit and before he could step into the opulent safety of his bullet-proof Mercedes, three Chinese assassins stepped forward and gunned him down at point-blank range. They were already speeding to Schipol airport before the first policeman had time to arrive at the body.

'His opponents had hired some killers from Hong Kong,' Toorenaar has told me. 'They flew in, they flew away. We now know who they are – if they are arrested anywhere in the world, they will be extradited to Holland. A "red notice" authorizing their immediate arrest has gone out from Interpol.'

I do not know the names of those three hired hit men, who are anyway mere cogs in a wheel of commercialized murder, but I *do* know the names of Chung Mon's three rivals, one based in Holland, one in Antwerp (Belgium) and one in Koblenz (West Germany), who Jan van Straten's Central Drugs Intelligence Unit at The Hague believes to have been the men who 'very likely' hired the killers. Two of them are today in prison in West Germany on major trafficking charges that are nothing to do with Chung Mon's murder. The third man (the one living in Holland) is still at liberty and has been charged with no offence of any kind. It is now unlikely in the extreme that any one of them will be charged with the murder of the once-powerful Chung Mon.

His personal empire did not last beyond his death. Neither his wife nor his son got their inheritance. The man who (according to Cees Koring) had told all his friends only a few months before his murder that he was going to invest $1 million of his own money in a lavish scheme to buy an island off the Hong Kong coast and build a gigantic gambling centre with the mysterious Ma as one of his partners, was suddenly found to have more debts than wealth. According to one story I have heard in Amsterdam, his daughter had to sell her horse to help pay for the sumptuous funeral.

Why was that? 'Some say he was extremely wealthy, others say he was as poor as a pauper when he died,' Cees Koring has written in *De Telegraaf.* A possible explanation – in my view, the most probable explanation – for this apparent contradiction is that Chung Mon had all the trappings of great wealth in those last triumphant years of his existence but that, just as the wealth with which he returned to Amsterdam originally was not truly his but came from the coffers of the 14K, so when he departed this world his wealth went back to the source from which his original working capital had come: the vast millions in the treasury of the 14K Triad Society.

The three rivals who had organized his murder also did not profit by his death. 'They were men of much lesser calibre,' I have been told by a DEA special agent in West Germany. 'They were younger, "good-time" guys, crazy about horse-racing. They were jealous of Chung Mon's success but they did not have his savvy.'

Within a few months, his successor from within the 14K – Godfather No. 2 – flew in from Hong Kong. This was Chan Yuen Muk, who, as we have already seen, soon antagonized everyone in the Chinese community in Amsterdam by his would-be strong-arm methods, so different from the older Chung Mon's more subtle 'father-figure' approach. Superintendent John Morris, who was then still in Hong Kong, told me in Paris how, in June 1975, not knowing what was soon to transpire in the Netherlands, he had Chan Yuen Muk called in for questioning and had him put on the watch-list. Round about that time also he was searched and found to have an opium pill on him. He was fined HK$500 – and soon afterwards he managed to get away to Holland.

Says Commisaris Toorenaar: 'Chan Yuen Muk was a very different sort of person from Chung Mon. The older man always denied any involvement with Triad Societies. He claimed he was just an honest businessman and he *did* have honest businesses, you cannot deny that. But Chan Yuen Muk used to boast that he was a 486!' That is the rank held by a *Shan Chu*, the highest-ranking Triad Society member.

When on the exact anniversary of Chung Mon's death, 3 March 1976, Chan Yuen Muk was also gunned down in an execution-type assassination by his Singaporean murderers at the behest of his own fellow Triad members, there was no one who mourned the passing of Godfather No. 2. A girl 14K member called Cheung Sau Fan tried to profit directly by it. Aged only nineteen, she had been sent as a courier to Hong Kong, where she had been born, to pick up half a kilo of heroin and bring it back to Amsterdam. When she was in the colony she heard about Chan Yuen Muk's death and decided that she would still come back with the heroin – but would keep it for herself. She must have thought the position following his assassination would have been so confused that no one would bother about a mere missing 500 grams. Sadly for her, she was wrong. As Toorenaar told a *De Telegraaf* journalist in May 1976: 'It was stupid of her. They found her immediately, of course, grabbed the heroin, took her for a ride to Akersloot [a town some distance away] and put a cord around her neck.' Such was the typical arrogance of Triad retribution, her killers did not even bother to remove the gold ring on her finger or the silver necklace around her neck.

Since Chan Yuen Muk died, there has been no Godfather No. 3 in Amsterdam – although as Toorenaar has told me with a smile, 'We were a little anxious on 3 March 1977 to see who might be shot down then!'

The situation has become fragmented, with the Singaporeans still, for the moment at any rate, ruling the roost in Amsterdam itself and the 14K driven out in some disarray into the rest of the country. Amsterdam has by now an estimated addict population of at least 10,000 people. In 1978 alone, according to one DEA informant, there were over twenty unsolved drugs-related murders. By now, the continuous presence of large-scale Chinese criminal elements and an endemic heroin problem have become an established part of the scene.

Holland today is a perplexed country with a great tradition of liberalism, where you have honest men like Hr Jan Visser, the Head of Customs at Schipol airport, musing about the perhaps undesirable consequences, from a humanitarian point of view, of the success of his own department. 'The price of our success,' he has told me, 'is that heroin is getting more and more expensive. I ask myself, what are we doing? Of course, we should try and catch as many smugglers as possible. But there are thousands of people who need their "shots" once or twice a day. Are we punishing sick or ill people?

'Shouldn't we try and improve them, and when they have this addiction, shouldn't you give it to them? I wrestle with this. Struggling against smuggling of drugs is a hopeless task. We know from history that the supply will always be there to meet the demand and, if you make the supply criminal, are you simply making it more expensive and possibly adulterating the supply?'

I do not agree with Hr Visser in his doubts about the value of his work. I side with the DEA special agent at The Hague who says: 'The Dutch, and others, try to say that drug addiction is a victimless crime, but that is nonsense. Society is the victim.'

I cannot believe that it is merely the coincidence of a large resident Chinese community that has made Amsterdam the drugs capital of Europe. The 14K began its operations there for many reasons, of which no doubt the country's geographical situation is among the most important, but a factor that has undoubtedly contributed to the Chinese criminals' success so that now, as we face the eighties, their position is solidly entrenched (even Jan van Straten does not claim they are beaten but only 'contained') is the liberal social climate in that country.

Amsterdam is a city where the policemen on patrol duty in the streets sport long thick hair that would be strictly non-regulation anywhere else in Western Europe or in North America; where scruffily dressed young cyclists systematically ignore traffic lights showing red against them, thereby putting their own lives and those of others in jeopardy; where faded blue jeans for young employees in offices (even in Hr Visser's Schipol Customs headquarters) are almost a rigid uniform of casualness; where the needs of the criminal are so tenderly minded that prisoners in jail enjoy visits from their wives for the purposes of sexual congress; where in the side street off the Rembrandtsplein, in the heart of Amsterdam's tourist area, you can find a shop calling itself 'the Satanic Information Centre';

and where, as you walk down Leise Straat past the smart shops, you will see young people with the tell-tale hollow eyes and the sunken cheeks of the heroin addict doomed to die before they are thirty years of age.

Every country gets the social problems it deserves and I believe that that is true of Holland and its heroin.

In the wake of the 14K Triads have come the lesser Triad Societies out of Hong Kong, such as the Wo Shing Wo, the Wo On Lok, the Wo Shing Yee, the Fuk Yee Hing and the Luen Ying S'he. As we have already seen, the Singaporean Triad elements have staked their claim in the market. The Surinamese, the black-skinned people from Holland's former Dutch West Indies colony on the northern coast of South America have formed links with the Chinese groups (rather like the black Mafia with the 14K in New York). Finally, home-grown, white-skinned Dutch criminal elements with connections in Bangkok or Indonesia, the former Dutch East Indies, so temptingly close to Peninsular Malaysia, have also recently scurried to join in this most profitable industry.

The fairest summary of the current Dutch position that I know is that given by this DEA report out of The Hague: 'The Dutch enforcement has greatly improved. The atmosphere of Amsterdam as an open city has faded from the front pages. However, seasoned criminal elements of all nationalities have been forced out of the flagrant attention-getting amateurish activities of the early 1970s and have developed sophisticated trafficking networks to continue the supply of drugs to the addicts in Holland and the United States.'

From time to time, reports appear in Britain that London is taking over from Amsterdam as the 'new' drugs capital of Europe. Says John Warner, DEA Regional Director, authoritatively in his Paris office: 'London is *not* taking over as the new transit centre. The statements of the Dutch police notwithstanding, Amsterdam is still the major distribution centre for all drugs reaching Western Europe from South-East Asia.' What then is the role of London – and the part played by Britain as a whole – in the Triad scheme of things?

12 Triads in Great Britain

London is less than one hour's flying time away from Amsterdam and the link between the Chinese communities in the two cities is as close as the tightly-packed airline schedule between the two airports. It is said that when the Chinese in Amsterdam weep, tears well up in the eyes of the Chinese in London. If you walk down Gerrard Street in London's Chinatown, you may well pass someone who was seen yesterday on Binnenbantammer Street, the equivalent centre of Amsterdam's Chinatown. This almost Siamese-twin linkage is no more clearly shown than in the story of Britain's only known Triad killing to date.

Wong Kam, a fifty-one-year-old Chinese restaurant owner, was quietly enjoying his regular (illegal) game of Mah Jong in a basement gambling club in Gerrard Street on the night of 3 February 1976 when four young Chinese men pushed past the 'bouncer' on duty at the door, rushed downstairs and, in front of about twenty cowering customers, launched a savage attack on him, demanding him to tell them the address of his son. The kicks were of such ferocity that the toe of one of their shoes split and the police were able to trace a shop in Leeds where the attackers had bought a new pair of shoes and to get the old shoes back, complete with blood traces in the split.

Why did they desperately want to know the whereabouts of twenty-three-year-old Wong Pun Hai? They wanted to kill him in revenge for the murder of a relation in Holland some two months previously, which they believed Wong Pun Hai and three other men were responsible for. And the reason for *that* murder? – their relation, Li Kwok Bun, had defaulted on a heroin delivery and the 14K had wreaked its customary retribution – eight bullets straight in the chest. The Amsterdam police were unaware that the murder had taken place and it was only two weeks after the attack on Wong Kam that the body was found mouldering beneath the dunes outside Scheveningen, near The Hague, with 1500 guilders (about £300) left contemptuously in the dead man's pocket.

Wong Kam's attackers wanted the blood of the man they believed was their relation's principal assassin but they had to be content with Wong Kam's blood, for despite the savageness of the attack – fourteen of his ribs were broken – he refused to betray his son and died as a result. The terrified onlookers were ordered to write down their names and addresses and told that they would meet a similar fate if they spoke to the police.

The four murderers fled to the home of a relation in Leeds and from there to Belfast where they split up, two flying to Holland, one to England and one to Wales. Eventually, by painstaking police work, they were all tracked down and charged with murder at the Old Bailey in November 1976. The jury finally convicted them on the lesser charge of manslaughter though the sentences ranged from five to fourteen years, the latter being more than most people would serve for murder now.

Several days after the killing, Wong Pun Hai walked into Vine Street Police Station to claim his father's body. He also said that he wanted to clear his name of murder. This was the first that the police authorities in either Britain or Holland had heard of Li Kwok Bun's death! Ex-Detective Chief Superintendent Gwyn Waters recalls vividly how young Wong turned up at the police station with no belongings whatsoever. 'It subsequently transpired that as a Chinese you never need anything. You never carry a spare shirt, a spare pair of trousers – you just go to another restaurant or another Chinese who you know and you leave your dirty shirt there, you take a clean shirt – and they'll give you enough money to get you to the next place. This was going on with all these people, with the four that went on the run as well. The amazing thing was they had the contacts spread across the whole of Europe, England, Wales, Ireland north and south, and Scotland; it really was quite fascinating how they could travel with no money.'

In due course, Wong Pun Hai led the Amsterdam police to Li Kwok Bun's body and far from clearing his name, he was put on trial with two other men for murder. My information is that all three were subsequently acquitted and Wong Pun Hai is now back in Britain running a fish-and-chip shop in the Midlands – yet another instance of the 'world of its own' quality of most Chinese crime in the Western hemisphere.

No one outside the Chinese themselves really knows the extent of Triad activity in Britain. Sensationalist stories occasionally appear in the British press implying that the 'yellow peril' is about to engulf us all in our beds while, on the other hand, senior police officers claim that there is no problem at all or, if there is, it is well in hand. It is admitted that, starting in the 1960s, a problem had developed by the mid-1970s. Horace Freeland Judson, an ex-London correspondent of *Time* magazine, describes in his book *Heroin Addiction in Britain* how he had been talking to a leader of the London youth underground late in 1968 when two addict friends came in with the news that 'Chinese heroin' was on sale in the East End of London. 'That was its first appearance among the addicts.' At that stage, it was merely a by-product of the internal demand from the growing Chinese community in Britain and it was only later that it caught on to any great extent with the local indigenous population. An anonymous Home Office source is quoted by Judson as giving this account of the new phenomenon:

How the contact arose between our indigenous junkies and this lot, we are not sure. One British addict told us he had been living over – or in – a billiard hall in London with some Chinese, who had this powder they said was heroin. They smoked it. He tried injecting it.

Then in August 1969, again for unexplained reasons, we just ceased to hear of Chinese heroin. Several explanations were suggested. One was that there had been two or three fatalities pretty clearly linked with Chinese heroin, which scared the kids off. Another was that the local Chinese themselves choked off the supply to the kids: the Chinese community is authoritarian, and possibly didn't like the police attention that was being attributed to it.

But in April 1970, the Chinese heroin was suddenly back on the streets. Where it has remained ever since.

The drugs problem of the mid-1970s, according to senior police officials, was effectively countered by the London Metropolitan Police Drugs Squad, especially during the years 1976 to 1978 when it was under the dynamic leadership of Superintendent Fred Luff. After cases like 'Jason' Ng and May Wong, the Chinese curtailed their activities in the heroin trade.

'I am convinced there is a large cache of the stuff that they have hidden away somewhere for future use,' Detective Sergeant Ken Beever, a keen young member of the squad, told me in the summer of 1978; 'but for the moment they have quietened down. We have beaten them.'

I got the same message from his then boss, Detective Chief Superintendent John Smith, in his room at New Scotland Yard in February 1979: 'I think as far as we can establish there is very little dealing by the Chinese or anybody else in Chinese heroin. And there hasn't been for the last year. There has, however, been a vast increase in dealing with Iranian heroin.'

I only hope that is right; but it is a matter of public record that in September 1978, only five months before Mr Smith's confident assertion, thirty-two kilos of heroin, the largest single consignment of Chinese heroin ever seized in Britain, with a street value of £6 million, was found hidden in the tyres of two Volkswagen cars on arrival at London's Royal Albert Docks in the holds of two freighters out of Penang in Malaysia. The haul was made by the purest chance, when an alert Customs officer, part of a newly set up mobile task force, wondered why a Volkswagen car was being brought into Britain at great expense from Malaysia, so many thousands of miles away, when West Germany, the country of manufacture, was only just across the North Sea. Mr Smith's drugs squad followed up this lucky find speedily and efficiently: with their Customs colleagues, they raided several buildings in the London area and nine people were arrested – a Belgian and eight Chinese Malaysians, one of them a woman.

In September 1979, exactly one year after that largely fluke haul of six million pounds worth of Chinese heroin, the Metropolitan Police Drugs Squad, again in working liaison with the Customs service, mounted an immensely successful joint operation called 'Operation Cyril'. Raids in London and Cornwall netted a total haul of four-and-a-half tons of high quality cannabis resin with a staggering street value of nearly £10 million. It was a magnificent culmination of three months' hard and difficult investigation by a joint police and Customs task force. But cannabis is a 'soft drug' which kills no one and its importation into Britain is a non-Asian affair with the participants speaking English or some other Western European language. Chinese heroin is a 'hard drug' and a killer, with its importation controlled by people from a totally different part of the world, with totally alien operating methods and speaking a language understood by hardly any serving British police officer.

Is there not, therefore, something disproportionate in the immense effort which went into landing a £10-million haul of cannabis resin and the virtual 'falling-into-their-lap' quality of the work that netted a £6-million catch of Chinese heroin that would, if not intercepted, almost certainly have destroyed, or helped to destroy, an unknown quantity of innocent young lives?

Police manpower is limited, budgets are not open-ended, the Chinese criminal world is almost an impenetrable secret community of its own. Choices have to be made. But with the greatest respect to Detective Chief Superintendent Smith, who is a keen, likeable senior police officer and continued as head of the Metropolitan Police Drugs Squad until November 1979 when he moved to take over a division in south London, one cannot help feeling that Chinese heroin, and all the many problems that it creates, has been put to the end of the list of priorities. He has said to me: 'I am certainly aware of what people say about Triad organizations. I am aware that, *if they exist* [my italics], then they seem to be involved in drug trafficking. And, therefore, I should be interested in Triad organizations – which I am!'

Yet the facts remain that the drugs squad inherited by his successor and former No. 2, Detective Chief Superintendent John Hoddinot, has been cut in numbers from what it was in Superintendent Luff's day. Luff's 'China section', an inner core of specialists within the squad, has been disbanded; the whole feel of the Metropolitan Police's activities on the Chinese heroin front nowadays is low key.

One gets a similar attitude from those in authority in Liverpool, the English city with probably the largest Chinese community outside London. 'When was the first time, to your mind, that the Merseyside police became aware of the existence of such things as Triads?' I have asked Superintendent Owen, former head of the local drugs squad. 'We have no knowledge of any criminal Triads working in the Merseyside area,' was his confident answer – despite the fact that probably the first known death of an addict from 'Chinese heroin' was in Liverpool, as far back as 1969.

Is this official police viewpoint valid – or a total misreading of the scene, a grievous miscalculation?

The Home Office statistics published in July 1979 showed a nineteen per cent rise in the number of known addicts to hard drugs, such as heroin, over the previous year. Mr Peter Cutting, chief of the Customs anti-drugs operations, commented to the press: 'We are on the verge of a drugs-inspired crime wave such as we have never seen before. You need to take heroin only three or four times to be hooked, and the evidence is that more and more people are experimenting. As this lucrative market widens, the price is likely to go up. More and more addicts will turn to crime to get money to buy a "fix".'

Granted that with the downfall of the Shah, Iranian heroin poured into Britain in greater quantities than ever before to help supply the market. But in August 1979 the Ayatollah Khomeini's government executed their first opium trafficker and there are now firm signs that Iran's new leaders will back up a further anti-opium decree of December 1979, and do all they can to restrict the trade in the future, as their effective hold over the country tightens.

Are the Chinese traffickers in Britain today really so quiescent as the authorities would have us believe? Even if they are, are they likely to remain so indefinitely? I cannot believe that the answer to either question is 'yes'. It would go completely against their track record and the way they normally operate.

I prefer the view put to me by a Customs officer whom I do not intend to name but in whose integrity and ability I have every confidence. He came to see me because he knew about the book I was writing and he wanted to talk to me. 'I feel,' he said, 'that in the Chinese society or in a Chinese area, if everything is very quiet and everything is going on peacefully, there is something going on; because the Chinese are never involved in nothing, they are always involved in something. It simply looks all above-board, but you can bet your bottom dollar that there is something beneath the surface because the Chinese, being a very close-knit community, keep things to themselves.

'It could be VAT forms, it could be drugs, illegal gaming, it could be anything. But the more placid and normal the appearance is, the more certain you can be that there is something going on.'

Consider also what a detective inspector has said to me:

'Crime is a statistic. Drugs aren't. So if you said to a chief constable, "You had last year twenty murders which have all been cleared up," he'll be very pleased with you, and with himself. But if you start getting drugs recorded as a crime, he is going to be swamped because the only time he realizes the problem is when he forms a special squad to look into it.

'So he forms a squad and he says, "Go out and do a job!" So they go out and all of a sudden for the next three months it gets publicity in the press and all the rest of it. The city which he covers gets the reputation of being a hotbed for drugs because it is splashed all over the press, and it's got to happen that someone will turn round to him and say, "What have you been doing for the last few years? Why has this suddenly cropped up?" and he'll say, "Well, I don't know. It wasn't there before." *But it was* – that's the point.

'It's like the tip of an iceberg. When you start scratching at the surface, things turn up and you have a hell of a problem.'

The apparatus of law enforcement is there, *and* with increasing effectiveness. We now have a far greater working co-operation between the various police drugs squads and the Customs investigation service, although – despite the existence since 1973 of a Central Drugs and Illegal Immigration Intelligence Unit at Scotland Yard – both the Customs and the police still persist in drawing up their own individual indices of suspected traffickers, with consequent totally unnecessary duplication of effort. It seems ludicrous that you can have the Customs investigation service, the Metropolitan Police Drugs Squad *and* the Central Drugs and Illegal Immigration Intelligence Unit all using time, effort, public money and limited resources in money and manpower on 'targetting' the same people. It does not happen all the time but it can and does happen on occasions.

At times, when you talk to different members of the various departments of the law, each one claiming the 'credit' for some particular exploit or sometimes, in the finest tradition of cricket, saying that the 'credit' should be borne by another department, it feels more of a school discussion on respective team performances than adult organizations fighting crime in the highly sophisticated world of the late twentieth century.

'The success of "Operation Cyril" and other recent investigations show that the joint operations between police and Customs are working extremely well,' Mr Gilbert Kelland, Assistant Commissioner (Crime) at New Scotland Yard, told a press conference in September 1979 after the successful capture of nearly £10 million-worth of cannabis resin. 'A bigger organization, such as a national drugs squad, would be more difficult to control, and it is not time for a national squad.' When will it ever be time? If, fragmented as our law enforcement effort is now, it can still have successes, how much greater might those successes be if we had a national force to contend with a national problem?

We might then not have the situation in Britain where, for instance, completely unknown to the average man – and, alas, to the average policeman also – Jersey, that delightful Channel Island closer geographically to the French mainland than to Britain, is, in the words of my detective inspector informant, 'a straight backdoor into the United Kingdom. Any person can come across here from Jersey, because it is an island where people are out to make money so that you get sailings perhaps every hour from France or the Continent, coming in there with no checks whatsoever, and then they get very little check coming over from there into Weymouth [on the English south coast straight across from the island].

'There are so many yacht basins round Jersey's coastline, it's just not true. And the Customs people, the immigration and the police all finish at six o'clock at night, because they don't get paid overtime!

'Another problem is that Jersey is a free state. They don't care who comes in and they are the third busiest airport in the United Kingdom, with direct air links to the Continent.'

The tragedy of the official police – and Customs – attitude to Triad activity in Britain is that, if only the authorities appreciated the reality of the danger, they could cope with it in exemplary fashion. I know that this is the view of many senior men in the DEA, and I can understand their feelings of frustration when contemplating the British scene today. Let me give just two examples of what rigorous British police enforcement *can* achieve when dealing with the Chinese secret criminal societies.

The first example is in Manchester, whose Chinese community, estimated to be within sixty and seventy thousand, is one of the largest outside London. 'We found out,' says

Detective Sergeant Derek Boone, 'that gangs of young hooligans, calling themselves Triads, were going to the Chinese film shows and making nuisances of themselves.

'Throughout the country in the bigger cities, there are late-night film shows where the people go, usually on Monday and Tuesday nights (in this city at least) – never on the weekends because they're all busy then in their restaurants and their other businesses. These shows start at about 1.15 in the morning. The set-up is that the Chinese film organizers travel about the country, taking their film with them, and they hire the cinema from the local people, so that the local people have nothing to do with the organization at all. They take their own cash, they put their own people on the ticket desk and they have their own projectionists, although sometimes they use a local projectionist.

'We found that a lot of these young hooligans were instilling a little bit of fear into the proprietors of the Chinese film shows and were going in without paying. That may sound a little tiny thing, but we looked at it as the thin end of the wedge. It is not a little tiny thing as far as the cinema man is concerned, because he is selling tickets at perhaps £2 a throw and if thirty or forty people are not going to pay – that's how many of these youngsters there might be – then it can involve quite a lot of money for the size of the business involved.

'We wouldn't have that here and, in fact, we found some difficulty with the Chinese proprietors themselves because they were terrified of not letting these people in free. So what did we do? We resorted to good old-fashioned police methods. We stayed up to one or two in the morning and we stood there outside the cinema and made sure that everyone going in there paid! If they wouldn't pay, they didn't get in – it was as simple as that.

'We feel that this has done a lot of good within our Chinese community by the simple presence of the police there. And also by making the self-styled leaders of these little groups of street thieves look small in front of the rest of them. That is just about the worst thing that can happen to them: "face" is vital to them.'

The second example of forceful police action concerns a man who is so notorious in the Triad world that I have heard him mentioned by police officers in Hong Kong and Amsterdam as well as in London, Manchester and Southampton. His name is Yau Lap Leun, but he is more commonly known as 'Georgie

Pai' meaning 'Georgie the Limping One' after the limp that he acquired, almost as a battle honour, in a fight back home in his teens in his native Hong Kong.

He was born on 13 July 1946 in Fanling, a small town way out in the New Territories almost on the border with China which even today hardly looks a suitable birthplace for a man who was to be, above all else, a supremely *urban* criminal. He came of Hakka stock, sturdy peasant people; but in the sixties, his parents, along with many other Hakkas from the New Territories, came to England under the easy immigration laws that then existed, allowing British passport holders from within the Commonwealth to enter the mother country as a matter of right. They came, as with many other honest, hard-working members of their ethnic group, to try and earn a better living for themselves than was possible in the then still primitive farming conditions of the New Territories. Like so many others, they opened a Chinese restaurant (in Glastonbury, Somerset, the legendary seat of that most English of mythical characters, King Arthur) – and regularly sent out money to their young son left behind in the colony.

Eventually, in February 1975, Georgie followed them over to England. By then, he was twenty-nine years of age, married to a Cantonese girl and with a considerable reputation in the gambling houses and ballrooms of Kowloon as a Triad 'enforcer'. Having joined the Wo Shing Wo, the largest Triad Society in the New Territories, as a schoolboy in his early teens, he was now a 426, a 'Red Pole': the same rank as that held by the Triad office-bearer whom I interviewed in my hotel room in Hong Kong, and, in a totally different era, as that held by Dr Sun Yat Sen in the old days of full Triad glory.

There is no evidence that I have been able to find either in Britain or Hong Kong to indicate that Georgie was sent here by superiors in the Wo Shing Wo to take over operations in Britain. The Wo Shing Wo is not *that* kind of Triad Society, with a defined structure and hierarchy, like the 14K. It is split into many groups which often battle with each other and has none of the overall, Mafia-type control that exists within the 14K. Where you have Wo Shing Wo Triad group members operating in harmony, as you sometimes do, in different countries of the world, it is because they fall into the first category of Triad conspiracy: the 'old school tie' international network of availability rather than a structured community with orders from 'on high' obeyed by those at the bottom of the line.

Even so, within a very short time of Georgie Pai's arrival at his parents' restaurant, and without in any way involving them or his wife in his criminal activities, he built up a core of about thirty Wo Shing Wo 49s and about fifty 'Blue Lanterns'* as a virtual marauding army of young strong-arm merchants exacting protection money from the owners of respectable restaurants and illegal gambling houses alike within the Chinese community, both in London and the provinces. It was the classic method of Triad operation in a new country: first, to batten upon their own people and set up a regular flow of money on a weekly basis, which serves both to pay for everyday living costs and to build up a working capital with which to branch out into even more rewarding activities, such as (quintessentially) trafficking in narcotics. It was at exactly this stage of moving in to the 'big time' of the heroin trade that Georgie Pai was caught.

After well over a year's highly profitable activities, in which from the illegal gambling clubs in London's Chinatown alone he was pulling in at least £250 a week (apart from protection rackets at restaurants, gambling clubs and Chinese film shows in places as far apart as Southampton in the south of England and Birmingham in the middle), Georgie became too arrogant.

One could hardly blame him for becoming somewhat contemptuous of the law. Arrested in his early days in Britain in July 1975, when involved in a fight at a Gerrard Street gambling club in which he was displaying, with his henchmen, his considerable skills as a Triad 'enforcer', he received a sentence of a two-months' *suspended* prison term and a £50 fine, despite having served two years in his native Hong Kong on six separate charges of wounding or other offences against the person.

Georgie did not even bother to renew his visa, a strict requirement under Britain's tightened immigration laws, and that simple error proved his undoing. In July 1977, the immigration authorities arrested him as an illegal immigrant for having outstayed his permitted time in the country. He was ordered to be deported back to Hong Kong and, after an unsuccessful appeal to the Home Office, he was due to be flown

* The figures are taken from Danah Zorah and Peter Watson's article that appeared in the 'Spectrum' feature of the London *Sunday Times* on 6 November 1977, when he was already in custody pending deportation.

back unwillingly to the colony when in November 1977 he was, at last, arrested by the police and charged with protection racket offences in Southampton and Portsmouth.

Superintendent John Wright of the Hampshire Constabulary, who commanded the team that finally broke Georgie, continues the story: 'In January 1976 two young Chinese were arrested in Southampton in possession of two guns. They were Luk Ming Pang, aged twenty, known as Steve Pang, and Kin Sang Yau, twenty-one, known as Eric Yau. They were both waiters, with Luk Ming Pang working in his father's restaurant in Southampton which soon figured in our main enquiries. They were both fined at Southampton magistrates court for illegal possession of the weapons and from then on we became interested in the Chinese community in Hampshire.

'To start with, we had a "softly, softly" approach and it soon paid dividends. In May 1976 Georgie Pai came to our attention when we became aware that he had arranged with another Chinaman, David Kung [this is a pseudonym because the man has not been charged with any criminal offence arising out of these matters], who then worked on the *Empire Gull*, a Royal Fleet Auxiliary vessel, to bring in guns for himself and Luk Ming Pang and Kin Sang Yau with which they were going to travel all over the country and put pressure on the Chinese in Birmingham, Manchester, etcetera, etcetera.

'The Royal Fleet Auxiliary vessels are a marvellous method of smuggling goods into a country, for they service ships in the Royal Navy all over the world. From that moment on, we took a particular interest in the Chinese on board the Royal Fleet Auxiliary vessels plying into Gosport. [This is the revictualling section of the Royal Navy's premier world-wide establishment at the Portsmouth dockyards.]

'From information that we received, it became apparent that Kung was also bringing in heroin for the use of Chinese in this country and to be transported on out of this country, *possibly to the United States* [my italics]. This figured very strongly in our enquiries. We interviewed every Chinese establishment in Hampshire, take-away restaurants, restaurants proper, where we knew the Chinese were engaged in gaming, to try and get a picture of what sort of pressure, if any, was being put on by Chinese young yobs, gangsters, Triad members, call them what you like.

'We were aware that "Triad", the name "Triad", was being mentioned but it was awfully difficult for anybody to really know whether any of these young men were genuinely Triad members or whether they were getting on the bandwagon. Certainly, there was mention of Georgie Pai being a "Red Pole" by the Chinese community in Hampshire.

'We spoke to all the Chinese community in Hampshire and we tried to build up confidence. And with a number we were able to do this but, with so many, clearly there was information they could give us but they were disinclined to do so.'

It was a long process. Slowly, the Hampshire police built up a comprehensive picture of a gang of protection racket hoodlums exacting 'lucky money', 'tea money', 'loans', call it what you will, from their terrified compatriots. 'Our biggest problem,' says Superintendent Wright, 'as in any organization putting pressure on certain sections of the community, was to infiltrate and to get in. But how could we do this? Because of the nationality problem – you can't even speak the language – you feel you're losing from the start. But in the end two or three people did come forward and gave us information, and it was fairly good information, as to what they were up to on the extortion racket – and also on the drug smuggling racket.'

A massive police operation was set up for 10 November 1977. 'Our hand was forced to a certain extent because we were interested in a chap who had taken over from David Kung on the *Empire Gull* and this fellow had had a heart attack and was due to be repatriated to Hong Kong after the vessel's next arrival, scheduled for that day, at Gosport. Pai was in prison on a deportation order, with his appeal just recently rejected, and we knew he was going to be kicked out of the country. So we thought: Well, now or never! . . . Now is the time to do it, otherwise all the work we've done till now will be lost for ever – even though, as we knew would happen, it meant that David Kung, at that time on the other side of the world, would get the tip-off and disappear, which he did.

'So the operation was mounted. Over a period of two days, nineteen suspects were arrested in raids that took place in London, the Home Counties and Hampshire. But at the very core of things, the arrival of the *Empire Gull* at its moorings in Gosport harbour, where police confidently expected to find a major cache of heroin, tragi-comedy took over. We had a team of police officers ready to board the *Empire Gull* with a Customs rummage crew. They set sail up the Solent to board it – and they couldn't get on the blasted thing because of the weather!

'This gale set in for about thirty-six hours and we just couldn't get on the damned thing. Although we kept it away from the press for as long as we possibly could, before we could actually get on that damned boat it had been on both the local radio and the local TV. The men had sat on board watching on their TV screens what we were up to!

'Needless to say, when we finally did get on board, we found absolutely nothing of any interest. No heroin, nothing. Those crewmen live on these auxiliary vessels. There are so many places to hide things on there, once they've been warned, it's virtually impossible to find them – and anyway they could always have thrown them overboard in the time they had.

'Without the drugs that we expected to find on the *Empire Gull*, the charges that we were able to bring against Georgie Pai and some of the others we had arrested were much less than they otherwise might have been.'

Eventually, out of the nineteen Chinese men arrested, only three – Pai himself and Luk Ming Pang and Kin Sang Yau, the two young waiters originally picked up for illegal possession of firearms – were put on trial at Winchester Crown Court in June 1978 charged with conspiring to demand money with menaces, i.e. running a protection racket. Trafficking in heroin was not a charge brought before the court. 'There was no evidence that we could present to a judge and jury,' says Superintendent Wright, 'although clearly it was our belief that Pai and his followers were involved in the importation of heroin.'

Even the trial did not run smoothly for the authorities. Time after time a Chinese witness called for the prosecution had to be treated as hostile and, with the judge's permission, cross-examined by prosecuting counsel in an effort to bring out his full story. Even with Pai and his two principal henchmen sitting in the dock, flanked by prison guards, their victims still remained terrified of what they might do to them – or to members of their family.

Finally, it took the jury just six hours to convict the accused on all charges, whereupon the judge sentenced Pai to two years in jail, Kin Sang Yau to twelve months and Luk Ming Pang merely to Borstal training. Why such light sentences? Having spoken at length to Superintendent Wright and having read reports of the evidence in court, it seems clear to me that the prosecution were lucky to get their convictions at all. The Crown case, *as it came out in court,* was paper thin. Stronger sentences might have provoked the defendants into appealing to the Appeal Court (Criminal Division) in London and that might well not have upheld the guilty verdicts.

Despite the bad luck of the police, the story still shows the good effects that resolute police action, rounded off by effective representation in court, can achieve. Georgie Pai was released from jail on 27 March 1979. He was immediately put on a plane and deported back to Hong Kong. At least Britain has been spared any further taste of the activities of this typical Triad villain reared in the back streets of one of its own colonies.

So much for the Triad impact on criminal endeavour in the Netherlands and in Britain. What has been the story in the rest of Western Europe?

13 Triads in the Rest of Europe

Time magazine, in its issue dated 7 March 1977, ran this story:

One day last week 1200 French police swarmed through two suburbs of Paris, stopping no fewer than 13,000 people for surprise identification checks. Nineteen were held for questioning. Object of the exercise: to demonstrate that the government was doing something, almost anything, about France's increasingly fearsome epidemic of drug abuse.

But when the dragnet operation ended, Minister of the Interior Michel Poniatowski publicly admitted what every government in Western Europe is discovering to its dismay: police alone are virtually helpless against the continent-wide plague of Asian heroin spewing out of Amsterdam.

The picture has not improved since. Writing nearly two years later, in February 1979, in the British medical journal *Nursing Mirror*, John Warner, DEA Regional Director for Europe and the Middle East, stated with grim authority:

We estimate there are about 250,000 drug abusers in Europe. The so-called overdose death rate for Europe is about 1000 per year and increasing. Heroin seizures in Europe now exceed those made in the United States and are in excess of 500 kilos per year.

As an example, by mid-October 1978 about 355 kilos of South-East Asian heroin and seventy-one kilos of Middle Eastern origin had been seized by police and customs authorities in Europe. When one compares this to 1972, when about ten kilos of heroin were seized for European consumption, and twenty-seven kilos in 1973, one can see the alarming spread of the problem.

Between 3 October and 9 October 1978, approximately eighty-five kilos of South-East Asian heroin fell into the hands of European law enforcement officers. The geographic distribution of the seizures during the week in question was as follows: London – 32 kilos; London

– 3.2 kilos (destined for the US); Amsterdam – 8 kilos; Frankfurt – 4.5 kilos; Brussels – 5 kilos; Milan – 19 kilos; Rome – 10.7 kilos. The nationalities of the couriers were Chinese Malaysian, Americans, French of Indian extraction, and Italian.

The gravity of the situation is unmistakable, however, neither the general public nor the governments in Europe have reached this realization. The only group of people who are aware are the law enforcement officers in the front lines who are facing the deluge of drug addiction, drug smuggling, trafficking and the crimes associated with it.

In West Germany, the presence of a million immigrant Turkish 'guest workers' in the country presents a special problem with their easy access to the opiates now pouring, in ever increasing numbers, out of the Middle East, not only from the newly re-cropped poppy fields of their own country but also from the Lebanon and even beyond from the virtually unpoliced wilder tracts of Afghanistan and Pakistan. The DEA special agent in charge in Bonn, who considers the West German narcotics police 'the most efficient in Western Europe', points out that Berlin has the fourth-largest Turkish population in the world – only three cities in Turkey have more Turks in them! They can get heroin into the country with ease but the trade is in the hands of individual entrepreneurs. 'There isn't the fantastic organization behind it that you find with the Chinese trade.' Berlin, situated in the middle of Communist East Germany, can hardly take over from Amsterdam as a courier centre.

A good-sized local Chinese community is necessary for the flourishing of full-scale Triad activity, with its pattern of initial exploitation of its own people blossoming into heroin trafficking, unlawful gambling, loan-sharking, etc. Although many cities in Western Europe have seen in recent years a rash of Chinese restaurants suddenly appearing, it has been on a sporadic basis and it is only in Holland and Britain that local conditions are appropriate for large Triad operations.

In September 1979, *Time* magazine reported that the West German police had already seized during the current year 116 kilograms of heroin, a higher figure than reported from all the other countries in Western Europe combined. However, most of this heroin was Middle-Eastern, not Chinese, and it is significant that the only major arrests made in West Germany of Chinese heroin traffickers – members of the Singaporean Ah Kong group – have been in Hamburg, the country's major seaport and the only German city with a Chinese community whose size can even begin to bear comparison with the Chinatowns of Amsterdam or London, or indeed Manchester.

Nevertheless, the absence of any substantial local power bases has not entirely ruled out Triad activities in other countries of Western Europe. Richard N. Gardner, United States ambassador to Italy, wrote in the DEA's magazine *Drug Enforcement*, February 1979:

Italy's place in the international network of drug traffic, prior to the suspension of opium gum-collection in Turkey, was primarily as a transit point for shipments of morphine base destined for clandestine heroin laboratories in the south of France. While this transit traffic has been discontinued, the abuse of drugs is rapidly becoming a fact of Italian life. Traffickers in No.3 and No.4 heroin from the Golden Triangle have found a market in Italy and now travel regularly to South-East Asia to buy kilogram quantities and to Amsterdam where heroin is readily available.

Recent evidence indicates the abuse of heroin has escalated alarmingly throughout Italy. In the first six months of 1978, thirty-five heroin-related deaths were registered. During all of 1977, forty persons died of heroin overdose, compared to thirty-one in 1976 and twenty-six in 1975.

Additionally the University of Rome Drug Abuse Programme estimates that as many as 40,000 individuals, ranging in age from fourteen to forty, are daily users of heroin. During 1977 more than 2500 heroin users, all but 100 of whom were Italians, came to the attention of judicial police authorities throughout the country.

Brussels airport, for instance, has seen an appreciable amount of Triad-organized trafficking. On one day in August 1977 sharp-eyed Belgian officials arrested two couriers working for the Ah Kong. The first was a Chinese Malaysian who arrived on a flight from Kuala Lumpur and immediately attracted attention because of the way he tottered through the arrival hall wearing high-heeled, thick-soled shoes and carrying a bright red portable television set. When stopped, a pound of heroin was found in his heels and 27 lb more in a dummy tube of the television set. (I must say that when I first read that report in the London *Sunday Telegraph* newspaper I wondered to myself how much was the *real* load on that flight, with the controller happily watching it go through as the police and Customs converged on this almost blatant decoy.)

The second arrest on that very same hot August day was of a

Dutchman who arrived by Soviet Aeroflot jet from Moscow but whose original departure point was in South-East Asia – where he had taken on board statuettes of Buddha containing 10 lb of heroin.

The story of Triad activity in the rest of Europe outside the Netherlands and Great Britain is basically a story of Ah Kong – and of its later offshoots. The DEA special agent in Singapore who was so helpful earlier, carries on the narrative:

'With the heyday of heroin building up, with a lot of countries in Europe gaining an addiction problem – whether a lot of them agree with me or not, this heroin is going over there so they're either lying or not realizing what their problem is! – a lot of independents started going to Ah Kong and asking if they could have their own small independent groups. Ah Kong said "Yes", and why not? For the way it would work would be like this:

'Most of these little independent groups were originally couriers for the Ah Kong. So a guy would go to one of the bosses and say, "Look, I've been bringing you two suitcases these last three trips. I've got two brothers and a cousin. Next time let me load all four of us up. You get half of it and we sell the other half ourselves?" "Sure!" says the boss: he's not losing anything, he's gaining something.

'So they arranged these small groups to do this. Which meant that besides selling their own heroin, Ah Kong were also getting a piece of everybody else's. So the more small, loyal independent groups they can muster up, the happier they are.

'Now that's if you go and ask permission like a good little boy. But if you do it two or three times on your own and then you try and slip a load past them or you try and set up on your own or you get your brother to do your dirty work for you and *Ah Kong* find out, then you become a rival group and, well, your couriers get robbed, beaten: it becomes a very messy business.

'Because of the military training of many of them in the Singapore Army, Ah Kong were super at ambushing other couriers. They could wait around at an airport or large railway station and nine times out of ten they could almost smell a courier or his controller: the way they acted, with their suitcases and all. They would take them off the area, strip them, tear open their bags, burn them with cigars, beat them up, stop them – and send them back with the message not to do it again.

'So the rival groups had two choices: they could either get

back in line with Ah Kong or quit. A third choice was to arm themselves and be ready for battle. You've had one major group do this: arm itself, get itself an army of Singaporeans who are of the same type. This is the first break-away from the traditional Singaporean cohesiveness and also the loyalties that go right back to the original Triads on Singapore island.

'This syndicate, the major rival syndicate, is in existence now also. It is part of our overall conspiracy investigation in the DEA. Does it have a name? No. It's just named after the person who runs it and right now that's something we can't give you because we are right on his heels – we really are!'

But what that DEA special agent did give me, and his information was subsequently enlarged upon by the DEA European regional headquarters in Paris, was the name of the boss of the only Ah Kong splinter group that did not go into rivalry with Ah Kong and even for a fruitful few years flourished alongside it. 'The name is Tan Suan Chin, although most people call him Johnny Tan, and he was one of the original seamen out of Singapore, a member of the See Tong, who shipped over to Copenhagen back in the mid-sixties. When he later went "independent", since he was one of the original five syndicate heads, they didn't seem to mind. It was a very friendly split-up.' It sounds almost like members of a corporation's board of directors agreeing to go their separate ways 'by mutual consent'.

Johnny Tan married a Swedish girl and set up home in Sweden where, among other activities, he masterminded the sudden flourishing of heroin there in the mid-seventies. In 1975, the drug was almost non-existent in that country, but in 1976 the amounts discovered had increased to more than 35 lb and in 1977 there were forty-nine deaths attributed to hard drugs in a country whose total population only amounts to eight million. By November 1978, the *South China Morning Post* in Hong Kong could run a news report from Stockholm about 'Sweden's busiest drug market being carried on right in the centre of the city, in front of the Parliament building', with heroin capsules selling at prices ranging from 350 to 500 kronor (£370 to £530) and some heroin users spending up to 2000 kronor (£1856) every twenty-four hours. The grisly credit for that achievement can largely be placed on the shoulders of Johnny Tan, born on 17 October 1946 thousands of miles away in Singapore.

This is how DEA European regional office in Paris received the news of his arrest at the hands of the Swedish police on 2 September 1977 from their local DEA office responsible for the area:

Subject: Singapore Chinese charged as leader of European narcotics ring.

The press has reported the arrest in Goteborg this week of a thirty-one-year-old Chinese from Singapore on charges of heroin smuggling. According to the papers, the Chinese is believed to be European chief of the 'See Tong', reportedly one of the most powerful Tongs in Singapore. The press also claimed that in the past three years Goteborg has become a major base of operations for narcotics smuggling in Europe, although reportedly the heroin has not been imported into Sweden for distribution.

2. According to the Goteborgs-Posten of September 9, the arrest of 'this seemingly serious business man' has attracted 'great attention' in European police circles, since he is allegedly a top figure in the narcotics smuggling field. The suspect, who has reportedly been operating an importing firm in Goteborg, was brought before an examining judge yesterday and remanded for further investigation. Two other Singapore Chinese have also been arrested in Goteborg in connection with the case and are scheduled to appear in court today.

3. In accordance with Swedish practice, the name of the alleged ringleader was not published. However, the press did report that he came to Goteborg in the early 1970s, and started a series of small Chinese restaurants together with some compatriots. Eventually he sold his interest in the restaurants and opened an importing business to serve as a cover for his illegal operations. Although he has applied for Swedish citizenship, it had not been granted at the time of his arrest.

4. Comment: The sudden increase in the number of Chinese restaurants in this port city in recent years has long provoked press and public speculation that they might be operating as a cover for the narcotics trade. While a number of long-established Swedish restaurants have been going out of business, in view of the depressed state of the Swedish economy, Chinese restaurants have been mushrooming, and far outnumber any other ethnic-type restaurants in Goteborg. This week's arrests will undoubtedly reinforce the general public impression that Goteborg has indeed become the 'Northern European headquarters' of the narcotics trade.

In fact, the DEA Paris office already knew all about Johnny Tan. His comparatively few years of successful trafficking had, in effect, received their *coup de grâce* just over a year previously when two Dutchmen had been arrested in Bangkok when a staggeringly large haul of 138.2 kilos of heroin was found concealed in two drums of aviation grease at Don Muang airport. 'What made the authorities suspicious,' says a DEA special agent, 'is that the stuff was being exported out of the country to Holland. Aviation grease is a rare commodity in Thailand. They normally import all the aviation grease they need. So what were these two large drums of the stuff doing about to be flown out?'

The two Dutchmen officially in charge of the consignment en route to Holland were arrested on the spot. Johnny Tan, who was there in the airport at the time, managed to get away. But one of the Dutchmen bought clemency for himself by pleading guilty (he got a sentence of fifty years in a Thai jail as against his confederate's seventy-five!): he told the Thai police, and the DEA, all that he knew. The result was that Johnny Tan was arrested in Holland, but, since he had not actually committed any crime in Holland itself and they could not bring a conspiracy charge against him in Dutch law, the Dutch police decided not to deal with him themselves but to deport him back to his country of origin, i.e. Singapore.

'So the authorities here geared up to receive him,' says the DEA special agent in Singapore, 'but it didn't work that way. Tan had married a Swedish girl and he had also applied for Swedish naturalization. So he was able to talk himself into being deported to Sweden as his "country of origin" instead of here where he ran the risk of being sentenced to death!

'So the tolerant, liberal Dutch put him on a plane to Sweden. But the Swedish police picked him up as he left the plane and, how they did it I still don't know, they put him on a heroin trafficking conspiracy charge, although the whole operation had taken place either in the Netherlands or Thailand!

'He was convicted and sentenced to ten years in jail, the Swedish maximum for trafficking in hard drugs and he is now serving that time in a Swedish prison. We thought it wouldn't hold up on appeal but it did.' In fact, the judgement of the Court of Appeals in Goteborg was pronounced on 23 May 1978.

The story of Johnny Tan is instructive. It proves yet again that concerted international law enforcement activity and tough supporting action by the courts can substantially disrupt even the most daring Triad-linked operations: once the authorities can actually bring themselves to admit that they have a problem.

As so often has been the case, the DEA played a leading role in the tracking down of this major trafficker. But what is the situation back home for the Americans? How stand the Triads in North America – on both sides of the 49th Parallel, that line on the map that separates the United States from its northern neighbour Canada?

14 Triads in the United States

Until only very recently, the story of the United States treatment of its ethnic Chinese minority was one of exploitation and discrimination. Although the great railroad that first linked the East to the West Coast in the late 1860s could not have been completed without thousands of early immigrant Chinese labourers, those men were denied the right to bring wives or womenfolk with them and once their usefulness was at an end and a whole network of minor regional railroads had been laid in the West, Congress passed a Chinese Exclusion Act, May 1882. This suspended all further immigration of Chinese labourers and stated that *no* Chinese resident in the United States was eligible for naturalization. Within seven years, an attempt was made to repeal the Act but the United States Supreme Court averred a power by Congress to exclude 'foreigners of a different race who will not assimilate with us'.

Chinese merchants were put in a different category. They were allowed to continue to enter the country and bring their wives with them but in 1924 – the year in which American Red Indians were granted the right to citizenship in their own country – Congress passed another Act decreeing that thenceforth no Chinese woman, whatever her husband's class or professional status, would be allowed permanent residence in the United States.

It seems extraordinary that when the Japanese bombed Pearl Harbor in December 1941 and brought the United States into war against the Japanese Empire alongside the armies of Chiang Kai Shek's Nationalist China, Chinese immigrants to the United States were still legally regarded as unfit for citizenship. Two more years passed before President Roosevelt signed an

Act repealing the Chinese Exclusion Act and granting naturalization rights to Chinese aliens. Yet it was prohibited by Californian law until 1948 for even a native-born Chinese-American to marry a white woman and that in a State which has the largest resident Chinese community outside mainland China or Taiwan – San Francisco.

There was even a time when a Chinese, even though a native-born American citizen, could not legally be hired by any corporation, nor could he or she testify in court. As Peter Fong, a Chinese-American senior DEA official, told me: 'The blacks were at one time declared second-rate by Congress by legislation. The Chinese were the first ethnic group to have themselves declared by Congress not only second-rate but undesirable!'

In California, a host of municipal ordinances were enacted to narrow the occupational options for the Chinese: for example, 'Every laundry employing one horse-drawn vehicle is to pay two dollars a quarter licence fee, those employing two such vehicles four dollars a quarter, and those using none fifteen dollars a quarter.' Since practically all of the Chinese delivered laundry by foot, this obviously hit the Chinese hardest. Licences for the transaction of any business or occupation were denied to any alien ineligible for citizenship. It was also ruled that aliens would be prohibited from taking fish out of any waters of the State for purposes of sale. Ordinances required that laundries must be constructed with stone or brick walls, and that laundries could not operate between ten o'clock at night and six in the morning.

It was Chief Justice Charles Evans Hughes, one of the greatest of American jurists, who said well over half a century ago: 'The security of the Republic will be found in the treatment of the poor and the ignorant; in our indifference to their misery and helplessness lies disaster.'

It is against this context that the phenomenon of the Triads in the United States has to be considered. As we saw in Chapter 3, during the turbulent years (1851–64) of the eventually unsuccessful Taiping Rebellion in Imperial China, some of the Triad rebels (at a time when the Triad Societies were still primarily honourable resistance organizations) managed to flee to the West Coast of the United States, where they set up branches of the Triad Society known as the Chee Kung Tong. That word 'Tong', which we have already met with in

Singapore, is the way in which Triad Societies in the United States have become known. As Peter Fong explains:

'When we talk about "Tongs" in the United States we are in fact talking of former "Triad Societies" that started a very long time ago back in the Far East. The "Tongs" in the United States were formed as benevolent societies in all the Chinese sectors in the major cities in the United States. "Tong" really means "town hall", "a large hall". The benevolent societies were formed to take care of the Chinese in America and, as a coterie, Asian-Americans, particularly Chinese, had a tendency to remain together; they were very close together. And these benevolent societies took care of everything: food, rent, whatever was needed. They took care of the crime rate: the Chinese in the United States had the lowest crime rate among all the ethnic groups – except in recent years when the youth gang wars started.

'They took care of their own. They exerted a strong influence on the social life of the community. We looked to them. Then as the Chinese assimilated, their influence became less. They still continued to exert great influence up to the time of my own generation, up to about the early forties, then they began to wane. They were losing it to the younger guys coming up. There were incredible gaps in communication between the Tongs and the younger generation of Chinese-Americans.'

And this is where the darker side of the story comes in. In 1951, the California Regional Office of the Bureau of Narcotics and Dangerous Drugs, precursor of the modern DEA, circulated a memorandum marked 'Restricted' for the guidance of narcotics officers. It began:

The investigation of criminal activity on the part of the Chinese population in the United States presents novel and complex problems which many officers may find unusually difficult.

As most of the American-Chinese criminals are members of one of the various 'Tongs', their tradition of secrecy is similar to that of the Mafia. Further, their social-psychology, or 'way of thinking', brought from the Orient, tends to make them contemptuous of Western manners, including law-enforcement. Chinese are seldom found in the civil courts of the US and a Chinese complainant in a criminal matter is rare. Most such disputes are settled through arbitration, or by force, by the Tongs, or Family Associations.

'There are five modern-day Tongs in the United States

today,' says a DEA special agent, born and bred in California but talking to me in his office in the US Embassy in London. 'The biggest is what we might call a combination, but it's the same leadership and the same management. It is called the Bing Kung or On Leong and it is a coast-to-coast secret society. Why it is the Bing Kung on the West Coast and the On Leong on the East Coast is anybody's guess. It seems to divide the country right in half* and it is called one thing on one end and the other on the other end. Bing Kung is the west end. You won't find any On Leong in San Francisco, for example, and you won't find any Bing Kung in New York – but it's the same apparatus.

'The second-largest single coast-to-coast Triad [*his* word] is the Hip Sing. The Hip Sing is a very powerful, very affluential – probably the most affluential – single secret society in the United States. They've got a big headquarters in San Francisco and they've got a big headquarters in New York and you can take it from me they talk daily.

'The third secret society, which is very affluential and influential, is the Ying On Tong, which controls the south-west, which includes especially places like Phoenix, Tucson, Los Angeles, Fresno, all the way up to San Francisco.

'The fourth is a small Tong in the San Francisco area generally and in the Los Angeles area called the Hop Sing. The

---

* The Triad I spoke to in my Canadian hotel room has this to add: 'I was president of the Hip Sing in Washington DC for a few years. Triads have very heavy control in North America of the Tongs. Denver is the dividing point not the Mason-Dixon Line. North of Denver belongs to the Bing Kung Triad [*his* word] from San Francisco. South of Denver is divided between the On Leong Tong and Hip Sing Tong.

'The Bing Kung were originally from Vancouver but then they spread down to San Francisco, Sacramento and Los Angeles. On Leong Tong is mostly businessmen. Most of the Tong was formed by members with the surname Wong: there were almost 20,000 Wongs in the On Leong Tong. It's just like Smith. Hip Sing Tong was originated by people with the surname Ng.

'At one time the Bing Kung and the On Leong were one Tong, but they split because there was too much trouble going back and forth. That is why Denver is made the dividing line.

'The Bing Kung and the On Leong are rich Chinese organizations but each had separate Hung Mon [a Chinese alternative name for Triad] flags. Hip Sing started as the poor man's society, the working man's society: no rich man wanted to join. That continues even up to today when, on the East Coast, business is in the hands of the On Leong and, on the West Coast, it is in the hands of the Bing Kung.

'But about fifteen years ago they decided to become friends and now when each one has a convention the other goes.'

fifth and the smallest of all these secret societies is the Suey Sing, which is again in San Francisco and Los Angeles.

'You've got to remember the derivation of these. Since the first Chinese came to California back in '49 in the days of the Gold Rush, the Tongs have been going through various permutations of name and evolving into these organizations today. The word "Tong" of course recollects the Tong Wars in the early years of this century and you think of the "hatchet men" and bloody fights in old San Francisco's Chinatown before the 1906 earthquake, but the word itself only means "assembly hall" or "clan association". It could mean "syndicate" but it usually means "clan" – and "clan" is a very important word when you consider words like Ku Klux Klan, and it is the same "tong" as in the name Kuomintang or Kuomintong, the KMT, the central political apparatus of the Republic of China, of Taiwan.

'The Tong Wars gave the secret societies a bad name and they grew up after that. They discovered they couldn't settle their disputes with hatchets – though that seems to be coming back these days. They grew up and they said, "Let's be part of the United States. Let's become civic-minded. Let's get involved in the civics of the United States. We won't call ourselves "Tongs" any more (except in the Chinese characters that are still up on the front door). We'll call ourselves "benevolent associations". So the Ying On Tong, for example, translates to Ying On Labour and Merchants Benevolent Association, which gives it an aura of civic responsibility.'

The Tongs of yesterday have evolved into the 'businessmen's benevolent associations' of today and, as such, they contain many honourable elements, far removed from knowingful participation in illegal or criminal activities, but alongside the decent citizens there are (I am assured by US law enforcement officers) criminal elements stretching right up to and including the leadership.

For instance, says my California-born DEA informant in London, speaking of one present-day 'businessmen's benevolent association': 'Regardless of what they call it, it still is a secret society run by an officership of bad people. Of course, there are honest, respectable businessmen in it as well, who would have no conscious part in criminality, but there is no possibility that a Chinese guy could run a business in the densely populated Chinese enclaves in places like San Francisco or New York without paying dues to one of these societies. And there's a lovely word for that in Chinese, "Deem Han Rou", which means "Dip into the fragrant oil" or "Give the fragrant oil", which means dues.'

This question of dues was confirmed by a US Immigration Services investigator at the Federal Building in downtown Manhattan, New York: 'I had a CI once – confidential informant – we used to call him "the electrician" because he used to do electrical work – didn't do it too well either, caused a couple of fires! We picked him up when he tried to enter into a marriage fraud – he was from Hong Kong – to get his papers to stay. It was a crazy set-up. He married a black woman: he spoke no English and she naturally didn't speak any Chinese. We broke the fraud very, very quickly. At the first interview he gave it up but then he came to work for me.

'First, we were going to use him for narcotics. But he was a member of the On Leong Association, and he was what they call a "Red Stick" man – he was the "enforcer". . . . He says, "I'm a liaison between the Association and the Ghost Shadows" [the name of a leading Chinese youth gang in New York's Chinatown]. What he meant by this was that if the youth gangs wanted to control a certain territory, they had to work through the Association. This was in about 1972 to 1976, when the Association had very good control over the gangs.

'The Associations in New York at that time – the Hip Sing as well as the On Leong . . . financed the gambling clubs, they took the profits of the clubs. If, say, a restaurant wanted to open up and they didn't pay their dues to the Associations and opened up anyhow, I guarantee the Association told the gang to tear that restaurant apart. Or go in and run up a bill and then not pay up, break the guy's windows or intimidate his customers or beat up his cooks.

'I'm not saying that I could prove in a court of law what I'm telling you, but, so far as I'm concerned, the On Leong Association, the Hip Sing, the major Chinese benevolent associations have their basis in criminality. They have a tie into it.

'It started off years ago when the associations were first set up to aid their Chinese countrymen from whatever province in China they were from, from whatever family they belonged to and that created a great smuggling circumstance where you could have someone say, "I have some people in Hong Kong". "Good. We'll give you the money. We'll get them here."

'So the association backs this little venture. When these people come here, well, now they're indebted to the association to pay whatever money has been spent on them. Now they were either given jobs in a restaurant, a tailor shop, a factory and had to pay over their salaries to the association. Or these were great people to send out on extortions, robberies, murders, break-ins, that type of thing.'

The Triad I spoke to in the Canadian hotel room takes up the story: 'The Tongs have acquired a great deal of wealth since the nineteenth century. The On Leong must have hundreds of millions of dollars. The Hip Sing I know has got forty million dollars in reserve. My predecessor, as president of the Washington DC Hip Sing, killed a guy; he committed a murder and served some time in jail. His family was raised in Washington by the Hip Sing for twenty-five years and every kid graduated from university.

'Why did he commit the murder? For the society. He killed a guy who had taken money out of the society, who had cheated the society. He took the gambling money and ran. I tell you there is big money involved in all this. We have a gambling house underneath my old headquarters in Washington DC and, if we made $2000 a week in the gambling house, we had to pay $200 to the Hip Sing headquarters in New York. The headquarters take ten per cent of the gross. They provide the fund for the benevolent work of the association.'

The Triad also said that he had taken part in a Triad initiation ceremony – 'with oath and with blood and all the ritual' – and that the initiations still took place today in America and Canada, and that this applied to the youth gangs too.

Says the California-born DEA special agent in London: 'Gambling is *the* money maker. It develops literally millions of pounds and millions of dollars of audit-free cash that usually goes through a money-washing cycle in Hong Kong or Taiwan and comes back in places like Reno, Nevada, for example, as legitimate Oriental investment money. By then it's as clean as a whistle but it's been created on the gambling tables of all these Chinese gambling clubs on Mott Street in New York or Gerrard Street in London.'

The profitability of gambling has carried on into the next

generation, as witness Lieutenant Martin Kennedy in police headquarters in New York City: 'Last year, we ran what they call a controlled pad and that's where gamblers gave us money believing we were corrupt police officers. This money was then turned in and retained as evidence against these people. We ran this particular operation to gather intelligence: we were watching everyone who was coming and going and, as they were being paid, they would come and go freely, believing that the cops are corrupt and you can do what you want.

'One of the places we had under observation was a location at 7 Division Street, down in Chinatown. This location made $247,000 a month – out of that they paid one youth gang leader, Michael Chen, $3400 a week: to him personally. He was then in charge of the Flying Dragons and he had six Flying Dragons living above the gambling house and they were all armed and they got paid $150 apiece a week. Not out of the $3400 – that was on top of it! So the kids between them were getting $4300 a week out of that one club!

'Now if I was a young Chinese criminal looking to put myself in a very, very lucrative business with minimal amount of jail time, I would say, "Why should I go into junk? Junk, if they catch you, they put you into jail for fifteen, twenty, twenty-five years. I'm disliked by the entire community. Nobody wants to have any dealings with a junk dealer. I'll become a gambler. I'll pay everybody off. I'll run a totally legitimate gambling house and, instead of making $4300 a week, I'll settle for $5000 a week tax-free – and everybody will look up to me!" '

But what about the Tongs and narcotics? What is their role in the international trafficking of heroin? This is what a senior DEA special agent, talking to me in an almost deserted New York Chinatown bar, has to say:

'Sure there is involvement! But the On Leong and the Hip Sing do it differently. Say I'm an On Leong member. I'd go to the On Leong's No. 1 man here in New York till he was voted out of office in January 1978 – I'd go to him and I'd say, "I'm going to do a dope deal. I can get the dope over here through my own connection, but can you help me with an Italian for distribution?" If the deal was right, they might do it or, if they didn't like you or they thought something was wrong with the deal, they'd tell you: "Go get your own Italian!"

'That's how the On Leong has always functioned. They've

always been a much looser-knit organization than the Hip Sing. They've always been the businessmen, the more prosperous section of the Chinese community. Whereas the Hip Sing have always been the ship-jumpers, restaurant workers, low level: their leadership has always been very much more conservative. They've kept things tightly within their own control.

'Their No. 1 man here for many years was named Sam Ong. He was the leader of his people. He was the George Washington of the poor people of Chinatown. Sam Ong I have a lot of respect for. He did things the American way. He wanted to bring his people up any way he could. One of the ways was narcotics for money.

'Now I'm a seaman. I've just come in from South-East Asia with 3 lb of heroin. I go to Sam Ong and I tell him I've got heroin. Sam Ong would take it from me and he would sell it for me – he would have his own connections with the Italians or the blacks or whoever – and then part of the money he would keep, sure, but part of it went to you and part to the Hip Sing. He always had in the forefront the welfare of his Hip Sing people. That's the one thing I've always respected him for. He died about five or six years ago.

'He was a crook narcotics dealer, but he took care of his people. As a result, the Hip Sing grew and prospered: since he died, they have gone downhill.'

This mention of the Mafia whetted my appetite for further information at ground-roots level as to the link (doubted in some rarified quarters) between Italian organized crime and the Chinese 'benevolent associations'. What exactly *is* the working relationship between the two syndicate-type operations?

'Look at the On Leong building on Mott Street and Canal [the American way of referring to a building on or close to the corner of Mott Street and Canal Street]. Right across the street from there is Italian organized crime in Mulberry Street in "Little Italy", right next door to Chinatown. That's the Mulberry Street crew where for a hundred years all they had to do was cross this street and make contacts with people interested in the narcotics business. They made these contacts and for years that's the way the Chinese did their business. Maybe they had two, three, four, five Italians that they trusted *and the Italians trusted them.*'

He names a notorious Italian criminal and continues, 'he did dope with the Chinese from the fifties to today. You would never, never hear of a Chinese guy being arrested and giving up an Italian. You would never hear of an Italian giving up a Chinese, never. You never hear of an Italian giving up an Italian!'

Traditionally there has been a great deal of hatred between Little Italy and Chinatown but this, I was told, is 'about Italian people who have lived all their lives in Little Italy and now they are being pushed out by Chinese immigrants. It's a different thing when you're talking about business, when you're talking about the organized crime Mafia and the Chinese and the 14K.

'A perfect example of this is two summers ago. The Flying Dragons, that's a Chinese youth gang, who are not allowed to come into the inner part of Chinatown, take up residence on the front of a building in Little Italy. There are ten, twelve kids who do not belong on that street: on the Italian section of Elizabeth Street in Little Italy. But they decide to settle there.

'They are there about six or seven days when the Italian kids come and say, "You don't belong here," and force them to leave. There is a full-fledged sit-down with the Italian leaders of Little Italy and the Mafia guys and the young buffaloes of the Italians are told: "Leave the kids alone."

'Is there a connection then?'

'It's very hard to prove: my agency has made cases involving Chinese and Italians; nothing spectacular. You never see cases where we could bust organized crime or bust the Chinese connection, but still we've made cases showing that Chinese have dealt in heroin to Italians.

'But hell, what is the Mafia? What is organized crime? The Mafia has always taken the stand that anyone who deals in narcotics is always like an outlaw of the Mafia. Now the real Mafia is into other things: prostitution, gambling, influence-peddling with the law, they're into the Teamsters. Narcotics, no – it's one area where any organization can be very vulnerable. So they always keep that on the side. [The earlier named Italian] is a full-fledged member of Italian organized crime, but he is like a section of his own. He is not with the other guys: when he gets arrested, if he ever gets arrested, and he turns, if he starts to co-operate, he'll never be able to talk about the big guys – that's to say, the guys who are in the Teamsters, who can elect the President. They always keep that separate.

'Narcotics to Italian organized crime is their life's blood. It always has been. Gambling, they get so much money from gambling – what do they do with it? They invest it in narcotics – it's such a fantastic profit.

'Now, within recent history, they've gotten out of narcotics. As a matter of fact, there has been word around that they have told many members of their organization "Get out of narcotics" and people have actually been killed for dealing in narcotics in the Italian organized crime section.

'One of the problems that has happened, therefore, is the Italians have been out of narcotics and the blacks have stepped in; and they have gained *fantastic* ground from the Italians. Money! Money buys power. These black guys now have fantastic power, and a tremendous thing has happened. The Italians have recognized this. I don't know how true this is, it has not been verified, but two summers ago there were murders in Harlem – unreported – I mean who cares if a black violator gets killed? Rumour had it that the Italians contracted one of their guys to go up there and knock off all these black guys who have gained so much control, just to put them in their place. They were getting out of place.'

If Tong involvement in the heroin trade on the East Coast, with distribution largely in the hands of the Italian and black Mafia, is considerable; then what must be its true extent on the West Coast where, if only for historical reasons, the position of 'benevolent associations' is, if anything, even more entrenched in the local Chinese communities?

The best possible pointer to the unfathomed depths of Tong narcotics activity on the West Coast is supplied by a confidential memorandum submitted by the BNDD's District Office in San Francisco in 1972 to Richard Kleindienst, then Attorney General of the United States, in reply to allegations of harassment made against it by the Ying On Labour and Merchants Benevolent Association, one of the 'Big Five', with its headquarters in San Francisco's Chinatown:

Although an aggressive investigation of Chinese suspect traffickers continues, and nothing less will be effective, every move has been after consultation with attorneys of the Organized Crime and Racketeering Section of the US Department of Justice, and where applicable, has been done with search and arrests warrants. The principal failure is not being able to devote more time and manpower to the investigation of these organized sophisticated criminals.

In support of that magisterial rebuttal of the charge of harassment of a respectable commercial organization, the memorandum gave a run-down on the track record of some of the then hierarchy of 'the Tong', as it persistently called the self-styled 'Benevolent Association'. Here are some extracts:

National President – a shrewd, experienced, professional financier of organized gambling and narcotic smuggling. He has been arrested four times for possession of narcotics, on the last occasion a Federal offence for which he was sentenced to five years in Federal prison.

National Treasurer – arrested two times for narcotic violations, on the first occasion for a Federal violation. He is presently under investigation by the San Francisco District Office, suspected of distributing heroin.

National Secretary – a heroin smoker, and undercover contact with him has been made at San Francisco to purchase small quantities of heroin.

Los Angeles Chapter President – recently convicted at San Francisco for importing one kilogram of heroin into the United States from Hong Kong. His previous criminal record includes an arrest and conviction for attempted bribery of a police officer.

English Secretary of the Tong – a glad-hander and a political machinator without equal. He also operates the Tong's Nam Fong Club at Oakland, which has remained untouchable by law enforcement authorities, and, which, according to one source, grosses about one quarter of a million dollars a year. The club operates on the premises of a Tong-owned building at Oakland. His arrest record includes numerous small gambling arrests. (He has managed to move a nephew [. . .] into [. . .] County District Attorney's Office, in which position he decides upon prosecution of Chinese violations.

The memorandum also states, in an introductory historical survey:

The one force upon which the Tongs (originally) relied heavily was the fear they were able to instil in the mass of Chinese immigrants arriving in the United States to work on the railroads or in the mines. It was natural, therefore, as the years went by, that second and third generation Chinese-Americans could no longer be coerced and frightened, and as a strict Oriental quota was established, the Tongs lost their potency, until in the late 1940s and middle 1960s, they practically became a thing of the past.

Ironically, the condition of Chinese immigrants that was created at the turn of the century was re-created with the relaxing of the Chinese quota in 1965. This Act opened the floodgates and Chinese immigrants poured – and are pouring – into the United States at a rate equalling the influx of pre-fire San Francisco days.

Since the Act signed by President Johnson on 3 October 1965, some 300,000 immigrants have flooded into the country from Hong Kong – in addition to tens of thousands of illegal entrants. Nearly half of them have ended up in the New York area. The rest have burst the seams of the existing Chinatowns of San Francisco, Los Angeles, Boston and Chicago. In New York, they have crossed the border into Canal Street into what used to be exclusively Little Italy. In Chicago, an entirely new Chinatown has had to be opened up in the western suburbs.

These new immigrants are different from the old. Sure enough, the greater number *are,* as before, hard-working, honest, seeking after the golden dream of happiness that has lured so many millions across the seas to the United States for a century and a half. But in their midst has come a minority of young tearaways straight off the back streets of Kowloon and Hong Kong island.

In the fifteen years that have passed since the new Immigration Act, these young men – some of them thirteen- and fourteen-year-old killers – have become known to the embattled police forces of the United States (and also of some Canadian cities) as 'the Chinese youth gangs'. Until 1965, the policemen of the 5th Precinct that takes in New York's Chinatown made fewer than ten arrests a year of Chinese youths under twenty-one: nowadays, the annual average is running at about 200. Until 1965, murders in San Francisco's Chinatown were almost unknown: by 1978 the local police had forty-five *recorded* homicides on their hands – and one cannot tell how many go unrecorded.

The gangs here called themselves different names in different parts of the country. In San Francisco and Los Angeles, they are the Wah Ching (meaning 'Chinese Youth') and the Joe Boys (named after Macao-born gang leader Joe Fong, who continued to run the outfit from Tracy Jail while serving nearly seven years of a life sentence for conspiracy to commit murder from 1972 to 1979). In New York, there have been the Ghost Shadows, White Eagles, Black Eagles, Flying Dragons, the Ching Yee, but they do not keep exclusively to their own home base.

In his opening speech, before a three-day joint United States–Canadian police conference on 'Chinese Street Gang and Triad Organized Criminal Activities' went into secret session at the New York City Police Academy in September 1978, Mr Herbert Stirs, New York City's Deputy Mayor for Criminal Justice, told the assembled roomful of detectives, investigators and policemen: 'In the past decade we have witnessed the rapid growth of these groups from local gangs to organized elements of international crime. Unfortunately, law enforcement agencies in North America have not always been able to keep up with the increasing mobility and sophistication of these gangs which now have no compunction about committing murder and other felonies in order to further the scope of their criminal activity.

'Hit men and extortionists can travel quickly between our great cities and just as quickly return to their place of origin before a police investigation can begin.

'Clearly, this new growth and mobility in Chinese youth gangs calls for a new response from the law enforcement agencies in the United States and Canada. If our police departments attempt to deal with this increasing problem individually, then city lines, State lines, and international borders will become sanctuaries for a growing class of criminals who have shown the potential of developing from 'youth gangs" into full-fledged adult criminal organizations, such as the Triads of Hong Kong.'

This mobility is astonishing. Suspects in extortions in Maryland and New Jersey have been arrested in Chicago and New York. A murder by a gang leader in San Francisco was solved by a tip picked up in a Hawaii bar. Teenage hit men from the Wah Chings in San Francisco have flown across the entire width of the country in an unsuccessful bid to kill Nicky Louie, the notorious Kowloon-born leader of New York's Ghost Shadows who has survived at least eleven attempts on his life and is still not yet twenty-five years of age. 'The gangs didn't ever get a foothold here. There were isolated incidents but the last that we knew about was in 1977. It's all finished now,' an investigator in the Chicago police assured me – ironically, the day after (as I later discovered) Nicky Louie had visited the 'Windy City' on one of his frequent visits to the local branch of his organization.

And perhaps the ultimate of all: 'It does seem to me that they have links with Hong Kong which they keep up,' says Ross Arai, head of the Asian Task Force of the Los Angeles police. 'We know that our leaders travel once a year back to Hong Kong but I'm never going to find out what happens. They may be a portion of the Triads. They may be trying to pattern themselves over here after them by going back to gain knowledge as to what should be done. They may talk to somebody over there that they respect as an elder and say: "This is what we are doing. What are we doing wrong? How can we better our organization in the States? Maybe when we get strong enough, we can join *your* organization?"'

The American public has little idea of the activities of the whole new wave of young criminals in their midst. Many of the youngsters have come in alone, leaving their parents behind in Hong Kong. 'They come here already street-wise, knowledgeable of the world of crime, of the underworld from whence they came,' says Sergeant John McKenna, head of the Asian Task Force of the San Francisco police. Others have come with their parents – such as fourteen-year-old John Lau [this is a pseudonym], described by Investigator Barney O'Riley of the Chicago police as 'a one-man crime wave' – who then run away from home, where often both parents are out working, with typical Chinese dedication, all possible hours to better their conditions. 'What makes you think that Chinese youth, with poor housing, social, educational and economic discrimination, might escape what the Irish and Italian children went through, or what black and Puerto Rican children go through?' asks an anthropologist, quoted by writer Berkeley Rice in an article in *Psychology Today* in May 1977.

These Chinese teenagers have a further problem. 'You'll find that they are in general not socially acceptable to the same age group that are born here,' says a Chinese-American DEA special agent in San Francisco, who himself looks no older than his late twenties. 'There is a stigma. The language barrier, education, social, they will not function well together with the Chinese kids who've been born in this country. The stigma will fester as they go through life in this age group so, they will gravitate towards and stick with their particular group, their particular youth gang. It is a form of discrimination within an already discriminated against minority.'

'Whichever way you look at it,' says a US Immigration Service investigator in New York, 'you've got young people that no longer have family ties or are subject to family discipline living in totally disoriented situations.'

But 'the youth gangs' are not limited only to youngsters in their teens. Says Lieutenant Martin Kennedy in New York: 'People say "youth gangs" and they figure fifteen-, sixteen-year-old kids. But that's not necessarily true. We find that the controlling members can be as old as twenty-five, thirty, forty years. What they do is get these youths to perform their acts for them, carry their weapons, even commit their murders for them because, under the age of eighteen, they're on Easy Street so far as the law is concerned.

'We have a case currently before the courts where we arrested an individual, whom we believed to be a major supplier of guns and ammunition to the gangs, and he's in his early forties. So you see we're also talking about adults in middle life.' After all, a sixteen-year-old who came over in 1966 would by 1980 be thirty years of age.

But what about these 'teeny-bopper' killers? 'Yes, of course, they exist,' says policeman Ross Arai in Los Angeles. 'You've got to look at the structure of these organizations. They're very well set up: I would put it equivalent to the Mafia here in the United States. They have their leaders, they have their national leaders, they have their city leaders, they have their lieutenants under the city leaders and these lieutenants are responsible for *x* number of members within their groups.

'And in each one of these groups that lieutenant will have one or two hit men that they train for the job. These individuals will be from the age of thirteen to seventeen, no older, because here in the United States they are still considered juveniles and cannot be tried as an adult.

'What happens to them? They *can* be tried as an adult, if the courts deem it so. But the majority of the time, because they are juveniles, the courts will not deem it so. These individuals will go to camp. They know that, even if they kill someone, they're only going to stay there until they're twenty-one and then they'll be out free again with a very high status assured to them within their own organization – they've got nothing to lose!

'I've arrested myself a Wah Ching kid who was only seventeen and who committed a homicide that was just like an execution. Some Wah Chings and the leader of an entertainment group visiting from Taiwan were sitting round a table in a restaurant. The Wah Chings were demanding a "donation" from him as the price of his group being allowed to perform in our city.

'He said no and this kid sitting on the opposite side of the table from him just drew a 9 mm automatic from his waistband and shot him dead. Executed him in front of everyone in that restaurant for not agreeing to pay the money. He went on the run for two months, then gave himself up to me. He was tried and convicted – and he's out again now! He's out on the streets. He'll kill again one of these days.

'But this is the way our laws are written, this is the way that society says it shall go.'

Says Lieutenant Martin Kennedy in New York: 'OK, the Triad Societies back in Hong Kong and before that in China, they were more than just a criminal element. At one time, they really believed that what they were doing was right. But now what happens is that, as the years go by, these Chinese-American kids that come over, what they do, they're not doing it because they believe in something. They do it, join a gang, for one reason and one reason only, and that is to make money and to be identified as someone, and that's it.

'You would not find these street gangs out in Chinatown anywhere just for the sake of killing or fighting, or anything like that, if there's no money involved. It's pure money. They will kill anybody for money, these kids, anybody, at a drop of a hat, even a cop.'

Within the space of a few weeks in New York's Chinatown, there was a grim tally of homicides and woundings: a shoot-out on Bayard Street between two rival youth gangs left five members of the White Eagles wounded. Two weeks later, a group of eight Black Eagles, wielding guns and meat cleavers, burst into a restaurant on Mott Street and attacked two nineteen-year-old Ghost Shadows. A few days later, a fifteen-year-old youth was shot and killed in front of his apartment house on Elizabeth Street by three members of the White Eagles. That same evening, two members of the Ghost Shadows entered the men's room of the Sung Sin Chinese Theatre and shot dead a nineteen-year-old youth. One week later, a group of Flying Dragons walked into the crowded lobby of the Pagoda Theatre and opened fire on two Ghost Shadows, killing one and wounding the other.

In San Francisco, fifteen-year-old Joe Boy was kidnapped by two car-loads of Wah Chings. Their purpose was to extract a membership list from him. They burned him with matches and beat him so fiercely that, later testimony revealed, they sent their women – their 'tough little bitches' – for ice cream to cool all of them off. The body of the victim was found mutilated and shot to death. But because a city parking meter collector, a Caucasian, had taken a licence number during the kidnapping, eleven Wah Chings were convicted.

Gang killings are almost always carefully planned public attacks. Afterwards, when the body of the victim is still sprawled in the street or slumped over a restaurant table, the killers often hold a victory celebration. 'Whenever we hear of a party in Chinatown we start looking for a body,' a San Francisco policeman has told Al Martinez, a *Los Angeles Times* staff writer.

So deep is the fear among merchants and residents and so rigid the Chinese tradition of silence in the face of authority – 'When alive don't go to authority, when dead don't go to Hell' is an old Chinese saying – that witnesses fade and assassination targets lucky enough to survive stand mute. When Nicky Louie, born Hin Pui Lui in the slums of Kowloon but by the mid-seventies unchallenged leader of the New York Ghost Shadows, was gunned down in a gang-land fight after his years of supreme ascendancy were over, Detective Neil Mauriello of the 5th Precinct (and probably the most knowledgeable policeman on Chinese youth gangs in the United States) leaned over his body lying in a pool of blood near the Bowery and said, 'Nicky, come on, you're gonna die, tell me who shot you', Louie looked up at Mauriello and said, 'Fuck you.'

Chinese-Americans who co-operate with the police and help them with information, out of public duty or for a more materialist reason, are called *Hon Chews* – 'bananas' – by the gangs, because they are considered yellow on the outside but white on the inside. 'I got to the restaurant where a young waiter who was one of my informants was killed by a hit man from out of town only half an hour after the murder,' Ross Arai relates. 'I counted thirty-two plates with half-eaten food on the tables – but there wasn't one witness left there by the time we arrived. Did we ever catch the guy? No, he is still free although I've a pretty good idea who he is. The next day we were contacted by just one witness, who was a Caucasian lady married to a

Chinese, and she stated that they were eating in the restaurant that night and saw it happen.

'So I immediately got some pictures of people together that I felt were involved. She was able to identify an individual that did the shooting and another individual who pointed out the target to him, but it wasn't enough for our DA's office. There was only one person who could identify the suspected killer, and that wasn't enough to bring him back from another State. For that, you'd need at least two eye-witnesses: there is no way you can put him on trial if you've only got one.'

But the San Francisco police knew that they had to catch the murderers who committed the famous 'Golden Dragon Massacre' in September 1977 if they were to retain any credibility with the city's Chinese population. Three masked Oriental youngsters had burst into the Chinatown restaurant of that name in the early hours of the morning and begun blazing away with a 12-gauge shotgun, a .38 pistol and an automatic rifle in a killing mission aimed at members of the Wah Ching gang dining there. They missed all the Wah Chings but shot dead five innocent customers and left wounded eleven others.

At first, local Police Chief Charles Gain uttered the usual police complaints about non-co-operation. He blamed the investigative impasse in which his men found themselves in a 'sub-culture of fear' in the Chinese community and blasted them publicly for 'an absolute abdication of responsibility'. 'This is a tragedy we are constantly faced with,' he told the press. 'Chinese persons will not talk.'

Slating honest people who are justifiably frightened accomplishes little. Many Chinese-Americans in the city exploded at what they considered 'racial slurs'. Said one Chinese spokesman: 'We can hardly believe that the SFPD has retreated to century-old stereotypes in their public statements.' He said that such statements 'were self-serving and gave the impression that they were trying to excuse themselves from their duties as law enforcement officers.'*

* At the same time one must have some sympathy for police officers like Chief Gain who feel that they do not always get maximum co-operation from the Chinese community itself. 'We have no problem at all about youth gangs in Chinatown,' Mr Joseph Mei, vice-president of the New York Chinese Consolidated Benevolent Association, told a *New York Times* reporter – the day after the Ghost Shadows allegedly shot up five members of the rival White Eagles in front of the Yuen Yuen snack shop in Mr Mei's own Chinatown.

Chief Gain responded with a twenty-one-member 'Gang Task Force' to attack the gang problem. 'We want to eradicate gangsterism in San Francisco,' he said, adding no less than realistically: 'It may take years to do it.'

At least, they made an impressive start. After an intense investigation, working with other law enforcement agencies and informants, six suspects, all under eighteen, were arrested in March and April 1978. Two were arrested as far away as Reno, Nevada. Guns tied to the shooting were pulled from the mud of San Francisco Bay.

In December 1978, a mild-looking, bespectacled youth named Melvin Yu, still only eighteen and said by prosecuting counsel to be the principal trigger-man in the 'Massacre', was sentenced by Superior Court Judge Walter Calcagno to five consecutive life imprisonment terms for the five first-degree murders and sixteen two-third years on each of eleven counts of assault with a deadly weapon. During the trial, testimony showed that Yu fired into the backs of some of his victims as they lay wounded on the floor of the restaurant. He was 'a marauding beast', said prosecuting counsel. Defence counsel urged upon Judge Calcagno, in a plea for mercy, that Yu had arrived in the United States at the age of twelve. 'The Golden Gate opened for him,' he said with court-room eloquence, 'and now at eighteen the prison gates open to slam behind him.' Replied the Judge: 'The court cannot forget what closed on five of the victims was five coffin lids.'

A similar call – 'Find this man at all costs!' – went out in New York City in July 1977 when in the early hours of a Sunday morning a young Chinese man walked into the Kuo Wan restaurant on Chinatown's Mott Street and said respectfully to its owner, Mr Man Bun Lee: 'Uncle, may I speak to you for a moment?' – then plunged a knife three times into his body, once just under the heart, once on the side and once in the stomach.

Man Bun Lee, ex-President of the local Chinese Consolidated Benevolent Association and, as such, former 'uncrowned Mayor' of Chinatown, had earned himself many enemies among the gangs. Born in Canton, he had come to New York in the years following Chiang Kai Shek's defeat and had built up a considerable reputation as an unashamedly pro-American Chinese post-war immigrant. He had criticized parents for their lack of control of their children: 'They work eighteen hours a day to get ahead, while their kids roam the streets. We try to tell the parents, don't spend all your time earning money. Look after your families.' He had consistently urged his fellow restaurant-owners and businessmen to go to the police when they were threatened. He had spoken out publicly many times against Nicky Louie and other local gang leaders. And now someone had walked into his own restaurant and stabbed him almost to death.

'We just had to catch that guy,' Detective Neil Mauriello has told me. 'The 5th Precinct, the New York City Police Department, the whole concept of law and order would have lost "face" completely if we hadn't got him.'

They 'got him' within two months. On 10 September 1977, twenty-seven-year-old Chik Keung Pang, a hired assassin from Hong Kong, who spoke not a word of English and who, according to Mauriello, was the victim of his own crime ('he only got $2000 for it. He didn't know whom he was hitting, how important he was.'), was picked up in some woods near Blaine, Washington, by an alert-eyed border guard. Pang was making his way towards the Canadian border – having jumped his Vancouver-bound flight from Hong Kong at San Francisco airport to commit his crime, he was now heading for Vancouver by the land route, almost certainly on his way back home again.

Brought back to New York, he was charged with attempted murder and eventually, in Detective Mauriello's words, 'plea-bargained out and is now serving three years to twelve, which means he has to do a minimum of three – normally more – and upon his release from prison, he will be immediately deported to Hong Kong, where we are under the impression here that the Hong Kong police will arrest him for possible Triad activities in Hong Kong prior to coming to America.'

Why was his job bungled? Why did not Man Bun Lee, a man in his fifties, die at his hands? Says Mr Lee, while showing me the scars on his body that he will carry for the rest of his life: 'I really don't know. Sometime I think he was maybe kind of scared or maybe he didn't want to kill me really. Also I was using all my strength to defend myself. Good thing I was so fat at the time. All the fat protect me. When he hit me first time, I didn't feel anything. The second stab I felt it – then I used my head in defence. I lost so much blood, but I never lost my conscious.'

Afterwards, Mr Lee was quoted as saying that he thought the

gangs were behind the attack. What does he think now? 'I don't know why he did it. Before he made his confession, he asked Captain Hoehl [then in command of the 5th Precinct] if he could see me. There were two reasons why he wanted to see me: one, to make sure whether I could identify him, two, maybe he feels inner guilt. I identified him, then went back to my apartment and Captain Hoehl then telephoned me again and said the boy was going to make a confession but he wanted to see me before he did so. Was I willing to see him?

'I said, "Why not?" So Neil [Mauriello] came down and collected me and took me up to the DA's office. He shook hands and said, "I am sorry, Uncle M.B." I said, "I don't know you. Why do you take my life?" He said, "Don't ask me why. I had my orders to do it. I am sorry. I hope you will continue to do the job for the Chinese–Americans in this country."

'In this country, the system is if you plead guilty, they don't want to know why. The case is closed. Some people say, if they can find out why, that will involve too many people and it would be a shock to the community. Some people believe that there are a lot of people involved in this case, including the so-called "big shots" in the Chinese community or even government officials from Taiwan, who knows?'

That last paragraph is not so far-fetched as at first it might appear, for it is well known and accepted in Chinatown – both in New York and in San Francisco – that the youth gangs are not lone agents. The ageing bosses of the Tongs employ them as their young 'enforcers' – as with the Immigration Service's investigator's earlier 'CI' – to help them keep control of their empire, to guard their gambling houses, to be 'look-see' boys keeping watch at the door for police and other 'undesirables'.

I asked my Triad informant, ex-president of the Washington DC branch of the Hip Sing, 'what the relationship was between the youth gangs and the Tongs.' His answer was straightforward: 'We hire these young guys to protect our gambling places.' 'They are just a smokescreen for the guys behind them,' says Detective Charles Henry of Homicide in New York's 13th Precinct, who attended the New York September 1978 conference on the Triads and international youth gangs and who has been called to several youth gang-related homicides.

After the 'Golden Dragon Massacre' in San Francisco, local Police Chief Charles Gain said cryptically to the press: 'We have reasons to feel these kids are no more than pawns or cannon fodder. . . . It's not just a matter of juvenile delinquency. This is a complex thing that involves adults without question.' *Police Magazine,* published bi-monthly by Criminal Justice Publications, Inc., a non-profit organization, tells of a significant case in San Francisco back in 1971:

After a group of Chinese youths started extorting money from businesses in the neighbourhood of one of the city's Tongs, the Tong took out an ad in one of the Chinese newspapers. It warned that if certain young people did not cease their illegal activities, they would be 'severely dealt with'.

A few weeks after the ad appeared, three young Chinese men were found dead – hogtied and dumped in San Francisco Bay.

That case, like numerous others, has not been solved. The theory on the streets is that the crime was committed by rival gang members, at the behest of the older 'criminal element' in Chinatown. But police investigators could not prove it. Information and witnesses are not forthcoming, leads could not be confirmed, cases could not be developed.

What about narcotics? What is the youth gangs' role to date in that field? My own theory, which I have trundled around various DEA offices throughout the world, is that the youth gangs of today are the drug traffickers of tomorrow. They have a superb built-in connection for distribution – and for source of supply. The theory has been generally accepted, and indeed there is already evidence that the youth gangs are participating in the heroin trade as runners: not yet in their own right as bosses, but as instruments of their masters, the criminal elements in the Tongs.

As New York's *Village Voice* journalist and researcher, Mark Jacobson, has written in a February 1978 issue of his newspaper: 'DEA people say the gangs are used as runners to pick up dope in the Chinese community in Toronto and then body-carry it across the border.'

In the future, and as they mature, their role could well become more entrepreneurial. Says a DEA senior agent in New York: 'These kids are all from Hong Kong. They don't have the connection. They might know a guy in Hong Kong, who knows a guy in Bangkok, but it still is at inflated prices. If you want your connection, you have to go to Bangkok.

'*But they can do it!* The black guys did it. These youth gang kids can do it more readily than the black guys. All they have to do is to go there with the money – and they have the money! – but they've never done it.

'Why? I have no idea. I don't know why they don't get into the business. My only idea is that this shows control of the Tongs over the kids. They do not want the kids to deal in heroin.'

Yet South-East Asian heroin has still not yet hit the United States in a really big way. The feared input in massive quantities to take the place of the fading Mexican supply has not yet occurred. 'Exactly!' says a senior DEA man, 'They don't consider the time is yet right. White heroin is already beginning to appear on the streets of New York but only in small quantities. The powers that be are biding their time until they think the time is right and then they want to come into the market themselves in a really big way – and they don't want the kids getting under their feet!'

Meanwhile, there have been some police efforts to solve the problem in New York's Chinatown. They are not on the level of those by Canadian police, which will be examined in the next chapter, and as Detective Neil Mauriello of New York's 5th Precinct says: 'Our problems were developing in 1967/8 and I would say their problems are less than a few years old. We should have been approaching our problems in 1970 the way they are approaching theirs. We came in at a very low level only in 1974.'

In the following year, police co-operation with the community was stepped up by a three-year $175,000 Federal Law Enforcement Assistance Administration grant to hire eleven citizens, fluent in Chinese and English, to set up an office in the 5th Precinct House 'in an effort to increase trust in the police and on the part of the residents of the Chinese community . . . and to increase the willingness of such persons to co-operate with the police'.

The 'Chinatown Project', its cost now absorbed permanently into the city's budget, still functions today out of the 5th Precinct House on Elizabeth Street. Its co-ordinator is a young Chinese-American policeman who is one of the only ten or so Chinese-Americans in the whole 30,000-strong New York City police force. The idea is to have a place to which Chinese people can come, talk to a Chinese receptionist, walk straight upstairs to the project's second-floor office and complain about anything they want – *in Chinese*. The project handles about 200 cases a month, but the policeman-co-ordinator admits that less than a third of these relate to criminal matters. He is quoted in an article in *Police Magazine* in July 1978 as saying, 'Family disputes, alien registration, social security, food stamps – you name it – they come in here.'

But why were there not more criminal complaints? Why were not people coming in to complain more about criminal activities within the community? *Police Magazine* is no leftist, subversive publication but even so, Rob Wilson, the writer of the July 1978 article, commented: 'Some community residents say the staff of the "Chinatown Project" has been too close to certain factions in the Chinatown establishment to be trusted by the majority.' He quoted a young Chinatown merchant, whom he named, as saying, 'The intention is great. But it's totally the product of the Chinese Consolidated Benevolent Association, and if the CCBA is into organized crime, how can it be good?'

Detective Neil Mauriello boasted to me in December 1978, with complete sincerity: 'We've closed down many of the gambling clubs. We've hit them hard. The gangs are retrenching. The thrust of law enforcement in Chinatown is informants – that's the name of the game – and we've never had such good information coming our way as now. The fact that we put inside the guy who attacked M.B.Lee. All this is working for us, and working well!

'I am a firm believer that we are going to solve the problems of the Chinese society in America. We are not going to live in a Triad Society, we are not going to let the Chinese people live in a Triad Society. We are going to get them to tell us everything that's going on in Chinatown. Chinese organized crime will not be like the Italian Mafia has become over the last seventy-five years. It will not. We will not permit it!'

Such enthusiasm and such dedication have to be admired. But how many Neil Mauriellos are there around? I saw him for the last time on a visit to New York in November 1979 and, alas, by then he was losing some of his passionate confidence. He told me that by systematically raiding all the known gambling clubs on the Precinct, he and his colleagues had managed to close down virtually *all* organized gambling in Chinatown between January and July of that year – 'but now it's starting up again'. By the time we were chatting in November in the detectives' room on the first floor of the 5th Precinct House, five clubs were functioning again – three along Mott Street, one on Baxter Street and one on Pell Street – all with their familiar 'look-see' boys hanging about outside in their near-uniform of fatigue jacket and blue jeans.

Nor was that all. 'We had a double murder down here last week,' said Mauriello. 'It was more like an execution. Two Chinese kids were picked up in a theatre, taken to a factory building down on East Broadway, made to kneel down and then shot in the back of their heads.' Cause of the assassination: a 'territorial dispute' between rival youth gangs, just as in 'the bad old days' of the mid-seventies.

In May 1980, while this book was at the printers and I was myself again in New York, a member of a youth gang was killed by a Chinese merchant in a shoot-out after a Chinatown shake-down attempt. The following letter appeared in the New York Post:

I am writing about the recent Chinatown shooting incident. It's long overdue that a Chinatown homicide incident was publicized. Being a resident of New York's Chinatown for all my sixteen years, I live in constant fear whenever these youth gangs come across me.

They extort from restaurants, rob clothing factories and residents of Chinatown, and are involved with narcotics and weapons. Residents do not want the incidents covered. The main reason for this is because everybody is afraid.

Chinatown incidents must be announced, even if it means sacrifices in the tourist trade. If enough attention is brought to bear, then maybe Chinatown will have peace again.

Please withhold my name.

So much for the American scene. How does Canada fit into the jigsaw? What is the role of Vancouver, the seaport city, to which Man Bun Lee's hit man was fleeing? What is the significance of Toronto, from where the New York youth gangs are said to be body-running heroin? There must be a reason why Canadian police officers attended the New York conference in September 1978, and indeed there had been an earlier one held in Toronto itself the year before. So what is the Canadian contribution to the over-all Triad scene?

15 Triads in Canada

The story of Triad activities in Canada is in many ways a carbon copy of what has happened in the United States, with Vancouver substituted for San Francisco and Toronto for New York – a tale of heroin and of youth gangs. The story even begins in the same historical fashion, with racial prejudice and discrimination against the early hard-working, honest Chinese immigrant community.

Mr Peter Stollery, a Toronto Federal MP and a distinguished journalist, in an outspoken article in *Toronto Life* in December 1976 writes bluntly:

> Canadians did not like Chinese. For fifty years, groups, many from British Columbia, protested the government's policies of allowing Chinese into Canada. Various methods were tried to restrain Chinese immigration. A head tax of $50 was introduced in 1885, raised, then raised again to $500 for every Chinese coming into Canada by 1903. Restrictions were placed on the number of Chinese per tonnage of any vessel entering a Canadian port. Still, the Chinese found ways of paying the tax and coming anyway. So in 1923, the government passed the Chinese Immigration Act and stopped Chinese coming into Canada altogether. I have read that fewer than twelve Chinese made it into this country between 1924 and 1939.

Mr Stollery quotes a now solidly established Toronto restaurant owner as saying: 'Things got better very slowly. In 1953, when I came, you couldn't be more than twenty-one-years old. My father was here and he brought me. I came from China and had to spend a year in Hong Kong because of paperwork at Immigration. My birthday is 10 January . Finally I had to fly over to beat the deadline and it cost me $1100. Imagine

$1100 to take a job for $20 a week, seven days, twelve hours a day at a downtown cafe.'

Such Chinese as did get in concentrated in two main Chinatowns: one in Vancouver, the largest seaport on the entire North American Pacific coast, and the other in Toronto, the country's largest English-speaking city (French-speaking Montreal is the only Canadian city with a population, as at the 1976 census, of more than a million). As with the United States, the immigrants came mainly from the two gateway provinces of Kwangtung and Fukien in southern China, and they came either directly across the Pacific into Vancouver or upwards from the United States itself where they had first settled. It is in fact even possible to pinpoint the first Chinese immigrant in Toronto as a man called Mark Moon who came up from New York before 1885 and opened a grocery store on York Street, in the centre of what is now Toronto's old Chinatown.

Despite prejudice and difficulties, those original settlers lived, if anything, a more lawful existence than most other ethnic groups. They constituted no problem at all to the forces of law and order. There *was* a Triad Society in their midst, but it was of the old Sun Yat Sen style, with generally a Canadian-born 489 in command. Perhaps it was tinged with illegality on the fringes (unlawful gambling houses, prostitution, opium dens – which were in any event legal in Canada until comparatively late into the twentieth century) but fundamentally it was (and is) an honourable organization, providing a link with 'home' back in China and playing a strongly protective role in the diaspora. 'If you had been here a week before, I could have taken you as my guest to a party to celebrate 120 years of the Society here in Canada,' my Canadian-based Triad informant told me.*

'The Chinese people that were here, that had come and raised families, were traditionally law-abiding people,' says Inspector Lew Dempsey of the Vancouver Integrated Intelligence Unit of the Royal Canadian Mounted Police. 'Going back to the fifties,

---

*In Toronto, Sergeant Bill Holdright of the Metropolitan Toronto Police says: 'It's not against the law to be a Triad in Canada. Therefore, there are businessmen who openly admit that they are Triads. Now, I don't have anything to suggest to me that, just because you are a Triad, that makes you a criminal but what I do believe is that members of Triad Societies are criminals, and there are a lot of people around the world that would suggest this. That's what we have in Toronto: we have Triads who openly admit that they are Triads but nobody will talk about the *other* Triads! They'll deny being involved in crime but they'll even talk about what rank they are.'

I can only recall one Chinese criminal in the area around Vancouver. It was unusual to find a Chinese criminal, even a Chinese heroin addict. Even in the sixties, there was only a handful of Chinese people that we knew were addicts.'

It was the same story in Toronto. 'The Elizabeth Street Chinatown of 1949 was a place of small cafes and sad old men waiting for women who would never arrive because of the racist immigration policies of the period,' writes Peter Stollery. 'The entire Chinese community consisted of no more than 6000 struggling souls making a scarce living from such service businesses as restaurants and laundries.' Says Sergeant Bill Holdright of the Metropolitan Toronto Police, seconded to the Chinese Intelligence Unit of a Joint Forces Operation with the RCMP: 'Outwardly it was a very quiet community. Everything was settled within that community. There had to be some kind of unofficial mayor or community leader who knew English and could speak for them. But they were decent people and caused no problem to anyone – and that continued right up to the seventies.'

But before then there had been a new wave of Chinese immigration. It came in greater volume than ever before and almost exclusively from one source alone: Hong Kong, then bursting at the seams with refugees from post-1949 Communist rule on the Chinese mainland. At first it was only a trickle: Canadian immigration laws, still blatantly racist in philosophy, permitted no more. But then in 1967 Canada followed the example of the United States two years earlier and re-wrote its immigration laws, virtually throwing open the floodgates to immigration from the Far East. Writes Peter Stollery:

The new wave that created the modern Chinatown in Toronto happened between 1967 and 1972 when 91,000 Chinese immigrated to Canada. During these halcyon days, almost anyone in the world who could get to Canada could stay, provided they could pass security and health standards. Between 1967 and 1972, in addition to regular immigration where people applied in their country of origin, about 150,000 people arrived in Canada on their own and said that this was the land of milk and honey and they wanted to stay. The media became alarmed and made this free immigration policy an election issue in 1972. After the election, when the Liberal Government was almost defeated, the right to apply in Canada for landed immigrant status was suspended.

In other words, the would-be immigrant could no longer apply at the seaport or airport of entry and almost literally knock at the door and ask to be let in. 'So ended the most enlightened period in Canadian immigration history,' comments Mr Stollery sadly. And it *had* been an enlightened period. That was the 'good side' of the whole operation. As Mr Stollery records:

With no small amount of wonder, I've watched our modern Chinatown in Toronto stretch out geographically and an incredibly vital community that some people estimate is now 60,000 strong. The Chinese community is no longer defined by its service businesses. New blood and new money from Hong Kong combined with local success stories have created a supply of Chinese-Canadian lawyers, architects, dentists, doctors, developers, computer experts, electricians, plumbers and stylish livers of the good life. There are those who suggest, and not altogether unreasonably, that within ten years Toronto's Chinatown will be the largest in North America. It's probably the largest by area already.*

The 'bad side' of Canada's recent Chinese population explosion is that the old days of Chinatowns as quiet, harmless enclaves, with colourful restaurants patronized by contented diners and shops sparkling with silk, jade and porcelain, have gone for ever. Youth gangs blazing away with guns and armed with choppers have burst onto the scene in Toronto; Vancouver has become not only the organizing headquarters of a massive illegal immigration network for both Canada and the United States but also a major entry point and distribution centre for South-East Asian heroin for British Columbia itself and for onward transmission to the rest of Canada and the United States; a new criminal post-1949 type of Triad Society called the Kung Lok, affiliated to the 14K in Hong Kong, has opened up its headquarters in Toronto alongside the respectable 120-year-old Triad Society already existing there; the same Hong Kong immigrant (and, like the police, I know his name) who started out the Kung Lok with a flag from 14K central headquarters

*Peter Stollery was writing in 1976. Sergeant Holdright and his Metropolitan Toronto Police colleague and friend in the Joint Forces Operation Intelligence Unit, ex-Hong Kong policeman Constable Michael King, estimate that today Toronto's Chinese population – legal and illegal – is running at 'probably over 100,000, probably by now greater than Vancouver's which has always traditionally been considered the largest in Canada.' (Michael King in fact resigned from the Metropolitan police in November 1979 to go into private business but, for the sake of convenience I shall continue to refer to him as 'Constable'.)

has set up a major heroin trafficking organization out of Toronto which, although Toronto itself almost miraculously has precious little addict problem, has already been the source of 'Chinese heroin' appearing on the streets of Boston and New York.* And all this in the space of less than a decade!

'The Chinese community itself here in Toronto tells us that ninety-nine per cent of the problem comes from the new immigrants, legal and illegal, from Hong Kong,' says Sergeant Bill Holdright. 'But I don't want you to put in your book that everyone that comes from Hong Kong is a problem. That isn't so. It's one per cent, we figure – less than one per cent.'

But what a one per cent! Even the notorious 'Five Dragons' came – with their vast wealth – to Canada, where they clearly saw both a 'safe haven' and a profitable sphere of business. Admittedly, they fled to Taiwan in a considerable hurry when they got wind of a ninety-minute CBS television documentary exposure, called 'Connections', that hit the nation's networks in July 1977; this brilliant exposure of their activities caused embarrassing questions to be asked in Canada's parliament as to how they got into the country in the first place, when already the Independent Commission Against Corruption in Hong Kong was on their trail.

Such are the limitations, and the *necessary* limitations, under which law enforcement agencies have to operate in a free society. The Canadian police had in fact arrested one of the 'Five Dragons', ex-detective Sergeant Hon Kwing Shum, and were holding him in custody pending extradition to Hong Kong when he challenged the legal validity of the extradition order in the Federal Court of Canada. The Court upheld his plea, he was released – and in the interregnum while the Canadian government waited to get its hearing before the Appeal Court, he slipped out of the country to Taiwan! I have seen for myself a beautiful apartment block in central Toronto owned by a company in which the main shareholder, either directly or

---

*He is referred to by pseudonym in *Sun Jee* ('New News'), a Chinese language newspaper in Hong Kong that Michael King, who speaks fluent Cantonese, has been kind enough to translate for me. I know also from another informant that he has recently opened up a gambling casino in, of all places, the Dominican Republic in the Caribbean. But, powerful though he is, he is not the only important Chinese heroin trafficker now operating out of Toronto. 'Those guys have got stuff pouring into Toronto that makes Lui Lok look like a beginner,' a DEA special agent told me in San Francisco in the autumn of 1979. 'There's so much money involved it's unbelievable.'

through nominees, is fellow ex-Hong Kong police sergeant Lui Lok, 'the six-hundred-million-dollar-man'.

'The families of some of the "Dragons" are still here,' says ex-Hong Kong policeman Michael King, 'and the income from their investments gets shipped out regularly to them in Taiwan. But how can you stop it? No offence has ever been proved against them in Canada.'

In its Third Report on Organized Crime in British Columbia, published in April 1979, the Province's Co-ordinated Law Enforcement Unit (CLEU) said grimly:

Organized criminals have also emerged from the Chinese population in British Columbia. Chinese groups are engaged in the importation and trafficking of heroin, in the fencing of stolen property, in prostitution, loansharking, bookmaking and gambling; all of which activities are often carried out behind the facade of legitimate business.

By the very nature of Chinese cultural ties, criminal activity is made to extend beyond the boundaries of British Columbia to the Chinese community at large. It is almost a commonplace that the heroin trade connects the Chinese to South-East Asia, North America and Europe, but other criminal activities have a similar international character, for there is a constant flow of visitors and immigrants between Asia, in particular Hong Kong, Vancouver, San Francisco and other major cities in North America. Such mobility and links across international boundaries make it difficult for the law enforcement authorities in British Columbia to control illegal activity, for suspects are elusive and temporary visitors only serve to confuse the situation.

In January 1980, the *Vancouver Sun* newspaper quoted Doug Ewing, the RCMP officer then attached to the Canadian Embassy in Bangkok as anti-narcotics liaison officer, as saying that more than ninety per cent of the heroin ending up on the streets of Canadian cities originated in the Golden Triangle.

Says Constable King: 'As long as you are born in Hong Kong and hold a British Commonwealth passport, you don't need a visa to come into Canada. You arrive at the airport, produce your return ticket, say you are visiting your aunt and want to be here for three weeks, the man stamps your passport – and that's it. You're in, and of course then you can just go to ground if you want to.' Many quite wealthy youngsters come from Hong Kong to study at high school or university in Canada: that means they will want official permission to stay longer than just a few weeks or months as a visitor. So they will need a visa – but 'even so there is no problem. We've picked up youngsters who've worked their way through to Toronto months after their student's visa has expired.'

In immigration terms, Vancouver is the soft under-belly of the United States. Huge tracts of the border are just open country, unfenced and unmanned, and at the airports, Customs and immigration formalities are at an absolute minimum. It was no coincidence that Chik Keung Pang, Man Bun Lee's assailant from Hong Kong, was picked up in the woods around Blaine in the State of Washington making for Vancouver.

The heroin problem in Vancouver and in British Columbia generally is one of gargantuan proportions. Speaking in March 1979 to the local Rotary Club in Victoria, the capital of British Columbia, Mr Malcolm Matheson, chairman of the Federal-Provincial Drug Strategies Committee, said: 'The heroin rate in the Province is more than five times the national average. The illicit trade ranks as the Province's fifth-largest industry, with an annual take of about $255 million. The risks are minimal and the profits enormous.'

He told his listeners exactly the same as senior police officers told me: 'The police estimate that more than sixty per cent of all crimes against property are committed by addicts. The extent of the problem shows up in other respects too. Between 1966 and 1978, there were seventy drug-related homicides in British Columbia.'

'It wasn't until the late sixties when all of a sudden we started having Chinese drug organizations here,' Inspector Lew Dempsey says, 'in other words, local Chinese people who had the contacts in Hong Kong to put their own heroin on the streets. This coincided with a time when, because of successful law enforcement, a number of the major Caucasian organizations had been prosecuted, taking them out of the picture and leaving the market-place open, so to speak. There was a void which, although not exclusively, was certainly substantially taken up by ethnic Chinese organizations with connections in Hong Kong.'

Inspector Dempsey and his colleagues would claim that they are coping adequately with their problem. 'The Greater Vancouver area takes about 1lb of heroin a day to sustain its addict population,' he says. 'That means it needs a total of 365lb a year just for itself – forgetting onward transmission to anywhere else. Now that's an awful lot of heroin. But we've had some good cases. Some of the top people have been knocked off. Good enforcement and other things have brought the quality of the heroin down from my days on the street, when you could get it at forty-five and fifty per cent purity, to now, when it's three to five per cent purity – *and* the price has gone up! Low purity and high price are always a good indication of the effectiveness of your law enforcement endeavour.'

Yet he admits: 'We've still got a problem. We're knocking off the top people as we go along but the heroin problem remains because you've still got the addict that is prepared to pay any price – and, if necessary, he'll commit serious crime to get the money to do so. We reckon that an addict today requires probably $1000 a day to support his habit.'

What about youth gangs? I was assured that in Vancouver they do not provide a problem. As one police corporal said to me: 'I don't know why but the Chinese gangs that we have in this city are much quieter than anywhere else that I know of. There's very little violence.' And when I checked this for myself with a friend in Vancouver's Chinatown, centred on Pender Street, that also seemed to be the general view in non-police circles.

But in Toronto the situation has been entirely different. 'Is Chinatown Becoming Crimetown?' was the heading of an article in a leading Toronto magazine in the autumn of 1977. 'Teen-aged thugs prey on Chinatown', 'Chinese gang run on fear, court told', 'Increase in Crime worried Chinatown', 'Chinatown fears rising crime' are some of the headlines in newspaper cuttings that Sergeant Holdright and Constable King have given me as background material for my researches. Giving evidence in a case of historical importance in February 1978, Sergeant Kenneth Cosgrove, a veteran of eighteen years in and around Chinatown for the Metro Toronto police, told the court on oath that gangs such as the local Kung Lok (the same name, it will be noticed, as Toronto's newly-established 14K Triad Society branch) are an extension of the Triads in Hong Kong. He said that Triad cells such as Kung Lok with its 150 to 250 members in Toronto had moved into the city 'in the last few years' working on much the same basis as the Triad gangs back home in Hong Kong.

'In the last year,' said Sergeant Cosgrove, 'about eighty per cent of the 125 crimes I have investigated in Chinatown have been the responsibility of the gangs, using no weapon except the psychology of fear. Many people in Toronto's Chinatown are recent immigrants and this great fear of gangs is instilled in them at birth because of the gangs in Hong Kong. Every once in a while their memories are refreshed by incidents in Toronto such as robberies or extortions.'

In the case in which Sergeant Cosgrove was giving evidence – the first ever to be brought in a Canadian court based upon the Chinese youth gangs' strong-arm extortion tactics – Chung Fai (Ronnie) Ma, a twenty-two-year-old Hong Kong immigrant, was charged, with others not in custody, with obstruction of justice. Some young Chinese men had burst into the apartment in St Catherine's, a district near Toronto, of a twenty-year-old Hong Kong-born high school student and his seventeen-year-old high school girl-friend, also from Hong Kong, and demanded the sum of $1008. Another twenty-two-year-old Hong Kong immigrant called Ah (Edward) Law, whose trial was due to follow in the next week, had punched the youth in the face, blacked his eye and made his nose bleed.

The student was told they would break his leg if he did not give them the money. One of the attackers, not charged in court, held a gun to the terrified couple while Law deliberately, and with Kung Fu skill, beat up his victim. Perhaps not surprisingly, he agreed to pay up and the money was duly handed over in two lots: one for $708 and the other for $300.

Why that strange amount? Why a total of $1008 and not a straight $1000? Sergeant Cosgrove told his enthralled listeners in court that 'it wasn't so strange in the light of the gang's superstitious belief in the powers of certain numbers, particularly the number 3. 1008 is not only reminiscent of the 108 original Triad monks, but is also divisible by three, the number which represents the three facets of the Triad – heaven, earth and man.'

How did 'Ronnie' Ma, the man accused in *this* case, come into it? When the news arrived in the Chinese community that the two young victims had actually told their story to the police and that a call had gone out to bring in their attackers, the gang had sent 'a delegation' (that is how Constable Michael King has described them to me), which included 'Ronnie' Ma, to see them. The couple had been terrorized into coming down to central Toronto, where they had sworn an affidavit saying that the money had been handed over voluntarily and that the story they had originally told the police was not true. Hence, the charge against Ma – the only man the police were able to trace – of 'obstructing the course of justice'.

But that was not the only significance of the case against Ma. For Sergeant Cosgrove also told the court how, on his arrest, the police had found in his briefcase Triad verses, written in Cantonese on Hong Kong hotel stationery. 'These verses, along with hand signals, are the identification they use so one member will know the other,' said Cosgrove. And he also gave the court in sworn testimony a highly detailed account of the traditional-type Triad initiation ceremonies, chicken blood and all, that were taking place among some of the gangs in Toronto at that time.

Both Ma and Law were convicted and received two years less a day and one year in jail respectively for their offences. Afterwards, Sergeant Cosgrove told a local reporter that members of the Chinese community who had been reluctant to talk about the Kung Lok terror tactics in the past were now coming forth and co-operating with the police. Asked why there had been a change, he said: 'I would think it would be because of the credibility established by the court system and police department that has aided in changing the attitude of the Chinese community.'

In fact, the Ma and Law trials were the first overt manifestation of a remarkable campaign of co-operation between the local police and the city's Chinatown population that had been then in existence for well over a year and provides still today a model for good policing in whatever part of the Western world a Chinese community may find itself.

No one is claimimg that the youth gangs in Toronto are conclusively beaten, that total peace now prevails in the city's Chinatown, but, at least, the reality of existence for the Chinese community in Toronto today is that their lot is no worse than anyone else's. Crime in Chinatown has been contained.

'In the mid-seventies,' says Constable Michael King, 'the RCMP heard these rumours of problems within the Chinese community, but nobody was complaining to the police, of course. So what the Metro Toronto police decided to do was send a couple of Chinese-Canadian policemen into the community – undercover – to see if there were legitimate problems that the Chinese community was facing and which we didn't know about. We wanted to find out if it was true. They *did* find out it was true. There *were* problems.

'They came back and told Inspector Lennox, he was head of Intelligence at the time, that something had gone wrong in the community. They wanted some more men to look into it. So this Joint Forces intelligence unit was formed, at first just with two sergeants and two constables, and I was lucky enough to be seconded to it.

'At that time, it was merely to see what the problems were. Was it smoke without fire or smoke with fire or what?'

This was from the police side – stretching out towards the community. Coincidentally, there came a call for help from the community itself – and this is what sets aside the Chinese community in Toronto from so many other ethnic Chinese groups in other cities. On a Sunday afternoon in January 1977, at the Chinese Community Centre on Hagerman Street, worried businessmen and community leaders called a meeting, attended by members of the Metro Toronto police, in which for the first time they talked openly about the armed robberies and threats to which they were being subjected by gangs of young men from within their own community. The principal of the Chinese public school, who had fled New York's youth gang violence four years earlier, warned, with reporters from the local press taking down his words: 'Toronto will be worse than New York if this keeps up.'

King and Holdright take up the story (and I am not differentiating between who said what): 'A number of the older people were willing to talk – to a degree. They weren't frank. They told us what they wanted us to know – same old problem, because they were talking to perfect strangers. They weren't accustomed to talking frankly about such matters before – why should they start now?

'We had to change their opinion of what the police were really like and we had to assure them that, whatever the problems they may have had in the past with the police, they weren't going to face these problems now. So our guys had to go out there and convince these people that we were serious and that when we said something, we meant to follow it through. If these people did not want to pursue these matters in the courts, we had to let them know that at this point we were more interested in the information about what was happening than pursuing the matter in the courts. So we wouldn't push them: whatever they said they wanted, we let it go at that.

'In a short period of time, it appeared that we were gaining the confidence of some of these people. They continued to help us by letting us know what was happening.

'Then it got to the point where arrests started being made. We were involved in the St Catherine's extortion case of the two high school students. We found out about it and we pursued the matter. We got in touch with the appropriate police, whom we assisted in their work, and we protected our witnesses. They came through with giving sworn testimony in court as to exactly what had happened to them.

'When these two young hoodlums were sent to prison for what they had done in St Catherine's, people in the community could see that here some people had come forward, complaining, telling what had happened to them – and that the law had done something about it. They could see that this criminal element is not untouchable, they're not so beyond reach as they thought they were. They were not! We started to pick them off one by one.

'A lot of things fell into our hands. The first arrest the unit made was an illegal immigrant: a gang member. He was from Hong Kong, had landed in Vancouver and got through to here: came as a visitor and then disappeared. He was here illegally for well over a year. Then we found him causing trouble in Chinatown. There was a chase, he was picked up, arrested, he admitted he was "an illegal" – and that was it!

'Word got out that we had picked up "an illegal" last night – and you'll be amazed how fast that kind of news can travel – and when within a week we had put him on a plane back to Hong Kong, that also got around pretty fast. They could see that we really meant business. But what they didn't know was that before he had gone back he had talked to us quite a lot: for the first time, we had a guy actually in the gangs telling us all that was going on – or, at least, all that was going on in the *other* gangs, not in his own!

'Anyway, that's how a whole series of deportations back to Hong Kong started. They went one after the other. Often the Immigration Service will issue warrants for people who are "out of status": in other words, no longer attending school as they should be, or out-stayed their visitor's time or whatever. They will issue a warrant for his arrest for him to be held for an immigration inquiry. A kind of court is then held and he can be deported back home by the Immigration Service itself – without going through the normal criminal courts and getting a judge's recommendation to deport him.

'We started to hang around the illegal Chinese gambling casinos in Chinatown and we talked with the kids that were hanging around the street corners. Through this we managed to gather a lot of intelligence information on criminal activities in our city and the gangs; and the people started to talk to us. We gained the credibility of the public. They were watching us: they saw we were serious, they saw us taking these kids off the streets and sending them back to Hong Kong.

'And this was done with universal approval. No one said that this was cruel. They thought this was good. We were actually physically shipping the trouble-makers back to where they came from.'

But even the success story in Toronto has almost inevitable limitations which show the dire problems faced by law enforcement officers trying to fight the Chinese secret criminal societies. One may lop off a tentacle of the octopus in one place only to find a new tentacle growing in another.

Sergeant Holdright knows who is the leader of the Toronto Ghost Shadows: indeed, he knows him personally quite well. I cannot name him because he has no criminal record and is, to the outward eye, a perfectly lawful immigrant from Hong Kong in his twenties. 'He's a gent and a professional,' says Holdright with a certain grudging admiration. 'It's always a pleasure to do business with a professional. I hate dealing with slobs. He doesn't make trouble any more in the community here. He keeps a tight rein on his boys. He doesn't make trouble in his own patch.' Explains Michael King: 'Bill has told him several times, "No messing on my patch". "Of course, of course," he says. So what do he and his boys do? They go out from here, use it as a base for their activities in the United States but at home they keep their nose clean.'

The notion of a 'safe haven', where you restrict your illegal activities to a minimum but keep it primarily as a base from which you go out on marauding expeditions or other criminal activity into other areas or jurisdictions is a time-honoured method of Triad operation. There is an old Chinese proverb, 'You don't eat the grass surrounding your rabbit hole.' Currently, for instance, Macao is a 'safe haven' for many of the lesser Triad criminals operating in Hong Kong – just as Taiwan is for the really important men. In just the same way, Ghost Shadows out of Toronto speed across the border into the United States and carry out virtual guerilla raids into the lushly profitable areas of the Chinese communities in Boston and Chicago, and even further afield into Illinois.

They are not only involved in the 'normal' activity of robbery and extortion in the United States, but they also form part of the drug-running teams now bringing 'Chinese heroin' in increasing quantities into the East Coast of the United States. 'The old routes are opening up again,' says a US Immigration Service investigator in New York. 'The stuff is coming out of Thailand, down through Malaysia and over to Amsterdam. The Amsterdam people sell it to Toronto, some of it by way of Montreal. From Montreal it goes through to Toronto and then it all comes down to the East Coast. Toronto makes a connection in Boston, where there is a sizeable Chinese community, and they smuggle it down. Boston may bring it to New York or they may distribute it out of Boston, that's what I don't know.'

'Two or three years ago in New York,' says James Judge, DEA public affairs spokesman in the city, 'eighty to ninety per cent of the heroin on the streets was "Mexican Brown". Right now, there is much more white in New York than brown. It's already taking up the gap in the supply caused by the success of the Mexican eradication programme and it's coming from South-East Asia by way of Europe.'

When I recounted this last remark to my Triad informant in Canada, he laughed outright. 'Asian heroin out of the Golden Triangle never stopped coming into the United States,' he said. 'What they did was, for a time, they shipped it into Mexico where they treated it by chemical process to make it look and "taste" like "Mexican Brown" – and then they brought it up into the States. It never stopped coming in.'

When I jibbed at this, he retorted that Mexico City has a large Chinese community, the largest in Central America: there are criminal elements there. 'There is no trouble about this,' he said. 'All the police and enforcement people only think about their own country. Only the DEA even begin to think properly, on a world-wide basis, and they have got troubles with their budget and have to explain all what they spend to Congress.

'This is a war that will last many years, maybe our lifetime, maybe over that. Heroin from South-East Asia never stopped coming into the United States. They ship it and they sell it, corner it sometimes. That story that you told me about the English policeman [he meant Ken Beever of the London drug squad] about the cache put away safely in England: he's right! It's there. That's the way these people operate.

'There is so much money it's unbelievable. When a criminal takes out money, he takes out only $100 bills. He can travel first-class, he can jump on a plane and go to Paris – wherever he likes. In the last three months, some guys from Europe have already been here several times and each time they came by Concorde!

'Law enforcement agencies can't afford it. They haven't got the money. Another thing is that the criminal can afford to wait. Once I make a kill of a quarter of a million dollars some place, do I need to worry? Of course, I don't. I sit back and smoke a cigar, wait a while and then make another big kill. One guy alone I know can bring out of the Golden Triangle eight tons of raw opium, whenever he wants. There is a fortune in this!

'Take Singapore. I was there not all that long ago. It is supposed to be a clean city now. For two years no one is supposed to have seen one ounce of heroin. Well, I said to the DEA there: "You want me to deliver two pounds of heroin to you right now tonight before eight o'clock? No problem. I'll deliver it to you at the Embassy!" Toronto, it's the same. OK the youth gangs are quiet now – more or less. But on the drugs side the Canadians just can't cope with the drug problem in Toronto: it's impossible, they're not geared to it. The Canadian authorities are not geared to an international conspiracy. The DEA can do it. Only the DEA in the world can stop the traffic – but they haven't the resources.'

Is this frighteningly pessimistic assessment of the world's South-East Asian heroin problem right?

Conclusion: A Losing Battle?

My considered judgement, worked out after two years of active research, is that there are two basic kinds of criminal Triad activity in operation throughout the world. Both stem from the teeming cities of the Far East, the forcing ground of Triad membership. Both operate on the basis of an ethnic Chinese international criminal network which gives criminals, through their shared Triad membership, availability to an 'underground' of criminal activity. The first is more loosely organized – the street gangs of Hong Kong or the youth gangs of the United States – and its members may not call themselves Triads even though their secret societies follow Triad traditions, structure and methods. The second, much more fearsome, is something more than just a network of old Triad 'university' friends. It is, I am firmly convinced, an organized international conspiracy with a strict hierarchy, operating from a central base in the Far East, with a Mafia-type control over its members, and an almost limitless capacity for criminal evil stretching across the world.

The Chinese criminal elements in communities throughout the world are as mobile as quicksilver. Any effective action against them by law enforcement agencies must be global. National efforts, even where these are efficiently made, are not enough. Because of limited resources, even the DEA, which does think globally and which is consistently impressive in its awareness of the international narcotics situation, has been forced to cut back. The DEA's specialization in this field is unique and has resulted in a rare sense of involvement and dedication. As a DEA special agent in Wiesbaden, West Germany, stated: 'We very honestly feel that we are involved in an international problem. It is very much our preference that DEA should be left very much in the background. Those who should know what we do, *do* know what we do and do know the importance of what we have been able to accomplish in Western Europe as well as in the Far East. Our primary purpose here is institutionalization: we need to build institutions that are effective and that are targeted against the international trafficking in narcotics. That's what we need, we don't want to blow our own horn.

'We will make cases, we will disrupt international heroin organizations a heck of a lot more effectively if we have the assistance of all our foreign colleagues and if we have their interest in the problem and their prioratizing the problem at as high a level as we do: that is the basic point from a recognition perspective. You've got to remember that drug trafficking is a secret business carried out in secret and by secret societies, so far as the Triads are involved, and they're probably more effective than their competitors because, let's face it, they've got a history going back hundreds of years. Yes, OK, I'll accept your expression: they are a different dimension in crime.'

In December 1979, Mr Peter Choi, senior narcotics information officer in Hong Kong, admitted to the press that with millions of passengers and packages coming through Kai Tak airport yearly, it was virtually impossible to know whether more drugs confiscated indicated greater enforcement success – *or a larger flow*. Traffickers do not issue annual progress reports.

Of course, there are individual success stories of police activity throughout the world. Not every major trafficker in Hong Kong, for instance, has managed to keep clear of the local police or, once caught, managed to escape to Taiwan. In May 1975, after a trial in which there were twenty prosecution witnesses and twenty-two police officers were commended for their work, Ng Sik Ho, a notorious *Chiu Chao* syndicate head, was convicted of narcotics offences spanning some eight years and sentenced to thirty years in jail. That was also the sentence imposed in February 1977 upon two fellow *Chiu Chaos*, Chu Kwan Kong and his wife Cheng Yuk Oi, believed to have sold more than 500 kilos of drugs valued at about HK$78 million (nearly £8 million) over a five-year span.

But those are the only prison sentences of such length imposed for narcotics offences in the colony and, in the 'Hong Kong

Narcotics Report 1977', the official Action Committee Against Narcotics repeated its standard warning from previous reports: 'Despite all the successes of recent years, the struggle against drug traffickers will, in all likelihood, continue to be an uphill battle. Given the immense profits involved in the drug trade, there will always be criminals who are eager to fill the places left behind by those who have been arrested or have fled Hong Kong.'

Sterling co-operation between Hong Kong and Bangkok authorities led to the arrest in March 1977 at Bangkok airport of Rita Nightingale, a twenty-four-year-old British girl from Hong Kong. She was arrested going through Customs on her way to board a plane for Paris after three days spent in the Thai capital with 7.7 lb of heroin in her suitcase. The case attracted a great deal of anti-Thai publicity in the British newspapers at the time. Miss Nightingale was presented, like her famous namesake, as a nurse and the Thai judicial system was held up to attack as biased, unfair and weighted against the British girl from the start.

In fact, as Peter Law, British and Hong Kong narcotics attaché in Bangkok at the time, who had many meetings with the arrested girl, has pointed out to me with some vehemence, Rita Nightingale was not a nurse but a hostess in a Japanese-owned nightclub in Hong Kong, and the judge was British trained with a British wife.

Rita, who has always protested her innocence, claimed that the drug must have been planted in her suitcase by her Chinese boy-friend and another Chinese man with whom she had flown from Hong Kong for her brief 'holiday' in Bangkok before flying to Paris on her way home, and the local police duly arrested those two men, but they were released with no charges being made because, says Peter Law, 'there simply wasn't any evidence against them'. These two men were 'suspected drug traffickers' and it was because Rita had been seen at Hong Kong's Kai Tak airport on her way out of the colony in association with these two men that the Hong Kong Preventive Service (as the local Customs were then called) tipped off their Thai colleagues. She was not stopped coming into Thailand because at that stage she would have had no heroin with her. But she *was* stopped going out, because, as Police Major-General Pow Sarasin has told me: 'The couriers do not start in Bangkok.

They always come in from outside, pick up their stuff here – and then go out with it.'

In August 1978, nine months after Rita's conviction and when the British outcry had died down, Ian Ward, the London *Daily Telegraph*'s highly experienced correspondent in the Far East, sent home a despatch in which, for the first time, he made public the full story of the earlier tip-off by the Hong Kong Preventive Service. He also recounted how, in April 1978, over a year after Rita's arrest, Chan Min Fai, one of her two Chinese travelling companions and an ex-croupier from, of all places, an Amsterdam gambling club, was jailed in Hong Kong for five years for *other* trafficking offences. His report continued: 'But I have been unable to establish whether or not Chan and Miss Nightingale were seen together or separately at the airport. If together, it would tend to question the validity of her story that she had never seen him in her life before the moment of arrest. If separately, it would add weight to her insistence that he was unknown to her.'

But, as Peter Law told me in Hong Kong: 'She denied flatly that she knew either of these two people *but she had been seen talking to them at Kai Tak airport.*' Incidentally, he also said of the ex-croupier, Chan Min Fai: 'He has Triad associations – in fact, *close* Triad associations.' (In fact, Rita Nightingale served only just over two years of her twenty-year sentence. In January 1980 she was freed from jail and returned to England after an 'act of clemency' by the Thai king.)

Another exemplary piece of international co-operation involving the British Customs, the DEA, the Thai and the Danish authorities led to the smashing in the late spring of 1978 of one of the most important American black gangs dealing in South-East Asian No.4 heroin with a Chinese source of supply in Bangkok. The twenty-strong Pretorius Gang, working out of Harlem and the Bronx in New York City, is cautiously estimated by the DEA to have netted at least a $10 million profit in its two-year span.

'I'd been monitoring the activities of the gang over here,' a DEA special agent has told me in Bangkok, 'because, as a source country, we monitor all cases of trafficking out of here that we know about, even if we haven't got enough positive evidence to put anyone inside. There was some information on this group but there was no substantive evidence on them and the hit at

Heathrow was the kick-off point.' That 'hit at Heathrow' was due to good old-fashioned Customs expertise on the part of an alert-eyed British Customs official named Peter Lawley. On Thursday, 16 March 1978, he noticed an attractive black girl coming through the green 'nothing to declare' channel at Heathrow's No. 3 intercontinental terminal.

There was no apparent way of knowing that she was just off a plane from Bangkok but Mr Lawley noticed a Bangkok label on her suitcase. He checked it and her handbag. Both were clean but there was a note written on the plane to her boy-friend in the Bronx telling him that she had gone through the Bangkok customs 'like a breeze'. In the ensuing strip search, two eighteen-ounce bags of ninety-nine per cent pure South-East Asian No.4 heroin were found taped to the back of her shins. She was a typical 'mule', as this type of one-off courier is known, and had been recruited in New York with two other black girls to go to Bangkok for a 'holiday'. Her fee was $5000 (£2500).

As soon as her personal cargo was discovered, she broke down and told the Customs as many details of the operation as she could. The two other girls were due in two days' time and also two black men who, as far as she knew, had set up the deal in New York. The men were later identified as Glenston Laws and Bobby Beutel, both thirty and both well known to the DEA as suspected members of the famous Pretorius Gang. The two other girls and the two men were subsequently picked up and they all pleaded guilty to drug smuggling charges. The girls got five years in jail each, Bobby Beutel, the original recruiter back in New York, ten years and Laws, a flamboyant character, nine years.

The year shorter sentence was partly because Laws co-operated with the authorities. On his way by car after a preliminary remand at a lower court, he told Customs men: 'Get me on to a plane to America and you'll get the biggest thing you ever had!' One of the two DEA special agents in London was called in and the talkative Mr Laws gave him enough information to arrest thirty-seven-year-old Charlie Pretorius and a dozen other leading members of the gang over in New York.

In October 1978, Laws stood trial with his confederates at the East District Court in New York, promptly pleaded guilty and went on the stand to give evidence that led to the conviction of

Pretorius and the rest of his henchmen. The judge imposed upon him the nominal sentence of 'special probation'. It is 'extremely unlikely', I am assured by a source within British Customs, that he will serve any of his time in jail – on either side of the Atlantic. So all the guilty people ended up in jail – except for the stool pigeon Laws and the original Chinese dealer in Bangkok who – but of course! – has not even been arrested.

There are many other individual success or semi-success stories of law enforcement agents throughout the world but do they really begin to have any real effect on Triad criminal activities? What is the likely future of such activities in the 1980s?

It *is* possible to defeat the Triads. It has already happened once in this century, for not all pre-Communist China's native Triads managed to escape to Hong Kong or Taiwan and out into the Western world. Thousands, if not millions, were left stranded under the new regime. Since my return from the Far East and after the United States' formal recognition of Red China, I have asked a Chinese DEA special agent based in Hong Kong whether these Triad Societies had been ruthlessly suppressed by the victorious Communists and whether there was any evidence that they might reappear now that Red China was opening itself up again to the world. His reply – 'There is no evidence at all that Triads may appear again in China.' What happened to those left behind when Chiang Kai Shek fled? Ex-Hong Kong Detective Inspector Walter Easey says:

'The one Triad Society in mainland China that I have details of is the Yi Kwan Tao, a large society in northern China around Peking. That had a membership in the region of two million in a very large part of Hopeh province.

'Peking was "liberated" in February 1949 and thereafter there was an investigation into the Yi Kwan Tao that took something over two years. Out of the total membership of two million, they arrested 120 of the leaders and put them on trial, of whom six received the death penalty – which was carried out.

'Now that sort of activity does two things: first of all, many of those people certainly deserved shooting or even being torn apart by wild animals in my opinion. Secondly, it encourages the rank and file to co-operate. It makes a very clear affirmation that the official policy is leniency to the rank and file and harsh treatment of the really senior people.'

It was a nation-wide application of that kind of policy that eradicated the Triads in their own original home territory. I am not advocating putting even the worst drug trafficker up against a wall and shooting him, but it does strike me as ironic that, in the rest of the world outside mainland China, the official policy of governments, even when they can be brought to admit that Triads actually exist, is exactly the opposite of the successful methods employed by the Communists: *we* have, all too often, shown leniency to the really senior people and harsh treatment to the rank and file.

There is, however, a double irony. By the early months of 1980 evidence was beginning to accrue that, although Triads had gone to ground or been annihilated during the thirty years of Communist China's virtual seclusion from the rest of the world, with the re-establishment of contact with outsiders, Triad criminal activities were being reactivated. Either Triads themselves were infiltrating back into mainland China from across its borders or the Triad seed was growing again in its original fertile soil; although it could well be a mixture of the two.

In November 1979, for example, the Hong Kong correspondent of the London *Times* sent back a report on the involvement of 'Chinese secret societies with Hong Kong and mainland connections' in the illegal smuggling of immigrants across the border into Hong Kong and Macao. In the following month, *Wen Wei Pao*, the colony's leading local Communist daily newspaper, quoted security authorities in Canton to the effect that call-girl rackets had reopened in the Chinese city 'under the management of unscrupulous traders and criminal elements from Hong Kong'. Shortly before Christmas, Nigel Wade, the London *Daily Telegraph*'s man in Peking, cabled a story about a new crime wave 'reported to be sweeping major cities' with a significant role being played by 'juvenile street gangs'. In March 1980 the London *Times* carried a news story about the start of co-operation between Chinese mainland and Hong Kong police in order to try and combat 'syndicates engaged in illegal immigration'.

It all seems remarkably *déjà vu*.

People get the governments that they deserve, people get the crime that they deserve, people get the villains that they deserve. Unless and until the law enforcement agencies of the world come alive to the problem that faces them and expend the time, budget and resources that are required, the 1980s are due to be the decade in which the Triads become as powerful a force for evil as ever the Italian Mafia has been in the past. One can only hope it is a lesson that it is still not too late to be learned.

Select Bibliography

By the very nature of the subject matter of this book, the bibliography cannot be very extensive. Most of the research that has gone into the previous pages has been personal 'on the spot' investigation. However, the following published books have been particularly helpful on various aspects of the subject and anyone interested in furthering his knowledge of the Triads in their cultural and ethnic setting could read them with profit and interest:

Triad Societies in Hong Kong by Inspector W.P.Morgan (Government Press, Hong Kong, 1960).

The Politics of Heroin in South-East Asia by Alfred W. McCoy (Harper Colophon Books, 1973).

Longtime Californ' by Victor G. & Brett de Bary Nee (Houghton Mifflin Company, Boston, 1974).

Chinese Americans by Stanford M. Lyman (Random House, New York, 1974).

The Rise of Modern China by Immanuel C.Y.Hsü (Oxford University Press, 1975).

A History of Malaysia and Singapore by N.J.Ryan (Oxford University Press, 1976).

Malaysia and Singapore: The Building of New States by Stanley S. Bedlington (Cornell University Press, 1978).

Index

Individual Triads are listed under 'Triads'
Chinese names are listed under the first part of the name unless the name has become Westernized; e.g. Mao Tse Tung, *but* Lim, David

Imp.